AFTER EARLY INTERVENTION, THEN WHAT?

Teaching Struggling Readers in Grades 3 and Beyond

RACHEL L. MCCORMACK
Roger Williams University
Bristol, Rhode Island, USA

JEANNE R. PARATORE
Boston University
Boston, Massachusetts, USA

EDITORS

INTERNATIONAL
Reading Association
800 Barksdale Road, PO Box 8139
Newark, Delaware 19714-8139, USA
www.reading.org

The International Reading Association attempts, through its publications, to provide a forum for a wide spectrum of opinions on reading. This policy permits divergent viewpoints without implying the endorsement of the Association.

Director of Publications   Joan M. Irwin
Editorial Director, Books and Special Projects   Matthew W. Baker
Production Editor   Shannon Benner
Permissions Editor   Janet S. Parrack
Acquisitions and Communications Coordinator   Corinne M. Mooney
Associate Editor, Books and Special Projects   Sara J. Murphy
Assistant Editor   Charlene M. Nichols
Administrative Assistant   Michele Jester
Senior Editorial Assistant   Tyanna L. Collins
Production Department Manager   Iona Sauscermen
Supervisor, Electronic Publishing   Anette Schütz
Senior Electronic Publishing Specialist   Cheryl J. Strum
Electronic Publishing Specialist   R. Lynn Harrison
Proofreader   Elizabeth C. Hunt

Project Editor   Shannon Benner

Cover   Design, Linda Steere; Photo, Image Productions

Web addresses in this book were correct as of the publication date but may have become inactive or otherwise modified since that time. If you notice a deactivated or changed Web address, please e-mail books@reading.org with the words "Website Update" in the subject line. In your message, specify the Web link, the book title, and the page number on which the link appears.

Library of Congress Cataloging-in-Publication Data
   After early intervention, then what? : teaching struggling readers in
grades 3 and beyond / Rachel L. McCormack, Jeanne R.
Paratore, editors.
      p. cm.
   ISBN 0-87207-009-3
   1. Reading--Remedial teaching--United States. I. McCormack, Rachel L.
   II. Paratore, Jeanne R.
   LB1050.5.A36 2003
   372.43--dc21

                                                                    2003004887

CONTENTS

SECTION I:

Understanding the Student: Exploring Cognitive, Cultural, and Linguistic Underpinnings to Literacy Learning

SECTION II:

Supporting Students in Grades 3 and Beyond as They Learn to Read

---

SECTION III:

Supporting Students in Grades 3 and Beyond as They Learn Through Text

FOREWORD

This book is both accessible and timely. We have reached a point at which there is wide agreement that good first teaching and early intervention are critical (though there are different views of what those should look like), but we also now realize that there are many reasons why difficulties for some students might persist or subsequently develop. Collectively this group of respected authors brings a remarkably diverse set of perspectives and possibilities to bear on the question of what to do when early intervention fails. The diversity is evident in the students represented, the contexts in which the teachers are working, and their instructional strategies and focus, making for a lively read.

The authors offer creative strategies for changing the ways unsuccessful students understand reading and writing and themselves as literate people. Some go directly at teaching about literacy, some teach about literacy in the process of accomplishing something else, like research. Some of the authors have expanded the usual ways of thinking about what we are trying to accomplish with students—what literacy is all about. Many of the authors involve the students in the planning and documenting of their learning lives. Although readers might find chapters that specifically address their particular students and context—an "off the rack" solution—for me, the value in the diversity of the chapters is that it reduces our tendency to interpret interventions literally, helping us explore trade-offs. Some of the chapters, for example, show how what works for some students does not necessarily work for others in the same group, highlighting the need for constant monitoring.

The book speaks to the very real problem of teaching children beyond the first two or three years of school what they need to know about print and productive strategies for using that knowledge. However, it also takes into account that more is acquired in becoming literate than mere knowledge and strategies. In the process of becoming literate, children construct literate identities relationships and epistemologies

(Collins, 1995; Gee, 1996). The authors demonstrate ways of changing how students use and understand the resources available to them—peers, computers, language, cultural experience, and books—and what it means to be literate.

But as the students in these chapters craft new literate identities, the teachers, too, are constructing new identities through the communities of practice they have organized. Each chapter provides us with a glimpse of small teacher-research communities bent on making a difference for students and in the process learning more about how to make a difference. While arranging for students to become more agentive in their literate practices, and in contributing to the meanings created in their classrooms, the authors offer teachers the same possibilities with their teaching. Indeed, the concluding chapter, focusing on helping children become researchers, is an excellent metaphor for the book, which offers examples of teachers involved in researching solutions to problems that matter.

While arguing that good first teaching and early intervention cannot be universally successful, these authors also provide excellent examples of why they are, nonetheless, important. They show the difficulties of finding appropriate reading material as discrepancies develop between interests and technical skills, the complex demands of collaborating among personnel in the classroom and various elements of the second system, and they provide evidence of the scar tissue that accumulates when literate identities sustain injury. Happily, they also offer a wide range of creative solutions.

Peter H. Johnston
University at Albany, State University of New York
Albany, New York, USA

REFERENCES

Collins, J. (1995). Literacy and literacies. *Annual Review of Anthropology, 24*, 75–93.
Gee, J.P. (1996). *Social linguistics and literacies: Ideology in discourses* (2nd ed.). London: Falmer Press.

CONTRIBUTORS

Kathryn H. Au
Professor of Education
University of Hawaii
Honolulu, Hawaii, USA

Kristina Farrell Dahlene
Title I Tutor
JA Parker School
New Bedford, Massachusetts, USA

Lisa W. Davis
Teacher
Collins Middle School
Collins, Georgia, USA

Douglas Fisher
Associate Professor of Teacher
    Education
San Diego State University
San Diego, California, USA

James Flood
Professor of Literacy Education
San Diego State University
San Diego, California, USA

Susan Florio-Ruane
Professor of Teacher Education
Michigan State University
East Lansing, Michigan, USA

Susan Franks
Associate Professor of Early
    Childhood Education
Georgia Southern University
Statesboro, Georgia, USA

Nancy Frey
Assistant Professor of Teacher
    Education
San Diego State University
San Diego, California, USA

Irene W. Gaskins
Founder and Director
Benchmark School
Media, Pennsylvania, USA

Eleanor Wiley Gensemer
Middle School Teacher and
    Language Arts Supervisor
Benchmark School
Media, Pennsylvania, USA

MariAnne George
Learning Coach
Rochester Community Schools
Rochester, Michigan, USA

Janis M. Harmon
Associate Professor of Literacy
    Education
University of Texas at San Antonio
San Antonio, Texas, USA

Nina Levorn Hasty
Elementary Teacher
Center for the Improvement of Early
    Reading Achievement
University of Michigan
Ann Arbor, Michigan, USA

Wanda B. Hedrick
Associate Professor of Literacy
    Education
University of Texas at San Antonio
San Antonio, Texas, USA

Kathy Highfield
Teacher
Holly Area Schools
Holly, Michigan, USA

Julie Jacobson
Teacher
San Diego Unified School District
San Diego, California, USA

Robert T. Jiménez
Professor of Bilingual and Literacy
    Education
University of Illinois at
    Urbana–Champaign
Champaign, Illinois, USA

Susan Keehn
Assistant Professor of Reading
    and Literacy
University of Texas at San Antonio
San Antonio, Texas, USA

Marcella J. Kehus
Berkley Public Schools
Berkley, Michigan, USA

Melanie R. Kuhn
Assistant Professor of Literacy
    Education
Rutgers, The State University
    of New Jersey
New Brunswick, New Jersey, USA

Diane Lapp
Professor of Literacy Education
San Diego State University
San Diego, California, USA

Joyce E. Many
Professor of Language and Literacy
    Education
Georgia State University
Atlanta, Georgia, USA

Miriam Martinez
Professor of Reading and Literacy
University of Texas at San Antonio
San Antonio, Texas, USA

Laura A. May
Reading Specialist
Channelview Independent School
    District
Channelview, Texas, USA

Rachel L. McCormack
Assistant Professor of Education
Roger Williams University
Bristol, Rhode Island, USA

Michael C. McKenna
Professor of Reading
Georgia Southern University
Savannah, Georgia, USA

Torry H. Montes
Language Arts Teacher
Mid-Pacific Institute
Honolulu, Hawaii, USA

Lesley Mandel Morrow
Professor of Literacy
Rutgers, The State University
    of New Jersey
New Brunswick, New Jersey, USA

Sharon O'Neal
Associate Professor
Southwest Texas State University
San Marcos, Texas, USA

Jeanne R. Paratore
Associate Professor of Education
Boston University
Boston, Massachusetts, USA

Taffy E. Raphael
Professor of Literacy Education
University of Illinois at Chicago
Chicago, Illinois, USA

Nancy L. Roser
Professor of Language and Literacy
    Studies
University of Texas
Austin, Texas, USA

Linda M. Six
Middle School Head
Benchmark School
Media, Pennsylvania, USA

Lynne Thrope
Reading Therapist
The Reading Room
El Cajon, California, USA

Karen D. Wood
Professor of Reading and Elementary
    Education
University of North
    Carolina–Charlotte
Charlotte, North Carolina, USA

In recent years, U.S. policy and funding initiatives, and as a consequence, much research at both national and local levels, have focused primarily on early intervention in reading, partially on the premise that if teachers strive to prevent reading difficulty at the start of children's schooling, remediation in the later grades will be largely unnecessary. For example, in 1999 during the Clinton administration, the Reading Excellence Act appropriated $260 million for the implementation of programs for children in kindergarten through grade 3 and essentially excluded children in later grades. The Bush administration has continued this emphasis on support for early reading success. The No Child Left Behind Act of 2001 supports administration of "screening and diagnostic assessments to determine which students in grades K–3 are at risk of reading failure, and provide professional development for K–3 teachers in the essential components of reading instruction" (U.S. Department of Education, 2002). The Act also authorizes awards to local school districts to "support early language, literacy, and pre-reading development of preschool-age children, particularly those from low-income families." Although the No Child Left Behind Act requires annual testing of reading achievement of all children in grades 3–8, no funding is allocated to support the instruction of children who continue to experience difficulty beyond grade 3.

Getting a good start in learning to read is clearly a worthy goal and one that reading professionals have long promoted. However, for many children, early intervention is insufficient. Children struggle in learning to read for an array of reasons, including language differences, learning and cognitive disabilities, and motivation and interest, some of which cannot be fully addressed during the early years of schooling. According to results from the 2000 National Assessment of Educational Progress (NAEP) (Donahue, Finnegan, Lutkus, Allen, & Campbell, 2001), 37% of fourth-grade students fail to achieve basic levels of reading competence. These results remained essentially unchanged from the results reported in 1998. The consequence of underachievement in reading in the intermediate grades is serious. In the oft-quoted words of Keith Stanovich, differential reading abilities may yield "'Matthew effects' in

1

literacy development: educational sequences in which early and efficient acquisition of reading skill yields faster rates of growth in reading achievement and other cognitive skills" (2000, p. 207). Beyond the effects on individuals' cognitive abilities, recent U.S. policies raise the stakes even higher, with many states now requiring that intermediate-grade children attain particular benchmarks on state reading assessments as a condition for promotion and, eventually, graduation.

In preparing this book, we hoped to accomplish two goals. First, we hoped to draw attention to the evidence that despite recognition of the importance of early reading achievement and good teaching, many students continue to need expert, intensive, and focused instruction in reading well beyond the primary school years—even after they have had the benefit of effective early instruction. Second, we sought to identify and describe effective practices for teaching intermediate- and middle-grade students who continue to struggle in reading. Drawing from both research and practice, the contributors (in most cases, researchers and teacher-researchers) share evidence of what works for students who are struggling as readers and writers in grades 3–8.

This book's chapters are organized into three major sections: Understanding the Student: Exploring Cognitive, Cultural, and Linguistic Underpinnings to Literacy Learning; Supporting Students in Grades 3 and Beyond as They Learn to Read; and Supporting Students in Grades 3 and Beyond as They Learn Through Text. Collectively, the chapters address the needs of students in a range of instructional settings, including general, special, and bilingual education classrooms, and in a range of learning contexts, including classroom, small group, individual, and tutorial. The selection of widely varying classroom settings was a deliberate response to our awareness that children struggle in classrooms in all types of settings and communities. In most cases, whatever the type of classroom in which the research was carried out, teachers will find the suggestions easily transferable to a range of classroom settings.

In Section I, we focus on the principle that understanding the student is the foundation for effective teaching, and to do so we juxtapose two chapters by authors who approach understanding students from two very different perspectives. These chapters are not intended to offer a broad and comprehensive view of student needs but rather to focus attention on two particular viewpoints. In chapter 1, Diane Lapp and James Flood focus on students' uses of literacy in school. They remind readers that the practice of diagnostic teaching, popularized years ago by Ruth Strang (1969), requires a deep and well-organized conception of how literacy is acquired and developed. They describe a diagnostic teaching model that they call "portable assessment," and they help readers learn to use it by sharing the reading profiles of two students: Anthony, a third grader, and Lajuana, a fifth grader.

In chapter 2, Robert T. Jiménez challenges readers to think beyond the classroom and to broaden their understanding of what it means to be literate outside of school. Through a collection of brief but penetrating case studies, Jiménez introduces readers to ways these students use literacy to accomplish important tasks in their daily lives. He suggests ways that teachers might more effectively come to know their students, and he argues that acknowledging and valuing what students know and do may stimulate in them "new insight and motivation to acquire higher levels of literacy."

In Section II, the chapters are unified in their focus on advancing the reading and writing abilities of struggling readers in grades 3–8. They are diverse, however, in what types of classrooms, schools, and approaches to learning they discuss. In some chapters, authors provide a comprehensive description of a program or approach to teaching and learning; in others, authors describe a strategy or practice intended to address a particular aspect of students' literacy development.

The section begins with a chapter by Nancy L. Roser, Laura A. May, Miriam Martinez, Susan Keehn, Janis M. Harmon, and Sharon O'Neal, who set the stage for our thinking about effective instructional strategies by arguing that developing reading fluency requires far more than rereading of familiar texts. Rather, they argue that it requires— and students deserve—instruction that invites thoughtful interpretation and purposeful rereading. Working in a bilingual fourth-grade classroom, they use the technique of Readers Theatre in combination with high-quality texts that are culturally and linguistically relevant to help children develop fluency without the loss of other aspects of effective instruction (interest, purpose, and engagement). The authors explicitly describe teaching procedures and plans, as well as the varied results for the 9- to 11-year-olds with whom they worked.

In chapter 4, Torry H. Montes and Kathryn H. Au take us into another linguistically and ethnically diverse fourth-grade classroom where, as a group, the students are characterized as struggling readers. Montes, the classroom teacher, sought a solution to her students' reading difficulties in the implementation of Book Club, an approach to reading and writing developed by Taffy E. Raphael and her colleagues (Raphael &

McMahon, 1994). Using numerous excerpts from children's book discussions and their own explanations of the process, Montes and Au demonstrate in this chapter how children learn, with expert teacher support, to view reading and writing as events that have purpose and importance in their own lives. Through the use of excerpts of superficial conversations as well as engaged student talk, the authors highlight the challenges they confronted along the way, and by so doing, they help educators to remember that there is no quick fix or easy solution to the reading problems of middle-grade students.

In chapter 5, Taffy E. Raphael, Susan Florio-Ruane, Marcella J. Kehus, MariAnne George, Nina Levorn Hasty, and Kathy Highfield expand on the Book Club model discussed in the previous chapter. They introduce an instructional approach that they call Book Club Plus—a combination of Book Club, as previously described, and Literacy Block, a time period during which activities related to the skills and strategies of reading and writing are taught and practiced. This chapter is distinct from the others in its detailed explanation of the process in which the teachers engaged as they planned an appropriate and comprehensive instructional approach for struggling readers. In contrast to other chapters in this book in which we expect that teachers will see descriptions of students who are very much like their own, in this chapter we expect that teachers will see themselves in the accounts of the instructional planning process. These authors remind readers of the complexity of teaching and learning, and of teachers' obligation to honor every student's intellectual ability by offering a curriculum that is worthy of every student's time and attention.

In chapter 6, Rachel L. McCormack, Jeanne R. Paratore, and Kristina Farrell Dahlene describe their work with students who often receive two instructional programs—one in the classroom and one with a special reading teacher. They share their experiences working with third-grade students in two classrooms, the first within a fairly typical suburban setting and the second within a fairly typical urban setting. In the suburban school classroom, children who experienced reading difficulty received extra help from a reading teacher who worked outside the classroom—a practice that was not open to change. In the urban school classroom, the children received extra help from a reading teacher who worked at the back of the classroom. McCormack, Paratore, and Dahlene provide a detailed account of what they did in each of these settings and of the learning outcomes for children. They conclude with a description of the particular instructional elements that they believe were critical in explaining children's learning success.

In chapter 7, readers encounter a school setting that they may find less familiar than those visited in the earlier chapters. Irene W. Gaskins, Eleanor Wiley Gensemer, and Linda M. Six describe their work in a seventh-grade classroom of only nine students at the Benchmark School, a school for struggling readers. What one is struck by as this report unfolds is not the smallness of the class nor the richness of teaching resources; rather, what stands out is the planful, thoughtful, cohesive, coherent, and intensive nature of the literacy experiences students have throughout and across the days, weeks, and months of the school year. The consequences of such high-quality and unified instruction are evident in the students' learning outcomes. The challenge for teachers who practice in different settings is to determine how similar teaching actions can be replicated in places where classes are larger, more diverse, and less rich in teaching resources.

In chapter 8, Douglas Fisher, Nancy Frey, Lynne Thrope, and Julie Jacobson remind readers that, for struggling readers, adequate achievement may be realized when teachers manage to not only provide expert instruction during the school day but also to extend the opportunities to engage in reading and writing beyond the school day. The authors describe a two-hour-per-day, three-day-per-week plan for an after-school reading club, and they discuss the array of factors they believe contributed to the gains students achieved.

This section concludes with a chapter by Melanie R. Kuhn and Lesley Mandel Morrow on the benefits of computer technology in supporting the literacy learning of struggling readers. In keeping with the focus of the other chapters in this section, Kuhn and Morrow provide specific examples of the ways various technologies may provide opportunities for struggling readers to advance fluency, vocabulary, background knowledge, and comprehension. In addition, they also emphasize the ways that various technologies can help students with poor reading abilities to access information in other ways besides reading. They describe the potential for multimedia presentations to provide an array of information in various forms, including, for example, video clips, audio interviews, and photographs, in addition to print.

The second half of the chapter by Kuhn and Morrow is an effective segue into Section III, where the chapters shift from an emphasis on practices that are effective in advancing the literacy knowledge of struggling readers to practices that emphasize advancing the content knowledge of struggling readers. In many ways, this is an arbitrary division—we are mindful of Alexander's (2002) contention that learning to read and reading to learn are inextricably intertwined; clearly students acquire content knowledge when they read any worthy text, and, by the same token, they advance literacy knowledge even when the focus is on "reading to learn." Our distinction, then, is one of relative emphasis rather than a point of separation.

In chapter 10, Wanda B. Hedrick, Janis M. Harmon, and Karen D. Wood remind us that as students advance through the grades, the difficulty of the task for struggling readers is compounded by both the need to read more, as texts become longer, and by the realization that what they are required to read is different, as instructional materials change from primarily narrative texts to primarily expository texts. Through a detailed description of their work in a fourth-grade bilingual classroom, Hedrick, Harmon, and Wood take their audience through a step-by-step plan for helping struggling readers to make the transition from reading and responding to narrative text to reading and learning from informational text. Although the authors developed the approach with particular attention to the needs of struggling adolescent readers, one suspects that nearly all middle-grade students would benefit from this explicit and thoughtful approach to content area instruction.

In chapter 11, Michael C. McKenna, Lisa W. Davis, and Susan Franks address essentially the same instructional need—helping students to read and learn from expository text—but they do so using a strategy that is substantially different from the collaborative model described in chapter 10. Recognizing that there are often contexts in which students work individually and independently, they describe how teachers might develop, introduce, and then use reading guides to help students acquire reading strategies to promote effective independent reading.

In the final chapter, Joyce E. Many encourages teachers to raise their expectations for struggling readers higher yet and focuses on effective ways to teach them to do "meaningful research." She defines meaningful research as "a transformation process leading to personal understanding." She relies on observations collected from children and teachers in grades 3–6 as they went about the research process to help her audience to understand how successful teachers teach, scaffold, and clarify the research process for children.

As we reflect on this collection of chapters, we note that they are unified by some long-held principles about effective teaching—

instruction is intense, explicit, strategic, and supported by knowledgeable teachers; curriculum is challenging and interesting; and student engagement is high, as are expectations for learning. Beyond these general descriptors, however, there are substantial differences in how these principles are assembled by individual teachers and teacher-researchers. The differences may be as important as the similarities, for they remind us that there are multiple pathways to success for struggling readers and that good teachers seek the particular approach or practice that represents a good fit for both teacher and learner.

—*JRP and RLM*

REFERENCES

Alexander, P. (2002, December). *Profiling the developing reader: The interplay of knowledge, interest, and strategic processing.* Paper presented at the annual meeting of the National Reading Conference, Miami, FL.

Donahue, P.L., Finnegan, R.J., Lutkus, A.D., Allen, N.L., & Campbell, J.R. (2001). *The nation's report card: Fourth-grade reading 2000.* Washington, DC: U.S. Department of Education, National Center for Education Statistics.

Raphael, T.E., & McMahon, S.I. (1994). Book Club: An alternative framework for reading instruction. *The Reading Teacher, 48,* 102–116.

Stanovich, K. (2000). *Progress in understanding reading: Scientific foundations and new frontiers.* New York: Guilford.

Strang, R. (1969). *Diagnostic teaching of reading.* New York: McGraw-Hill.

U.S. Department of Education. (2002). *No Child Left Behind Act of 2001, executive summary.* Available: http://www.ed.gov/offices/OESE/esea/exec-summ.html

Understanding the Student: Exploring Cognitive, Cultural, and Linguistic Underpinnings to Literacy Learning

CHAPTER 1

Understanding the Learner: Using Portable Assessment

Diane Lapp and James Flood

The smiling mother leans into the crib of her newborn and softly tells him a soothing bedtime tale filled with princes and pirates and blue skies.

The young father watches with amusement as his 1-year-old baby picks up her tattered copy of Dorothy Kunhardt's *Pat the Bunny* and promptly puts the corner of the book into her mouth. The father takes the book from his daughter's mouth, opens the pages with care, and begins to read each page diligently with his baby.

The 2-year-old sits quietly on the bookstore floor with a copy of Richard Scary's *Cars and Trucks and Things That Go*. As he turns the pages, sometimes two at a time, he puts his lips together and blows air through his mouth in such a way that he sounds like a truck with a somewhat troubled muffler.

The very tired 4-year-old, who appears to be fully asleep, has one more spurt of energy as she tells her equally tired mother, who isn't reading every word of *Goldilocks and the Three Bears*: "You skipped the part about Goldilocks sitting in the Mama Bear's chair. Read that part, Mommy."

The 5-year-old points proudly to the word *hat* as he reads Dr. Seuss's *The Cat in the Hat*, telling his equally proud grandfather, "That says 'hat.'"

The 7-year-old, sitting with his teacher, pulls out his copy of Arnold Lobel's *Frog and Toad Are Friends* and reads the entire first page to his attentive teacher without missing a word.

Two 9-year-olds enjoy sharing their responses with one another during buddy reading of *Dinosaur Dinner: Favorite Poems by Dennis Lee*.

The 11-year-old listens to the audio narration as he intently reads along in *Harry Potter and the Sorcerer's Stone*.

The 13-year-old reads and writes about sea life as she prepares for her oral report titled "Fossil Fish Found Alive."

T hese snippets of family and school life are a small sampling of the experiences that children encounter as they grow toward competence and independence in literacy. It would be a wonderful world indeed if all children were able to have the experiences illustrated in these vignettes, but it is a sad fact that they do not. Children come to school with various types of literacy experiences. As the cultural and linguistic demography of public schools continues to change, teachers are faced with the ever-growing complexities of educating diverse populations of students who come from homes where early literacy experiences may not be a part of the daily routine. Rosow (1992) notes this when she introduces readers to Irma, a child from a home where the adults do not have the educational or experiential knowledge needed to provide school-related early literacy experiences. Like Irma, many children come from homes where loving adults do not view themselves as being providers of early literacy education because they believe that the school is responsible for providing these experiences (Lapp, Fisher, Flood, & Moore, 2002). Parents of children like Irma do not realize that their children's limited early literacy experiences may result in an achievement gap with lifelong consequences for future employment and earnings (Carnevale, 1999; Coleman et al., 1966; Jencks, 1992; Murnane & Levy, 1996; National Institute of Child Health and Human Development, 2002; Ogbu, 1994; Salus & Flood, 2002).

How can a child like Irma find her way to the opportunities associated with early literacy and subsequent school success? This is a question that haunts all of us. Although no single factor alone accounts for student achievement gaps (Lee, 2002), we believe that a child's schooling is the one factor that educators have power to control. Educators have the power to provide a positive school environment that can promote literacy development for Irma and all the children like her.

In this chapter, we focus specifically on students whose struggle with reading has extended well beyond the primary grades. Many of these students have had limited early literacy experiences. As we focus our discussion on struggling readers, we propose a model in which students' reading skills are assessed and analyzed before instruction is planned. Toward this end, we recommend a technique that we call "portable assessment."

What Is Portable Assessment?

Portable assessment enables teachers to regularly assess their struggling readers. The practice is portable because teachers (a) reliably depend on their own knowledge of language and reading development as a guide in their analysis of students' needs; (b) are knowledgeable about diagnosis and assessment in general and about running record procedures in particular (Clay, 1979); and (c) use for assessment the materials that students are already reading as part of their classroom programs. Portable assessment frees teachers from the constraints of time-consuming formal assessments that may or may not provide the information they need to plan appropriate instruction. It allows for frequent assessment that pinpoints needs as they occur.

What Do Teachers Need to Know to Conduct a Portable Assessment?

As we begin our discussion of literacy assessment and instruction for struggling readers in grades 3–5, we maintain that it is important for every teacher to have a mental model of the ways in which literacy develops in children from the beginnings of their lives. The model shown in Figure 1.1 is one way of organizing this knowledge of language and literacy development. Here, we divide literacy skills into oral skills and written skills. As the vignettes at the beginning of this chapter suggest, literacy develops in systematic ways that are influenced by the experiences children have during their early years.

In section A of Figure 1.1, we list the early literacy development of children before coming to school. It has been documented widely that the early literacy experiences children have prior to school greatly influence their school performance (Adams, 1990; Gillet & Temple, 1994; Strickland, Ganske, & Monroe, 2002; Sulzby & Teale, 1987). Because of the variance that occurs in before-school experiences, children come to school with a wide range of literacy abilities. Differences in the literacy achievement of children with greater and fewer home literacy experiences often continue throughout their school careers (Anderson, Hiebert, Scott, & Wilkinson, 1985; Dickinson & Smith, 1994). It is critical that teachers acknowledge the differences that exist at the beginning so they will be able to teach to each child's developmental stage without thinking that children are "disabled."

FIGURE 1.1

A MODEL OF LITERACY DEVELOPMENT

Section A: Before School—The Foundation

Oral Language ———————————————————— Written Language

Communication— Early	Conversation	Writing	Reading
Crying	Socializing through language	Scribbling	Emergent Stage
Cooing	turn taking	Drawing	*Pre-alphabetic phase*
Babbling	language rituals	Copy environmental	looking at pictures
Experimenting	listening	print	pretend reading
with sounds	Phonemic awareness	Random letters	attending to words and
Experimenting	rhyming	Early invented	letters
with words	segmenting	spelling	development of
Generating	substituting	Transitional spelling	concepts of print
sentences			(Functions of print)
Learning syntax			
Learning semantics			

Section B: During School—Developing Concepts/Vocabulary (More Formal Instruction)

Vocabulary	Expanded voices	Alphabetic Writing	Early Stage	
Development	Registers	Standard	*Phonetic cue*	
Complex syntactic		Orthography	*reading phase*	
structures		Composition	Learning the	
Complex semantic		words ⟶	alphabetic code	
development		phrases ⟶	Alphabetic Synthetic	Sight Word Development
		sentences ⟶	phonics	
		paragraphs ⟶	c/a/t/	
		full texts ⟶	Developing Stage	
		Audience and	*Cipher or full*	
		purpose	*alphabetic phase*	
		Organization	Onset and rime	
		Coherence	Analytic phonics	
			Chunking	
			1. one-syllable words	
			2. two-syllable words	
			3. three-syllable words	
			Fluent Stage	
			Strategies	
			rereading	
			fixing/	
			crosschecking cues	
			inferring	
			visualizing	
			summarizing	

From Lapp & Flood, 1993, 2001

In section B of Figure 1.1, we identify how literacy continues to develop throughout a child's school life. Because of the range of literacy skills that will exist among students at any grade, it is very important that teachers continuously observe and assess student performance, identify strengths, diagnose needs, and plan instruction. Lipson and Wixson (1991) define this diagnostic teaching as "thoughtfully planned" instruction that includes "our best guesses" about what is needed for each student (p. 31).

Although diagnostic teaching is essential to the literacy growth of all children, for the purpose of this chapter we will be concentrating on struggling readers, whom we define simply and straightforwardly as students who are not reading grade-level materials with fluency and comprehension.

Are you thinking about your students and wondering how many of them qualify as "struggling"? McCormick (1995) and Vellutino et al. (1996) suggest that about 10% of school-age children have mild reading difficulties, 12% have moderate problems, and 3% have serious reading needs. These estimates are supported by the National Assessment of Educational Progress (2001). As explained by Campbell, Hombo, and Mazzeo (2000) and Loveless and Diperna (2000), data indicate that about 25% of the school-age student population have some type of reading needs, and 42% of fourth graders and 31% of eighth graders are not able to literally comprehend grade-level texts and relate them to their life experiences. Substantial differences in performance also exist when students are grouped by race and ethnicity (Lee, 2002).

These data underscore two important points: (1) In any given classroom there will be a range of reading proficiencies, and (2) this variance necessitates continuous diagnostic assessment and instruction. Teachers need to spend a great deal of time with the assessment data before they plan instruction. However, sometimes teachers are so overwhelmed by the multiple needs of their students that they rush to "fix" them with a "splash" approach to both assessment and instruction. An example of this recently occurred when an exasperated teacher, who is one of our graduate students, came to our office with a plea for help. She had just finished administering 25 running records, one for each of her third graders. She also had completed a retelling assessment and queried children for additional information about what they had read. She told us she had questioned them to determine what they knew about the topic before the assessments were conducted. Doesn't this sound thorough? You're probably wondering why she was exasperated. Hadn't she done a comprehensive job of assessing each child's reading performance? Yes, but she wasn't sure how to analyze her data—she wasn't sure about the instruction that was needed for her children based on their assessment results. She was eager to begin teaching but wanted to be sure that she was planning appropriate instruction that would ensure student growth.

As we spoke with this graduate student, we reviewed a process of continuous diagnostic teaching that focuses on ongoing assessment and instruction that can be used by every classroom teacher to monitor reading performance. Here is how portable assessment works:

Assess:

• Identify the literacy behaviors that the student has mastered. Use performance instruments such as running records (Clay, 1979), retellings (Morrow, 1988), and questioning (Raphael, 1982) to collect your data about student performance. This will help you to determine the next steps in instruction.

• Identify areas in which the student has needs.

Diagnose/analyze: Analyze the data to pinpoint the areas of strength and need.

Teach: Plan the next steps in instruction based on the identified areas of strength and need.

How Do Teachers Use Portable Assessment? Two Stories From the Classroom

In this section, we illustrate the ways in which two teachers used portable assessment to diagnose their students' strengths and needs.

Anthony's Story

Anthony is a third grader. He entered first grade without having attended kindergarten and with very limited literacy experiences. Anthony is from a home where he is provided with an abundance of love and care from a mother with limited literacy skills and limited knowledge about the concepts and importance of early literacy experiences. When Anthony entered first grade, he could not recognize any letters of the alphabet and was not aware that he or anyone else had a last name. He had a very good sense of humor. Once he was introduced to books, he enjoyed being read to, and he quickly became very interested in books about many topics. He also showed a real curiosity about words and dictionaries but was reluctant to engage in extensive conversation.

With excellent classroom teaching and numerous hours of individual tutoring during grades 1 and 2, Anthony acquired many of the early literacy skills he needed to be prepared for third grade. At the beginning of his third-grade year, Anthony's teacher, Ms. Moore, assessed him as being capable of reading second-grade texts. She made this determination based on three pieces of data: (1) her observations, (2) his score of 16 on the Developmental Reading Assessment (DRA), and (3) his second-grade level score on the San Diego Quick Assessment.

To determine where to begin third-grade instruction, Ms. Moore asked Anthony to read "Pet Show," a second-grade story that was part of his independent reading program. She began with an assessment of his background knowledge about pet shows and concluded that he did indeed know what pet shows were. As he read, Ms. Moore conducted a running record with a retelling. When he finished, she encouraged him to share his thoughts about the story. She then questioned him about the setting, characters, dialogue, and the problem/solution of the story. The text of the story follows:

Pet Show

Rex is getting a bath.
"Rex will go to the pet show," Jack said.
"He will win the cleanest dog prize," said Dan.
Then Rex ran in the mud.
Jack and Dan took him to the pet show anyway.
Later Dan said, "I knew Rex would win a prize."
"Rex won the dirty dog prize!" Jack said.
The boys laughed. Rex barked. (Lapp & Flood, 2000, p. 78)

The running record in Figure 1.2 illustrates Anthony's successes and errors as he read the text.

FIGURE 1.2

ANTHONY'S RUNNING RECORD

√ √

√ √ √ √   bath
                                          ─────
                                          ball

√ √ √ √ √ √ √ √

√ √ √ √   cl   –   party   √ √
                   ────   ─────
                   cleanest   prize

√ √ √ √ √

√ √ √ √ √ √ √ √   away
                                     ─────
                                     anyway

√ √ √ √ √ √   wa, wa | √ √   APP
                   ───────────   ─────
                   would (would)   prize

√ √ √   -   √ √ √ √
                 ─────
                 dirty

√ √   laugh   √ √
            ─────────
            laughed

APP = appeal for help

After Ms. Moore collected these data, she analyzed his performance with an eye toward what she knew about Anthony and what she
knew about children's language development (refer to Figure 1.1 on
page 13).

As shown in the running record, when Anthony came to the word
bath, he said "ball." His decoding skills broke down, and he reverted
to one of his earlier strategies of matching the initial letter in the target
word to others he had previously seen in print. He continued anxiously
and said /cl/ when he came to the word *cleanest*, "party" when he came
to the word *prize*, and "away" when he came to the word *anyway*. He
tried unsuccessfully to sound out the word *would*. Ms. Moore listed
Anthony's strengths and needs:

- enjoyed reading the text
- never lost interest in trying to read the text
- automaticity is increasing
- confidence as a reader is increasing

- focused on initial consonants whether the word is monosyllabic ("ball" for *bath*) or multisyllabic (/cl/ for *cleanest*, "party" for *prize*)
- focused on first letter and said incorrect sight word "away" for *anyway*
- didn't recognize common chunks of words
- rushed through the text, didn't stop when the text didn't make sense
- didn't seem able to monitor his comprehension
- didn't pay clear attention to the pictorial cue
- didn't stop to fix his miscues
- didn't integrate the meaning, the structure, and the visual cues contained in the passage
- is not yet fluent in phrasing

Ms. Moore concluded that Anthony fluctuates between the early developing and fluent stages of reading (refer to Figure 1.1 on page 13). As she thought about Anthony's performance, she designed the following instruction for him:

- She would encourage him to read whole texts so he could gain fluency and an understanding that the primary purpose of reading is to comprehend and enjoy texts. Activities that support this included (a) practicing reading with appropriate-level readers; (b) engaging with Ms. Moore in Neurological Impress Method (NIM) (Heckelman, 1966), in which she can model how a fluent reader sounds while he orally reads along with her; (c) partnering for choral reading; and (d) reading independently.
- She would reintroduce and model how to use the cueing systems in order to make sense of the text.
- She would provide word-study activities that would help him to develop his automaticity when reading decodable and sight words. Her activities included the following:
    1. Practicing the decoding of one- to three-syllable words, focusing on all word parts
    2. Reading the charts in the room daily by reading the phonetically regular word wall and the sight-word wall
    3. Copying words into his Tricky Word Book (e.g., *people*) and his Sight Word Book (*the*, *what*)

After a few weeks of instruction, Ms. Moore made instructional and grouping alterations based on additional observations of Anthony's performance during retellings, oral reading, conversations, and question-answer responses. She observed that Anthony

- knew all the appropriate sight words;
- hesitated when encountering an unfamiliar one- or two-syllable word and attended to familiar chunks that would help him read the word;
- used visualization and matching of the text and pictures as a support for comprehension on a more regular basis;
- offered more consistent text retellings, including minor points as well as major points, but left out character motives and resolution;
- rushed, and didn't fix up regularly; and
- lacked fluency.

Ms. Moore adjusted her instruction in many ways. She

- continued to build fluency through neurological impress, partner reading, and reading along with tapes;
- discontinued direct instruction of common sight words;
- focused more on "tricky" sight words such as *people*, *balloon*, *brother*, *community*, and *neighborhood*;
- focused on chunking of words with three or more syllables;
- placed more emphasis on comprehending character motivation, setting, and cause/effect and text-to-text relationships; and
- discussed metacognitive strategies that would help when not understanding (e.g., selecting a less difficult text on the same topic, checking the dictionary to get a needed definition).

Lajuana's Story

Our second story is about Lajuana, a fifth grader who eagerly reads with good comprehension and fluency. She enjoys reading series books and rarely has trouble engaging herself during independent reading time. However, she tends to experience difficulty when she reads informational texts. Her teacher, Ms. Ryan, has assessed her overall reading level as fourth grade based on several measures, including her observations, the DRA, the San Diego Quick Assessment, and the Scholastic Achievement Test 9 (SAT9).

Unlike Anthony, Lajuana is from a middle-class, two-parent family. But, like Anthony, she entered first grade with limited school-related early literacy experiences.

Based on her understanding of how an almost fluent reader performs (see Figure 1.1 on page 13), Ms. Ryan had been encouraging Lajuana to read more widely; she had invited Lajuana repeatedly to read informational texts. During independent reading, when Lajuana was reading "Rosa Parks," a fourth-grade passage, Ms. Ryan conducted a running record. Before she began, she assessed Lajuana's background knowledge about Rosa Parks's contribution to U.S. history and discovered that Lajuana knew the details of Rosa Parks's story and seemed ready to read the following text:

Rosa Parks

On December 1, 1955, an African-American woman named Rosa Parks was riding the bus home from work. A white man was standing up on the crowded bus. The driver demanded that Parks give up her seat. At the time, the law in many places in the south said African Americans had to give up their seats to white people. Rosa Parks refused to give up her seat. She was tired of giving in to laws that were unfair.

Parks was arrested and found guilty of disorderly conduct. Four days later, the Rev. Dr. Martin Luther King, Jr., organized a bus boycott. African Americans did not patronize city buses for over a year. Finally, the court ruled that African Americans no longer had to give up their seats to white people. (Lapp & Flood, 2000, p. 13)

When Lajuana retold the text, it was quite clear that she did not understand much of what she had read in the second paragraph. Her retelling was exclusively about Rosa Parks's refusal to give up her seat. When she was questioned by Ms. Ryan about the whole text, it became clear that she did not know the meanings of the words *boycott* and *patronize* and that she was not sure of the meaning of *disorderly conduct*. Her problems with comprehending the text were not decoding problems; they were vocabulary problems and a lack of background knowledge about the Civil Rights Movement. Her running record in Figure 1.3 clearly shows that her decoding skills were good.

FIGURE 1.3

LAJUANA'S RUNNING RECORD

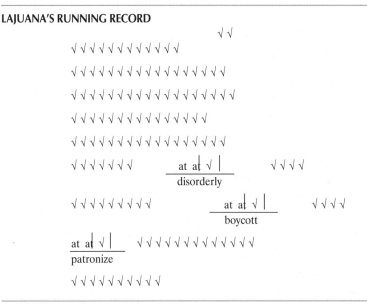

at = attempt

As Ms. Ryan analyzed Lajuana's reading needs, she found that Lajuana was in the fluent stage of reading (see Figure 1.1 on page 13), but her comprehension was limited because of her lack of vocabulary and concept knowledge. She also did not seem to attend to the chronological structure of the second paragraph of the reading passage. Ms. Ryan suggested the following instructional plan:

- Teach concepts/vocabulary before asking Lajuana to read the text (in this example, discussion of the U.S. Civil Rights movement may have been helpful).

- Model for Lajuana how to set a purpose before beginning to read by previewing the title, headings, etc.

- Help Lajuana to make a mental image of the information being read by identifying/visualizing graphically the main idea and supporting details.

- Model for Lajuana how to secure less difficult texts on the same topic and also other support materials (e.g., dictionary, Internet, encyclopedias) as a means of building background knowledge and vocabulary.

• Teach underlying structures of nonfiction, noting format, text organization, subheadings, charts, photos.

• Use a graphic organizer to help Lajuana sort and understand information as she reads; in this case a timeline may have helped Lajuana understand the story (see Moss, 2002).

• Model for Lajuana metacognitive thinking while reading to be sure that the passage is making sense.

Conclusion

The instructional scenario played out in the course of a teaching day by an effective teacher is complex and never the same for any two children. Teachers are with their students daily and, therefore, have the opportunity to make continuous diagnostic observations about how their students are currently performing compared with their performance on similar tasks encountered in the past. A teacher who is skilled at conducting ongoing evaluation has the data needed to inform the next steps in the child's instructional plan.

After assessment and the creation of a diagnostic instructional plan, the teacher's next responsibilities begin with helping students to understand how, when, and why reading is important and to provide them with a framework for implementing comprehension strategies as they read. Effective teachers recognize that students who have an understanding of strategic reading have a vested interest in making connections, visualizing, asking questions, formulating and reformulating predictions, gaining meaning that is personally significant, and satisfying and stimulating their own curiosity.

We are especially concerned about the instructional needs of students whose early literacy experiences are minimal or nonexistent. We have argued that such children need skilled and ongoing assessment by teachers knowledgeable about reading development. However, we acknowledge that classrooms are very busy places where teachers rarely have time to conduct time-consuming formal assessments that may not provide useful instructional information. We contend that portable assessment may be an answer to the demands of ongoing classroom assessment for every child, especially those who struggle with learning to read and becoming a proficient reader.

REFERENCES

Adams, M.J. (1990). *Beginning to read: Thinking and learning about print*. Cambridge, MA: MIT Press.

Anderson, R.C., Hiebert, E.H., Scott, J.A., & Wilkinson, I.A.G. (1985). *Becoming a nation of readers: The report of the commission on reading*. Washington, DC: National Institute of Education.

Campbell, J.R., Hombo, C.M., & Mazzeo, J. (2000). *NAEP 1999 trends in academic progress: Three decades of student performance*. Washington, DC: U.S. Department of Education, Office of Educational Research and Improvement.

Carnevale, A.P. (1999). *Education = success: Empowering Hispanic youth and adults*. Princeton, NJ: Educational Testing Service.

Clay, M.M. (1979). *The early detection of reading difficulties* (2nd ed.). Auckland, New Zealand: Heinemann.

Coleman, J.S., Campbell, E.Q., Hobson, C.J., McPartland, J., Mood, A.M., Weinfeld, A.D., et al. (1966). *Equality of educational opportunity*. Washington, DC: U.S. Government Printing Office.

Dickinson, D.K., & Smith, M.W. (1994). Long-term effects of preschool teachers' book readings on low income children's vocabulary and story comprehension. *Reading Research Quarterly, 29*, 104–122.

Gillett, J.W., & Temple, C. (1994). *Understanding reading problems: Assessment and instruction* (4th ed.). New York: HarperCollins.

Heckelman, R.G. (1966). Using the neurological impress method. *Academic Therapy Quarterly, 1*, 235–239.

Jencks, C. (1992). *Rethinking social policy: Race, poverty, and the underclass*. Cambridge, MA: Harvard University Press.

Lapp, D., Fisher, D., Flood, J., & Moore, K. (2002). "I don't want to teach it wrong": An investigation of the role families believe they should play in the early literacy development of their children. In D.L. Schallert, C.M. Fairbanks, J. Worthy, B. Maloch, & J.V. Hoffman (Eds.), *51st yearbook of the National Reading Conference* (pp. 275–286). Oak Creek, WI: National Reading Conference.

Lapp, D., & Flood, J. (2000). *Comprehension Plus, grades 1–6*. Parsippany, NJ: Modern Curriculum Press.

Lee, J. (2002). Racial and ethnic achievement gap trends: Reversing the progress toward equity. *Educational Researcher, 31*(1), 3–12.

Lipson, M., & Wixson, K. (1991). *Assessment of reading and writing disability: An interactive approach*. New York: HarperCollins.

Loveless, T., & Diperna, P. (2000). *How well are American students learning? Focus on math achievement* (Brown Center Report, Vol. 1, No. 1). Washington, DC: Brookings Institution.

McCormick, S. (1995). *Instructing students who have literacy problems* (2nd ed.). Englewood Cliffs, NJ: Prentice-Hall.

Morrow, L.M. (1988). Retelling stories as a diagnostic tool. In S.M. Glazer, L.W. Searfoss, & L.M. Gentile (Eds.), *Reexamining reading diagnosis: New trends and procedures* (pp. 128–149). Newark, DE: International Reading Association.

Moss, B. (2002). *25 strategies for guiding readers through informational texts*. Colorado Springs, CO: PEAK-APD Press.

Murnane, R., & Levy, R.J. (1996). *Teaching the new basic skills: Principles for educating children to thrive in a changing economy*. New York: The Free Press.

National Assessment of Educational Progress. (2001). *NAEP 2001 Reading: A first look—Findings from the National Assessment of Educational Progress* (Rev. ed.). Washington, DC: U.S. Government Printing Office.

National Institute of Child Health and Human Development Early Child Care Research Network. (2002). Early child care and children's development prior to school entry: Results from the NICHD study of early child care. *American Educational Research Journal, 39*(1), 133–164.

Ogbu, J.U. (1994). Racial stratification and education in the United States: Why inequality persists. *Teachers College Record, 96*, 264–298.

Raphael, T. (1982). Question-asking strategies for children. *The Reading Teacher, 39*, 186–190.

Rosow, L. (1992). The story of Irma. *The Reading Teacher, 41*, 562–566.

Salus, P., & Flood, J. (2002). *Language: A user's guide: What we say and why*. Colorado Springs, CO: PEAK-APD Press.

Strickland, D.S., Ganske, K., & Monroe, J.K. (2002). *Supporting struggling readers and writers: Strategies for classroom intervention 3–6*. Portland, ME: Stenhouse; Newark, DE: International Reading Association.

Sulzby, E., & Teale, W.H. (1987, November). *Young children's storybook reading: Longitudinal study of parent-child interactions and children's independent functioning* (final report to the Spencer Foundation). Ann Arbor, MI: University of Michigan.

Vellutino, F.R., Scanlon, D.M., Sipay, E.R., Small, S.G., Pratt, R., Chen, R., et al. (1996). Cognitive profiles of difficult-to-remediate and readily remediated poor readers: Early intervention as a vehicle for distinguishing between cognitive and experiential deficits as basic causes of specific reading disability. *Journal of Educational Psychology, 88*, 601–638.

CHILDREN'S LITERATURE CITED

Brett, J. (1992). *Goldilocks and the three bears*. New York: Putnam.

Dr. Seuss. (1957). *Cat in the hat*. New York: Random House.

Kunhardt, D. (1940). *Pat the bunny*. New York: Golden Books.

Lobel, A. (1970). *Frog and Toad are friends*. New York: HarperCollins.

Prelutsky, J. (1999). *Dinosaur dinner: Favorite poems by Dennis Lee*. New York: Dragonfly Press.

Rowling, J.K. (1998). *Harry Potter and the sorcerer's stone*. New York: Scholastic.

Scary, R. (1997). *Cars and trucks and things that go*. New York: Golden Books.

Walker, S.M. (2002). *Fossil fish found alive*. Minneapolis, MN: Carolrhoda Books.

CHAPTER 2

The Interaction of Language, Literacy, and Identity in the Lives of Latina/o Students

Robert T. Jiménez

Saúl grabbed my attention when he told me that he was tutoring an older sister who was studying to be a nurse. I was intrigued because Saúl was receiving services in a bilingual special education classroom serving grades 4–6. Saúl attended school in a large district that served almost 30,000 pupils, of which about 7,000 were Latina/o. His particular school served 517 students, and 290 of these were Latina/o. A school district-appointed psychologist had determined that Saúl, a 12-year-old, was reading in Spanish at a beginning third-grade level and described his reading as "weak and deficient." Ironically, Saúl explained that he was helping his 20-year-old sister to relearn the Spanish language, a language she no longer felt comfortable using:

> Como mi hermana, le explico, así como palabras en español. Es porque estaba tomando una clase de español. Ya se le olvidó casi todo el español pero, ya, ya se lo sabe más. Cuando tenía tarea de español, le decía las palabras, que significaban. Yo, y mi papá, le decíamos. [Like my sister, I explain to her, like words in Spanish. It's because she was taking a Spanish class. She has already forgotten almost all of her Spanish but now, now she knows a little more. When she has Spanish homework I tell her the words, what they mean. I and my father, we tell (this) to her.]

Although unique, Saúl's story parallels that of other students I got to know while conducting a study of the biliterate development of intermediate-grade Latina/o students in the midwestern United States. These other students, like Saúl, reported using

Adapted from Jiménez, R.T. (2001). "It's a difference that changes us": An alternative view of the language and literacy learning needs of Latina/o students. *The Reading Teacher, 54,* 736–742.

Spanish and English both orally and in writing to accomplish what I considered to be sophisticated and worthwhile objectives.

Over the course of one school year, I observed, taught, and interviewed students in four bilingual education classrooms, one of which was a bilingual special education classroom. As in the case of Saúl, I discovered that the students I was interviewing often responded to my questions in ways that I had not anticipated. In fact, they often described participating in literacy activities that I would not have predicted. Researchers, educators, and policymakers, on the other hand, often depict students like Saúl as passive recipients of their instruction (Snow, Burns, & Griffin, 1998). Factors such as students' language proficiency, their class backgrounds, and/or their ethnic/racial heritage are frequently cited as reasons for their low academic achievement (August & Hakuta, 1997).

As a result, educators often ask the question of what can be done to better promote the school literacy development of Latina/o students, rather than the equally compelling question, How is literacy already meaningful to these same students? Although the former question is not irrelevant, it assumes that neither the students themselves nor their families will be the major determinants of whether and how this literacy development occurs. Saúl's revelation encouraged me to consider the possibility of multiple literacies: the idea that literacy can take on forms other than those typically expected in schools. Guerra (1998), for example, documents the ways that adult Mexican immigrants creatively use oral language and engage in writing letters and personal autobiographies. I concluded that the literacy promoted by U.S. schooling may not always be the literacy desired or needed by students from culturally and linguistically diverse communities. Saúl's interview inspired me to imagine a literacy curriculum or program that would envision or place Saúl, a student diagnosed as having learning disabilities, in the position of tutor to a college student.

In this chapter, I make a case that one of the reasons that schools are not as successful with the literacy development of Latina/o students is that school literacy, whether it be in Spanish or English, envisions forms of literacy that some students do not recognize. In other words, many Latina/o students want and need to develop both their Spanish and English literacies, but they need to accomplish tasks for which typical school curricula and instructional activities fail to prepare them. Students from recent immigrant backgrounds or working-class families may be among those who find school literacy least relevant to their needs. The problem faced by educators—namely, low academic achievement for many Latina/o students—is not due to these students' motivation nor to their ethno-linguistic backgrounds, but should instead be attributed to a lack of information concerning who students are and what they want and need to accomplish through literacy.

On the other hand, many of the assumptions made concerning the literacy learning needs of Latina/o students, as well as the instructional methods employed to supply those needs, are often inadvertently alienating. This alienation results, at least in part, because of the disconnection between school-based literacy and the realities of students' lives. These realities include tasks not envisioned in curriculum materials that are grounded in mainstream assumptions and practices. In this chapter, I will explore what some of these alternative literacies might look like by asking Latina/o students to describe their lives, their involvement with literacy, and the various roles that they themselves play in both learning and teaching these forms of literacy. A goal of my work, then, was to identify and describe literacy practices familiar to many working-class Latina/o students, practices that to them are, quite possibly, every bit as important and meaningful as is the storybook reading and personal writing of the type so familiar to mainstream educators. I determined that a good place to start was with what the students had to say concerning who they were.

The Interaction of Language and Identity

A frequent source of confusion for mainstream educators concerning Latina/o students stems from a failure to recognize the high level of diversity within the group. For example, a recurring question concerns how best to refer to Latina/o students. Typically, scholars encourage as much specificity as possible (Darder, Torres, & Gutiérrez, 1997). In other words, if the student is from Guatemala or from Nicaragua, he or she should be recognized as being of Guatemalan or Nicaraguan origin. Students, however, are frequently found in more complex settings, settings in which various communities are represented. For example, one might have in the same classroom students from Puerto Rican, Mexican, and Central American backgrounds (see Nieto [1992] and Giménez [1997] for more in-depth discussions of this issue). Furthermore, one's current geographical location, generational status, political awareness, and social class can all influence self-identification. For example, many individuals of Mexican origin living in the Southwest who are second, third, or fourth generation consider themselves Chicano. However, umbrella terms such as *Latina/o* (although used in this chapter for lack of a better alternative) can obscure the evolving and ever-changing reality of students' identities. Anzaldúa (1999) insightfully critiques the shortcomings of these umbrella designations, as well as those based on national origin, primarily because all of them fail to account for the complex and multifaceted identities that many Latina/o students bring with them into school. In other words, while the terms *Latina* and *Latino* are useful as a starting point, they need to be clarified and made more specific when referring to a particular individual.

All the students who participated in this research project were first- or second-generation immigrants who lived in the midwestern United States. Of the approximately 85 students, 30 had been born in the continental United States, 1 on the island of Puerto Rico, and the remaining 54 in Mexico. None of their parents had been born in the United States. Even though they themselves are immigrants, their experiences span a range from having spent most of their lives in the United States to being very recent arrivals. For example, the students I met during this project averaged 6.6 years of residence in the United States, but some reported having spent 12 years in the country and some 1 year or less. Their ages ranged from 9 to 12.

The combination of the aforementioned facts makes these students somewhat different from their parents and quite a bit distinct in comparison to mainstream students of European American origin. Their specific identities show influences from their experiences in the United States and what they consider to be their countries of origin.

Ferdman (1990) has claimed that identity is rooted in one's membership in specific ethno-cultural groups and that this membership has consequences for "becoming and being literate" (p. 182). This fundamental aspect of one's identity, ignored so often in classrooms as being too incendiary and too volatile a subject for open class discussion, at the same time has a huge influence on the types of schooling available to students, their later educational opportunities, and even their career possibilities. These contradictions are understood well by many students, and for this reason Ferdman encourages educators to actively recognize students' ethnicity. Ethnicity, however, is in itself a highly complex domain that involves, among other factors, students' biculturalism, various degrees of biracialism, and at times biethnicity. In other words, ethnicity encompasses a vast domain of potential influences and is much greater than the sum of any collection of parts. Ferdman's insight also can be extended to recognition of students' evolving sense of identity.

The importance of identity and its influence on students' under-standing of—and stance toward—literacy was brought home to me in a very concrete manner when I asked Petra, a fourth-grade student in a general bilingual classroom, how reading in English was different from reading in Spanish. I did not anticipate that she would discuss her identity with me. Her comments, however, are revealing in terms of the importance she placed on the relationship of identity to literate development:

> Pues, como yo soy, yo nací aquí, y soy de padres mexicanos, era difícil para mi aprender el inglés. Es una diferencia que nos cambia porque en in-glés hay palabras que uno no entiende, y en español, como yo soy [de habla] española, son más así las en español que en inglés. [Well, since I am, I was born here, and I am from Mexican parents, it was difficult for me to learn English. It's a difference that changes us, because in English there are words that one does not understand, and in Spanish, well, since I am (a) Spanish (speaker) there are more like that in Spanish than in English.]

Of interest to me was her comment that she was born in the United States but that her parents were Mexicans. This combination of events, she explained, is a "difference that changes us." Petra used this understanding of her unique identity as cause for explaining why there were so many words in both English and Spanish that she did not know. This is a common struggle faced by many bilingual Latina/o students (Jiménez, García, & Pearson, 1996). I found it fascinating that she was able to verbalize in such a specific manner how her iden-tity influenced her literacy development. Perhaps most interesting is the connection she established between identity and language. I was espe-cially intrigued that she seemed to have an incipient sense of an iden-tity different from those of both her parents and her mainstream counterparts.

How we use language, our dialect, the range of our vocabulary, and the content of our speech are but a few of the ways we define our-selves and others. Educators' failure to recognize students' ethnicity has been theorized to have negative consequences for student achievement because, in essence, this failure is a refusal to accept the students for who they are (Delpit, 1995; Diller, 1999; Ladson-Billings, 1994). It seems reasonable to assume that active recognition of students' more complex identities might facilitate their interaction with literacy.

In the next section, I touch on a few of the distinctive ways that the participating students in my study used language.

Recognizing and Affirming Students' Creative Use of Language

The fact that many Latina/o students are bilingual to varying degrees is a source of constant confusion for many educators who are socialized to view English monolingualism as the norm. All the students involved in this project, with only one exception, indicated that Spanish had been their first language. Because their school district had been a pioneer in the field of bilingual education and had actively advocated native-language instruction, students averaged 4.2 years in a bilingual class-room. Almost 200 of the approximately 517 Latina/o students enrolled in the participating school were receiving bilingual education services at the time of the study.

Even so, according to Hakuta (1986) and Crawford (1995), the frequent use of two languages strikes many mainstream U.S. residents as odd, perhaps schizophrenic, and even a bit un-American. This atti-tude persists despite the fact that at least 50% of the world's population may be bilingual (Baker, 1996). But few things in life are as personal as the content and the manner of our speech. One need only reflect on the last time someone pointed out a grammatical error or nonstan-dard linguistic feature in our own speech to be reminded of this truth. Consider the following excerpt from a story retelling narrated by Lito, a student in a fourth-grade general bilingual classroom, after he read the story *Nuestra Señora de Guadalupe (The Virgin of Guadalupe)* (1980) by Tomie dePaola:

> Um, que está...la virgencita le,um, la virgencita told the...la virgencita le dijo al hombre que...um um he could go to the side to get some flowers for he could be on the...and um...she says go to the other side...she says, váyate para el otro lado, y um llevaron las flores y véte and, y, he said okay and he left, dice he went to the village and showed the...the roses, flowers. [Then] she disappeared.... [Um, that there is, the little Virgin (told) him, um the little Virgin told the...The little Virgin told the man that...um, um, he could go to the side to get some flowers for he could on the...and um...she says go to the other side...she says you go to the other side and um, they carried the flowers and go and, and, he said okay and he left, it says he went to the village and showed the roses, flowers. (Then) she disappeared....]

Lito's retelling includes many of the key features of the story. Through the use of his background knowledge and the information found in the text, he was able to demonstrate comprehension of the story. However, because of his frequent code-switching between languages (Zentella, 1981), his account might be interpreted by some as an indication of a failure to become proficient in either Spanish or English. Although such an interpretation is plausible, it overlooks the fact that Lito includes almost the same information in both languages. In other words, he doesn't simply switch between languages because of a lack of vocabulary, nor does he simply translate. Instead, he reiterates some of what he considered to be important information in both Spanish and English. In fact, he appears to have switched into Spanish for the purpose of quoting textual information. (The use of code-switching to quote another is described by McClure [1981].) The book was written in Spanish, and Lito's retelling reflects this fact. Lito's ability to create a coherent account using two languages rather than just one, often within the same utterance, is an indication that he not only determined that his interviewer was bilingual but also that he appreciated the opportunity to demonstrate this dual language proficiency. This was something I never observed him doing when interacting with monolingual English speakers.

Baker (1996) likens the bilingual person to an athlete trained to both run and swim. He contends that it would be unfair and misleading to compare such an athlete with another who focused all of his or her training solely on swimming. Likewise, bilingual students should be recognized as having dual language abilities and viewed in that light rather than compared only to Spanish or English monolingual students. In the case of Laura, who is discussed in the next section, I explore some of the specific ways the participating students reported using literacy.

Latina/o Students Explain Their Language and Literacy Needs

I began this chapter with a brief glimpse at what was a somewhat unusual and unexpected use of language and literacy on the part of one student. More commonly, Latina/o students who are recent immigrants or the children of immigrants engage in a number of language and literacy transactions that are complex, demanding, and even stressful. Perhaps the most common of these transactions places the student in the role of language broker (McQuillan & Tse, 1995; Valdés, 1996). The language broker translates but often also interprets—and serves as a bridge between—individuals who are limited to a monolingual world in either Spanish or English. Laura briefly explained her job with respect to language brokering:

> Como por ejemplo cuando voy a la tienda y voy con mi tía y ella no sabe como decirle y yo debo...yo debo de decirle, y lo que me dice mi tía, le digo...le digo a la señora...mi tía me dice una cosa que le diga...yo se la digo y...y...diciendo lo que me diga la señora, se lo digo a mi tía. [Like for example I go to the store and I go with my aunt and she doesn't know how to speak to him/her and I have to, I have to say it to him/her and what my aunt says to me, I say it, I say it to the lady...my aunt says something to me that I say...I say it to her and...and saying whatever the lady says, I say it to my aunt.]

One can easily imagine the rapid pace of such a transaction, the need to satisfy the English speaker unaccustomed to accommodating speakers of other languages, and the importance of accurately relaying the message to both parties. Some of my Latina/o university students have conveyed to me their occasional discomfort in similar situations and how language brokering reversed some of the traditional roles of parent and child. Furthermore, they described how they were often asked to perform this function as intermediaries between English monolingual educators and Spanish monolingual classmates at school because no bilingual personnel were employed.

For Laura, oral language was the focus, but at other times students explained that the role of language broker extended to the translation of documents such as bills and other complex texts. For example, Gil described assisting his parents when I asked him the question, "What is reading?" I had expected to hear him describe the sorts of literacy that students are asked to engage in at school. Instead, he explained,

> Es muy importante...tienen algo que está en el libro y si, este, no sé leer, pues, ¿cómo le voy a entender...? Y cuando te dan como así...algo que tienes que pagar...y no tienen números y solamente así como en letras...y no vas a saber que vas a pagar. [It's very important...they have something that is in the book and if, uh, I don't know how to read, well, how am I going to understand it...? And when they give you something like that...something that you have to pay...and it doesn't have numbers and it only has it like that in letters...and you are not going to know what you are going to pay.]

Tremendous responsibility had been placed on the shoulders of this 9-year-old boy, whose parents, and perhaps other adult family members as well, depended on him to assist them with crucial transactions. Failure at such a task has far greater consequences than failure to accurately decode a fictional account of the type that constitutes much of what students are presented with in schools. Yet, instruction designed to facilitate Latina/o students' skills as language brokers is rare. Finding ways to give students credit for these skills could provide them with new insight and motivation to acquire higher levels of literacy. Literacy curricula and instructional methods that are created, modified, or otherwise structured so as to affirm the unique identities of these students would be an exciting educational innovation.

In this last section, I briefly discuss one student's account of the instruction he imparted to a younger brother. The majority of the students I interviewed related similar information concerning their younger siblings.

Seeing Latina/o Students as Reading Teachers

Perhaps the least surprising uses of literacy on the part of the participating students were their reports of teaching younger siblings. Although such a use of literacy is not unexpected and might be found in the homes of students from just about any ethnic background, these students reported using an instructional method very much like that described by Eve Gregory (1996), who described the literacy learning of Asian immigrant students to Great Britain. In her book, Gregory provides multiple examples of how immigrant students in London insist on first hearing words, then asking for these words to be repeated, and finally repeating the words themselves. Such an approach appears to be associated with traditional instructional methods in many non-Western cultures. Christopher described his interaction with his 6-year-old brother in ways that Gregory would probably regard as familiar:

Interviewer: How is José Luis doing in school?

Christopher: Not too good. He doesn't know how to do his homework. I'm teaching him how and I read it. I tell him to read a book, and then he reads it, and then I read it again.

Several other students who participated in this research project reported similar types of interactions with their younger siblings. Gregory encourages teachers to recognize these somewhat different approaches to text. Further, she explains that a failure to understand these distinct approaches can leave parents and others who care for the children without a firm understanding of how to help their children succeed with school literacy. In her words, the school curriculum and instructional approach "leave them [the parents] floundering" (p. 44).

In the preceding sections of this chapter, participating students shared their understanding of identity, language, and uses of literacy. It seems as though there is much more to learn concerning how these three domains interact, combine, and influence one another. In the next section, three conclusions concerning instructional applications will be presented.

Instructional Recommendations

Freire and Macedo (1987) assert that educators have the duty to provide students with "the right to express their thoughts, the[ir] right to speak, which corresponds to the educators [sic] duty to listen to them" (p. 40). The student voices presented in this chapter, when taken in combination, present a different way of thinking concerning literacy instruction and development. This information was shared by Latina/o students for the benefit of those interested in their literacy development. The instructional recommendations presented here were designed to facilitate and promote students' multiple literacies.

The first recommendation is that students should be recognized for who they are on their own terms. At one level, this means acknowledging their specific backgrounds and national origins, but at another level it means recognizing that they are "both and" rather than "neither nor." Some of these students may be left with the feeling that the attainment of a full command of both Spanish and English literacy is an insurmountable task because of who they are and what they have experienced. Petra's concern with encountering lots of unknown vocabulary is a case in point. Making students aware of both the challenges as well as the special advantages of bilingualism is one potentially productive approach (Jiménez, 1997). At a deeper level, this recognition includes an understanding that terms such as *bilingualism, biculturalism,* and *ethnicity*—all important facets of these students' identities—are abstractions and umbrella terms, useful at times but potentially mis-leading if used uncritically to label and categorize rather than as start-ing points for gaining insight into students' complex identities.

Petra's awareness that there are many words in English that are not part of her vocabulary and Lito's creative use of two languages to comprehend text are examples of practices that many monolingual English speakers would interpret as problematic. Such language prac-tices need to be identified and reinterpreted in an intellectually thoughtful manner. For example, Lito's hybrid language practices can be understood as a reflection of the richness and enhanced commu-nicative abilities available to the bilingual individual. These ways of us-ing language are also indications of broader patterns of community practices. The creation of an inventory of publicly displayed texts found within local businesses, churches, and the surrounding community could be used to stimulate the thinking and perceptions of educators responsible for the literacy instruction of Latina/o students.

Second, it is clear from the interviews that these students should be viewed as individuals who want and need to read and write. Reading and writing are a part of their lives in indispensable ways. They need it to help their parents and extended family members, they need it to help their younger siblings, and they need it to fully develop their own iden-tities. In fact, some of the literacy engagements they report may be much more sophisticated than that expected in school (McQuillan & Tse, 1995). Recognition of these realities is a starting point for begin-ning productive conversations with Latina/o students concerning their own literacy learning. Because no two students are identical, it may be necessary to find out how literacy is used in each community, in each student's life. Becoming aware of some of the different ways that read-ing and writing are important to students in specific classrooms requires dialogue, a genuine two-way flow of information. Finding time to lis-ten to students, providing them with time to interact with one another, and opening dialogue with members of students' communities can pro-vide educators with insights that counteract negative portrayals of Latina/o students that are so pervasive in our larger culture. Cummins (1986), in his discussion of interactive empowerment theory for stu-dents from language minority communities, argues that students will succeed to the extent that community participation is encouraged as an integral component of their education.

With some effort, the language and literacy activities employed successfully by struggling students outside of school can be identified and brought into the classroom. For example, the juxtaposition of Saúl's tutoring of his older sister and the difficulties he experienced with literacy in school is a powerful stimulus for considering alternative scenarios. Students themselves can be recruited to record their encounters with text in both their languages. They can also bring in examples of when and how spoken language is employed in their daily activities. Small notepads could be used to record oral language, and disposable cameras could capture examples of publicly displayed texts. This information can then form the basis for discussions that compare and contrast these uses of language and literacy with those found within the school. Students' awareness of these differences could then be used to discuss how school-based literacy is useful within their daily lives. Students might also suggest ways to expand the curriculum beyond mainstream, monolingual language and literacy practices. Teachers from mainstream backgrounds or from a higher socioeconomic status would also have a chance to learn from their students in ways that are respectful and intellectually challenging.

The third recommendation is that students should be encouraged to fully develop those literacies that traditionally have not been a part of the school curriculum. For the students involved in my research project, that meant serving as language brokers of both oral and written text and as teachers of their siblings. These activities depend on the students' bicultural and bilingual development. Depriving students of these abilities by insisting on monolingual/monocultural programs of forced assimilation does fundamental damage to their sense of self and their identity as members of the Latina/o community.

One way to implement this recommendation would be to analyze the school curriculum and determine the extent to which the activities, goals, and textual selections match the lived experiences of the students. How relevant are these components to the students' interactions with two languages, both in their oral and written forms? Information gathered from the first and second recommendations can be used to make these determinations. Finally, students themselves can contribute to curriculum design by discussing how well the school curriculum meets their language and literacy needs. In other words, they ought to visually display what it is they need to do with language and literacy next to that of the official school curriculum. For example, students like Christopher, who are expected by their families to play important roles in teaching literacy to younger siblings, ought to receive information that allows them to engage in these activities successfully.

Conclusion

Finding ways to adequately convey to mainstream individuals how important knowledge of both Spanish and English is to many Latina/os is difficult. Marc Anthony, the Puerto Rican salsa musician, recently compared the attachment to both languages to what a parent of two children feels. To abandon one for the other is at best undesirable and at worst unthinkable. Hopefully our schools and other societal institutions will begin to understand, value, and actively promote this crucial facet of Latina/o identity.

REFERENCES

Anzaldúa, G. (1999, October). *Nos/otros: "Us" vs. "them," (des) conocimientos y compromisos*. Paper presented at the Territories and Boundaries, Geographies of Latinidad conference, University of Illinois at Urbana-Champaign.

August, D., & Hakuta, K. (1997). *Improving schooling for language-minority children*. Washington, DC: National Academy Press.

Baker, C. (1996). *Foundations of bilingual education and bilingualism*. Philadelphia, PA: Multilingual Matters.

Crawford, J. (1995). *Bilingual education: History, politics, theory, and practice*. Los Angeles, CA: Bilingual Educational Services.

Cummins, J. (1986). Empowering minority students: A framework for intervention. *Harvard Educational Review*, *56*(1), 18–36.

Darder, A., Torres, R.D., & Gutiérrez, H. (1997). *Latinos and education: A critical reader*. New York: Routledge.

Delpit, L. (1995). *Other people's children: Cultural conflict in the classroom*. New York: New Press.

Diller, D. (1999). Opening the dialogue: Using culture as a tool in teaching young African American children. *The Reading Teacher*, *52*, 820–828.

Ferdman, B. (1990). Literacy and cultural identity. *Harvard Educational Review*, *60*(2), 181–204.

Freire, P., & Macedo, D. (1987). *Literacy: Reading the word and the world*. South Hadley, MA: Bergin & Garvey.

Giménez, M.E. (1997). Latino/"Hispanic": Who needs a name? The case against a standardized terminology. In A. Darder, R.D. Torres, & H. Gutiérrez (Eds.), *Latinos and education: A critical reader* (pp. 224–238). New York: Routledge.

Gregory, E. (1996). *Making sense of a new world: Learning to read in a second language*. London: Paul Chapman.

Guerra, J.C. (1998). *Close to home: Oral and literate practices in a transnational Mexicano community*. New York: Teachers College Press.

Hakuta, K. (1986). *Mirror of language: The debate on bilingualism*. New York: Basic Books.

Jiménez, R.T. (1997). The strategic reading abilities and potential of five low-literacy Latina/o readers in middle school. *Reading Research Quarterly*, *32*, 224–243.

Jiménez, R.T., García, G.E., & Pearson, P.D. (1996). The reading strategies of Latina/o students who are successful English readers: Opportunities and obstacles. *Reading Research Quarterly*, *31*, 90–112.

Ladson-Billings, G. (1994). *The dreamkeepers: Successful teachers of African American children*. San Francisco: Jossey-Bass.

McClure, E. (1981). Formal and functional aspects of codeswitched discourse of bilingual children. In R.P. Durán (Ed.), *Latino language and communicative behavior* (pp. 69–94). Norwood, NJ: Ablex.

McQuillan, J., & Tse. L. (1995). Child language brokering in linguistic minority communities: Effects on cultural interaction, cognition, and literacy. *Language and Education*, *9*(3), 195–215.

Nieto, S. (1992). *Affirming diversity: The sociopolitical context of multicultural education*. White Plains, NY: Longman.

Snow, C., Burns, M.S., & Griffin, P. (1998). *Preventing reading difficulties in young children*. Washington, DC: National Academy Press.

Valdés, G. (1996). *Con respeto: Bridging the distances between culturally diverse families and schools*. New York: Teachers College Press.

Zentella, A.C. (1981). Language variety among Puerto Ricans. In C.A. Ferguson & S.B. Heath (Eds.), *Language in the USA* (pp. 218–238). Cambridge, UK: Cambridge University Press.

CHILDREN'S LITERATURE CITED

dePaola, T. (1980). *Nuestra Señora de Guadalupe*. New York: Holiday House.

Supporting Students in Grades 3 and Beyond as They Learn to Read

CHAPTER 3

Stepping Into Character(s): Using Readers Theatre With Bilingual Fourth Graders

Nancy L. Roser, Laura A. May, Miriam Martinez, Susan Keehn, Janis M. Harmon, and Sharon O'Neal

Raúl:	Mi madre dice que a veces la gente no se puede ir a México porque son ciudadanos allí. [My mom says sometimes people can't go to Mexico because they are citizens there.]
Teacher:	Funny, because citizens of the U.S. can go.
Raúl:	Porque Ud. tiene papeles y puede regresar. [Because you have papers and can come back.]
Yesenia:	That's what I can't do. I can't go to Mexico because I don't have no papers.
Carla:	Siente triste porque sus amigos están allí. [He (Jorge) feels sad because his friends are there.]
Lisa:	Let's write what he wants.
Ricardo:	To be a Chicano.

The 21 fourth graders in Laura May's bilingual classroom in Texas were reading and talking about the experiences of Jorge, an immigrant child from *My Name Is Jorge on Both Sides of the River* (Medina, 1999). Through choral readings and rereadings, followed by thoughtful talk, Laura was leading her students toward deeper understandings of Jorge as a literary character—with traits, needs, feelings, ideas, and goals. The book's poems, written in English and Spanish, reflect the daily experiences and trials of a child whose Spanish-speaking family emigrates from Mexico to the United States. Laura's class was learning to orally interpret Jorge's experiences—experiences that many of them shared—in a kind of biliterate binationalism.

All of us (teacher-researchers and university researchers) hypothesized that when students "step into the shoes" of characters, actually trying on characters' traits, predicaments, and goals, the students may register gains in language proficiency, literary understanding, and reading level. Laura's classroom was one part of a larger, collaborative research effort exploring children's understanding of character across several school sites and multiple grade levels. Our intent was to give her students an opportunity to become fluent, flexible, and appreciative readers of texts that featured characters who shared some of their own experiences.

So, with funds from a small grant ($750), we stocked the classroom with culturally relevant picture books and chapter books in English and Spanish, as well as Readers Theatre scripts based on those books. We wanted to make sure that each child, regardless of language proficiency or reading level, would have repeated opportunities to "try on" language—to listen to and read books; to talk over the characters and their dilemmas; and, finally, to read and reread the scripts, interpreting characters' thoughts, feelings, and actions with their voices. At the end of the school year, we inspected the children's pretest and posttest scores for shifts in reading level and rate, and we interviewed them to determine their understanding of the concept of character. We also compared the children in Laura's classroom with those in the bilingual classroom next door. This chapter summarizes what we learned.

Learning From Other Studies

To design our study, it seemed important to learn from at least three strands of related research. First, we needed to be knowledgeable about the influences of the use of culturally relevant children's literature in bilingual and English as a Second Language (ESL) classes; second, we needed to understand the effects of meaningful practice (such as rehearsal for a Readers Theatre performance) on language and literacy learning; and third, we needed to learn more about the value of character discussions as one key for helping children make sense of the deeper meanings of narratives.

Incorporating Culturally Relevant Literature
We looked first to researchers who have examined the effects of culturally relevant literature on children's learning (see, for example, Au,

1998; García, 2000). Educators such as Bishop (1992), Harris (1992), and Yokota (1993) argue persuasively that if the literacy achievement of children from diverse cultures is to be improved, then the children must find themselves within the literature they read. A number of researchers have documented that children of color seek out and respond more deeply to literature that features characters of the same ethnicity (e.g., McGinley & Kamberelis, 1996; Smith, 1995). There is also evidence that language learners participate more fully in discussion and comprehend better when they are able to relate texts to their personal lives (Droop & Verhoeven, 1998; Thornburg, 1993)—as long as the texts themselves are worthwhile. Researchers such as Moll (1988, 1992) have shown that children acquiring a language not only need access to talk and to manageable texts, but also opportunities to bring what they know to purpose-filled uses within social contexts. There is much to learn about the supports and strategies that bilingual students require and use (Jiménez, García, & Pearson, 1996; see also chapter 2 in this book). For example, we still do not understand fully the residual effects of literacy teaching on students' efforts to balance two or more cultures (García, 2000).

Providing for Fluency Through Readers Theatre

To understand more about fluent reading, we looked first to researchers who have inspected the critical effects of practice on achieving oral reading fluency (Allington, 1983; Dowhower, 1987, 1994; Hoffman, 1987; Rashotte & Torgesen, 1985). Although investigators may define fluency somewhat differently (Strecker, Roser, & Martinez, 1998), fluency seems to be most often characterized as reading with accuracy, adequate rate, and (for oral reading, at least) prosody—or the musicality that includes appropriate stress, pitch, and juncture (National Institute of Child Health and Human Development, 2000; Strecker et al., 1998). However, since Samuels's (1979) seminal work on the effect of practice on rapid and automatic word recognition (or automaticity), even the best-intentioned teachers and researchers have sometimes interpreted the route to fluency as being repetition or repeated readings of the same passages until some standard of rate and accuracy is achieved (Koskinen & Blum, 1986).

As a way of avoiding practice that may not be as purposeful, interesting, or engaging as effective teachers demand (Guthrie et al., 1995), we looked toward the techniques associated with Readers

Theatre for help with making practice more meaningful for bilingual learners (Martinez, Roser, & Strecker, 1998/1999). Readers Theatre is an interpretive reading activity in which readers use their voices to bring characters to life. Unlike conventional drama, Readers' Theatre requires no sets, costumes, props, or memorization. Instead, it is a form of what Worthy and Broaddus (2002) call performance reading. Performance reading, according to the researchers, "encourages students to read at a rate appropriate to the particular text rather than to simply read faster" (p. 337).

And, unlike repeated readings that focus on how rapidly and accurately students move through a passage, Readers Theatre focuses on how meaningfully a text is interpreted orally. In an earlier pilot study, after only a few weeks with Readers Theatre scripts, we had observed second graders making significant gains in fluency, as well as becoming enthusiastic participants in both reading practice and performance (Martinez et al., 1998/1999). We anticipated that practicing for live performances with Readers Theatre might give purpose (and motivation) for Laura's bilingual fourth graders to read stories and chapters more than once. We wondered whether students learning to read better in two languages could be effectively boosted in ways that made more sense to them.

Understanding Characters as a Gateway to Understanding Stories

As bilingual children learn to read ever more fluently in both their first and second languages, it is essential that they remain eager, comprehending readers. It is yet unclear whether improved comprehension is a precursor or a by-product of fluent reading. That is, does a fluent reading of a text reflect a deep understanding, or does reading fluently directly contribute to understanding—or both? Regardless, we were interested in helping children achieve both, and Readers Theatre, because of its focus on bringing characters to life, seemed to be an especially promising instructional strategy for achieving both fluency and deep comprehension.

Langer (1995) proposes that literary meaning making involves, among other things, knowing how to "step into" and "move through" story worlds (pp. 16–17). We have argued elsewhere that it is when readers have deep understanding and identification with story characters that they are best able to negotiate the intricacies of plot (Martinez, Keehn, Roser, Harmon, & O'Neal, 2002). Cullinan and Galda (1998) also describe characters as the driving force of stories, and Emery (1996) has observed that "character states, such as their desires, feelings, thoughts, and beliefs, are the glue that [binds] the story together" (p. 534).

A number of studies suggest that even young children focus on characters in stories. For example, Wollman-Bonilla and Werchadlo (1995) suggest that nearly one quarter of first graders' literary responses in journals focuses on understanding characters. Hancock (1993) found that sixth graders, too, wrote extensively about characters in their journals, expressing empathy; offering advice; making judgments; and attempting to understand characters' feelings, thoughts, and motives. Lehr (1991) found that when children talked at length about characters and their internal motivations, their talk frequently became the pathway through which they were able to discuss story themes. We hoped that the bilingual fourth graders in this investigation would be able to use the inspection of character as an entree to narrative and literary meaning making. We intended to introduce characters worth knowing and then to work beside students to explore the feelings, beliefs, and motivations of those characters as a way of plumbing story depths. All this would lead to students' interpreting their understandings for the benefit of others through well-rehearsed performance reading.

The Context

Laura's classroom was in an urban Title I school during the 2000–2001 school year. Approximately 92% of the school's 750 students were considered economically disadvantaged. The school had five fourth-grade classes, two of which were designated as bilingual. Two thirds of the school's total population were Hispanic, and just over one quarter was African American. Fewer than 10% of the students were Anglo. The school had been designated "low-performing" by the Texas Education Agency three years prior to Laura's initiation of Readers Theatre, but it has since been raised to the level of "acceptable" based on an increase in test scores. In Texas, as in other states, teachers and principals are under pressure to ensure that students pass state-mandated tests in reading, writing, and math at the fourth-grade level. Students who are recent immigrants from Mexico, or who are not yet proficient in spoken English, take the test in Spanish instead of English. These students' scores are not included in a school's report. Nonetheless, the tests are administered to each child at grade level, meaning that regardless of the student's achieved reading level, the state assessment is administered at the grade level to which the child is assigned.

Both the bilingual fourth grades in Laura's school were taught by Anglo teachers who speak Spanish as a second language and who have had three or four years of teaching experience. The fourth graders were assigned to the two bilingual classrooms by their third-grade teachers, who worked together to achieve an even distribution of ability levels and language proficiency. Each bilingual fourth grade (Laura's, as well as Stephen's, the class next door) had 21 students at the beginning of the year. All the bilingual students came from homes with Spanish as the primary language, and all the children's parents had been born in Mexico. Five of Laura's students were recent immigrants, and almost all their initial classroom work was accomplished in Spanish. Twelve students had been in the United States since second grade, and one student had enrolled in a U.S. school at the beginning of third grade. In addition to Hispanic students, Stephen had two African American children in his classroom who spoke only English at the beginning of the school year.

In both fourth grades, some students arrived after the preassessments, and others left before the postassessments. Because of student mobility, by the end of the school year complete records were available for 17 of Laura's students and for 19 of Stephen's. Table 3.1 summarizes the pretest levels in English and Spanish for those children for whom complete data were available at the end of the study. Note that some children were assessed in two languages, but others only in Spanish.

TABLE 3.1

FOURTH GRADERS' ENTRY READING LEVELS IN ENGLISH AND SPANISH

		Level in English Reading		Level in Spanish Reading	
	Levels	Readers Theatre class	Comparison class	Readers Theatre class	Comparison class
Number of scores at each level	pp/P	4	6	5	2
	1st	3	4	1	3
	2nd	4	3	3	2
	3rd	3	1	1	1
	4th		1	6	5
	5th			2	4
	6th				
	7th				
	Total	14	15	18	17

Even as the time for the state test grew nearer and the intensity of test preparation increased, the life of the two classrooms went on, and the doorway that connected them carried the voices of teachers and students from room to room. Laura and Stephen shared similar teaching philosophies. Their classroom routines for language arts differed somewhat, however. Although each had a two-hour block designated for language arts, and both placed students into homogeneous groups based on their reading levels, in Stephen's classroom the groups rotated among activities. These activities included (a) free read or DEAR time; (b) practice with standardized test preparation; (c) participation in response activities (writing, crafting, filling in graphic organizers); and (d) teacher-led guided reading instruction. By contrast, Laura opened the language arts period by reading aloud in English or Spanish to the whole class from one of the culturally relevant texts (see the end of this chapter for some titles). She then led discussion and taught a minilesson aimed toward helping her students make meanings—both plot centered (monitoring for understanding) and literary (reaching for ideas, images, and feelings). Next, she assigned a text and its accompanying Readers Theatre script to one of her five homogeneous reading groups (a group for whom the script would be at an independent or instructional level). All students then worked in their groups to rehearse their own Readers Theatre scripts. The second hour of her language arts block was designed to provide a variety of whole-group activities including free read or DEAR time, writing activities, word work, and standardized test preparation. At the end of each two-hour block, one of the five groups performed a script its members had been rehearsing for the four previous class days.

Although the same set of approximately 50 culturally relevant stories, poems, and legends were added to both classrooms, the two teachers used the texts differently (and brought in additional books). Stephen incorporated the new texts into his read-alouds and encouraged at-home reading. It was only in Laura's classroom, though, that the children were introduced to Readers Theatre and its potential for effecting literary understandings and literacy growth. One of this chapter's authors (most commonly Nancy Roser, a university researcher) worked in Laura's classroom three or four times per week during language arts, observing, taking notes, tape-recording discussions, coaching "rehearsals" of Readers Theatre scripts, clarifying English meanings for children, learning Spanish meanings from children, and planning instruction with Laura.

Getting Started With Readers Theatre

We hoped Readers Theatre would help us work toward several goals simultaneously: First, we wanted students to read texts that were fine examples of literature. Second, we wanted them to read within the range of their instructional reading levels—which, with practice, would become independent, fluent reading. Third, we wanted to ensure that time devoted to reading instruction maximized students' active participation in the actual reading of text. Fourth, we wanted to offer texts that were both relevant to and reflective of the children's lives and culture. Fifth, we wanted the instruction that accompanied the literature to focus on deep understandings of the stories rather than the (potential) artificiality of "expressive" oral reading. That is, instead of admonishing, "Make it sound like somebody is talking," we wanted to work to make certain that students had ways to understand how characters might sound in a given situation and why.

Introducing Interpretive Oral Reading

To get started, we chose shorter, more manageable poems—beginning with "Jorge" (Medina, 1999), the character who struggles with learning a new language and new customs and who struggles against prejudice. Laura's class gathered around the overhead projector as she read a projected Jorge poem aloud, and then we waited silently to see how (and whether) children would respond. After the talk about the poem, the whole class read as one voice and then in parts, offering impressions and "noticings" after each reading. Then, Laura read again, asking her students to notice how she used her voice. The students talked most frequently from "within" the poem—making conjectures about its meanings and importance—but they also talked about the way the poem sounded as Laura (or they) read:

C1:	[You] did it a little more hard each time.
Children:	[agreement]
C2:	Said like scared.
C3:	A little harder first and then softer...
C4:	...to sound like Jorge
C2:	Sounds like scared, like sad.
C5:	Then stronger.

Ricardo:	It was *you* making it sound sad.
C4:	The words are sad, so that's why you're making your voice sound sad.

Indeed, it had been Laura making it sound sad. Ricardo's realization that readers act out stories signalled his initiation into intentional literary meaning making. To prepare the poem for Readers Theatre, we had typed the poem as one might prepare a script, inserting character names beside appropriate lines to divide the poem into voices: Jorge and Mrs. Roberts, Jorge and Tim, Jorge, Juan, Christina, Julisa, and more. Figure 3.1 shows the poem in Spanish and English just as it appears in the book, with the addition of the roles we marked.

FIGURE 3.1

JORGE POEM IN SPANISH AND ENGLISH MARKED WITH CHARACTER ROLES

Me llamo Jorge		**My Name Is Jorge**	
Personajes:	*Jorge* *Niña*	*Characters:*	*Jorge* *Girl*
Jorge:	Me llamo Jorge. Sé que mi nombre es Jorge. Pero todos me llaman... 　　　　　　—Chorg.	Jorge:	My name is Jorge. I know that my name is Jorge But everyone calls me... 　　　　　　—George.
Chorg. ¡Qué feo sonido! ¡Como un estornudo!		George. What an ugly sound! Like a sneeze!	
¡CHORG!	Y lo peor de todo es que hoy en la mañana una niña me llamó,	GEORGE!	And the worst of all Is that this morning A girl called to me,
Niña:	"Chorg"	Girl:	"George"
Jorge:	Y volteé la cabeza.	Jorge:	And I turned my head.
	No quiero convertirme en un estornudo.		I don't want to turn into a sneeze!

Medina, J. (1999). *My name is Jorge on both sides of the river*, p. 6.

Medina's poems revealed not just Jorge's reactions to his mispronounced name but also his feelings of being "dumb" in his new country, his fear of tests, the loss of someone dear to him, his uncertain patriotism, and the clash of customs he experiences. Students read and reread in parts, but Laura also invited them to think about what Jorge wanted most, what he was feeling in each poem, and what kind of character/boy he seemed to be. The poems lent themselves to some sobering talk. Laura collected the children's ideas about Jorge on a language chart:

Samples of Language From Discussion of Jorge

Speaks Spanish

Mexican-American

Is a boy

Probably has black eyes/black hair

Skin is brown

Just arrived from Mexico

Shy

He's bilingual

He doesn't like to turn into a sneeze

George is a funny name

His name is Jorge, not George

He doesn't know what George means

He doesn't like the way it sounds

Jorge likes Spanish more than English

Later, Laura's minilessons would help children sort Jorge's feelings ("sad," "nervous," "scared") from his qualities ("kind," "loves his family") as well as try to understand what Jorge really wants ("people to call him Jorge," "the teacher to know that he doesn't do bad things and that he's good"). But on this first day, she was most intent on encouraging the free flow of talk—whether in English or Spanish—and finally returning to the poem to let the deepened understandings seep into the way in which the students read.

As talk subsided or focus strayed, Laura invited the class to read the poem again. Immediately after rereading, students had more ideas to share. For the first two weeks of introducing Readers Theatre, each day meant reading new poems together, talking, changing parts, and reading again. The conversation excerpt that appears at the beginning of this chapter occurred in response to the poem reprinted on the next page.

Jorge Poem by Jane Medina Marked With Readers Theatre Roles
"Yanquis/Yankees"

Jorge: Miguelito
               and Chucho
               are citizens.
               After the flag salute
               they sing,
Miguelito: "This is my country,
Chucho: land of my birth."
Jorge: I won't sing that song,
               now that I know the words.
               I look at my shoes
               and kick the carpet
               a little.

The conversations about "Yanquis/Yankees" were both thought-ful and poignant. Turns marked with an (S) were spoken in Spanish:

Teacher: It's interesting Jorge didn't want to...
C1:   Maybe his sister is Chicaña.
Teacher: What's Chicaña mean?
C2:   His parents are born in Mexico.
C3:   They come to Texas to get money.
C4 :   I feel better from the flag from here. Because I was born here, I feel closer to the American flag.
C5:   I feel confused because most of my family was born there.
C6:   I feel more comfortable with Mexico because I was born there.
C7:   I feel closer to the Mexican flag because most of my family is there.
Teacher: But you were born here?
C7:   I have heard some white people don't celebrate Christmas...[discussion about differences in celebrations of The Day of the Dead, Christmas, and Halloween in Mexico and the United States].
Teacher: So, I think that some of us feel a little bit the same way as Jorge?

C8:   (S) Because he feels closer to where he was born...

C4:   I'm different. I don't feel like Jorge because I was born here.

C5:   No.

C9:   I was born in the middle [reference to an earlier anecdote of a child born in the middle of the Rio Grande as his mother crossed from Mexico to the United States]

C10:   (S) When I'm here, I miss Mexico, and when I'm there, I miss here.

On the day following her students' discussion of a character's and their own divided national loyalties, Laura held small flags of Mexico and the United States in front of the children. She then gave each a copy of the U.S. and Mexican Pledges of Allegiance. Together, the class said both—one version in English, the other in Spanish. "Now," she asked, "what were you thinking and feeling as you said these pledges?" And after the students talked, Laura circled back to the poem "Yanquis/Yankees" to help students think more about Jorge's reticence to sing to his new country.

Besides serving as an introduction to Readers Theatre, these poems seemed to be doing more: First, they provided impetus for readers to *work out word meaning*:

C1:   What are Yankees?

C2:   The World Cup.

C3:   The favorite baseball team.

C4:   All the people in the U.S.

C5:   (S) Ms. K. has a banner that says "Yankees."

C6:   (S) *Yankees* mean citizens.

C7:   (S) All [of them] read English and Spanish.

C6:   (S) *Yankees* might mean citizens.

C8:   Miguelito and Chucho are yanquis.

C3:   [shows pictures of Yankees from newspaper]

Teacher: The New York Yankees won the World Series—just what you were saying, Silvano.

C4:   Persons. Citizens are people.

Teacher: What do we know about Jorge from this?

C9:   Miguelito and Chucho are yanquis (citizens).

Teacher: What about Jorge?

C10:   (S) [It] means two things.

Teacher: (S) I think you're right. What does it tell us?

C10:   (S) That he wants to be a citizen.

Second, the poems also seemed to encourage students to *work for literal understanding*:

C1:   How is Miguelito related to Jorge?

C2:   His friend.

Teacher: All agree?

Children: Yes.

C3:   He feels bad because his friends are citizens and he's not.

Third, the poems encouraged *inferences*:

C1:   He didn't want to make a promise to the flag of here.

Teacher: What kind of promise?

C1:   What was that...loy...

Teacher: loyal. Go ahead.

C1:   He's from over there, and he doesn't want to make a promise for here.

Finally, the poems seemed to encourage students to *speculate and problem solve*. The following conversation followed a reading of a poem titled "The Test," in which Jorge, trying to hide his tears of frustration while taking a test that is "too hard for me," senses the presence of his *abuelita* (grandmother) behind him:

C1:   He loves her and thinks of her.

C2:   He thinks Mrs. Roberts looks a lot like his abuelita.

C3:   (S) Maybe he lives with his grandmother and wants to make her proud....

C4:   (S) Maybe his grandmother died and she had been helping him on his test and now she died....

C5:   His eyes were turning black.

Teacher:	[reads appropriate part] Why?
C5:	Maybe he's trying not to cry.
C6:	Maybe he's feeling his grandmother's spirit.
C7:	Maybe he's worried he's not going to pass the test.

During these reading and poem talk sessions, the text was always in front of the students via the overhead projector. It was frequently referred to as the need for clarification arose. Thus, the first experiences with Readers Theatre occurred with the whole class and with short, eminently "talkable" poems. As the students were becoming comfortable with choral reading, with reading in parts, and with voiced interpretations, they were also divided into pairs to rehearse a previously introduced script of a Jorge poem (with two characters). Each pair then "performed" on a voluntary basis before the class. Soon after, small groups of children rehearsed poems with three or four roles. After two and one half weeks of Jorge, the class was ready to take on lengthier scripts.

Choosing Quality Texts

We chose children's books in English and Spanish that included Mexican or Mexican American protagonists, settings, or referents (see Figure 3.2 for a partial listing). For example, we used *The Bossy Gallito* by Lucía González (1994), *The Skirt* by Gary Soto (1994), *My Name Is María Isabel* by Alma Flor Ada (1993), and *Going Home* by Eve Bunting (1996). We verified the quality of the books, not just against respected review sources, but with a local expert in multicultural children's literature. We removed from the list any titles that reviewers judged to be stereotyped portrayals or less than high-quality literature. Although the students in both classrooms were predominantly first- or second-generation Americans from Mexico, we also included books from other countries in which Spanish is spoken.

Writing Readers Theatre Scripts

Each of the texts (in English and Spanish) was turned into a script for Readers Theatre. We developed guidelines for script writing that allowed little tampering with the original language. Direct quotations became character lines. We assigned important descriptions and

FIGURE 3.2

EXAMPLES OF TITLES USED FOR CULTURALLY RELEVANT READERS THEATRE SCRIPTS

The Adventures of Connie and Diego/Las aventuras de Connie y Diego (María García)
Abuela (Arthur Dorros)
The Bossy Gallito (Alma Flor Ada)
The Bossy Gallito/El gallito bossy (Lucía González)
Carlos and the Carnival/Carlos y la fería (Jan Romero Stephens)
Carlos and the Squash Plant/Carlos y la planta de calabaza (Jan Romero Stephenns)
A Chair for My Mother/Un sillón para mi mama (Vera Williams)
Chato and the Party Animals (Gary Soto)
Chato's Kitchen (Gary Soto)
Coyote: Un cuento folklórico del sudoeste de estados unidos (Gerald McDermott)
A Day's Work (Eve Bunting)
Faith and the Electric Dogs (Patrick Jennings)
Faith and the Rocket Cat (Patrick Jennings)
Friends From the Other Side/Amigos del otro lado (Gloria E. Anzaldua)
A Gift From Papá Diego (Benjamin Alire Saenz)
Going Home (Eve Bunting)
The Gold Coin (Alma Flor Ada)
The Gullywasher/El chaparron torrencial (Joyce Rossi)
Isla (Arthur Dorros)
Juan Bobo (Carmen Bernier-Grand)
La leyenda de Mexicatl/The Legend of Mexicatl (Jo Harper)
Mediopollito/Half-Chicken (Alma Flor Ada)
My Name Is Jorge on Both Sides of the River (Jane Medina)
My Name Is María Isabel (Alma Flor Ada)
The Skirt (Gary Soto)
Something Special for Me/Algo especial para mi (Vera Williams)
The Three Pigs/Los tres cerdos: Nacho, Tito, y Miguel (Bobbi Salinas)
Too Many Tamales/Qué montón de Tamales (Gary Soto)
The Upside Down Boy/El niño de cabeza (Juan Felipe Herrera)

"gluing" narrative to one or more narrator roles. When absolutely necessary, we added to the narration some key details that appeared only in the illustrations. On occasion, we shortened the narrator's portion a bit—to ensure that the script kept moving—and, of course, we made certain that the original text of the book or story was shared with the whole class before the script was assigned to any "repertory group" for rehearsal.

Over time, we found that four to six pages of script typed in a 14- to 16-point font size seemed most accessible to the students. We learned, too, that four to six roles seemed to work well, so that students did not have to wait too long for their next speaking turn. Finally, we found that using different-colored highlighters to mark the speaking parts of characters ahead of time smoothed the performance of the routines.

Forming the Groups

To decide the language of reading instruction, we relied on the children's oral English proficiency—their ability to use conversational English with peers. We next determined the students' reading levels and rates, using informal inventories and timed readings of unrehearsed text. In Laura's class, as mentioned earlier, there were five repertory groups—four that would rehearse and perform in English, and one in Spanish. (Children who could read even a limited amount in English were assigned to English language scripts.) Each of the readers in a repertory group had approximately the same instructional reading level as the rest of his or her group.

Establishing the Routines

Because there were five classroom groups or repertory companies, each day of the week began with Laura's introduction of a new narrative. Regardless of the repertory group to which a student belonged—or whether he or she would read in English or Spanish—all children gathered on the story rug to be introduced to and discuss the new story of the day. Following the story and discussion, Laura taught comprehension minilessons, many of which were designed to draw attention to understanding the nuances of characters, their relationships, and their changes. The reading, talking, and instruction were also useful in encouraging the children's eventual reading on their own.

Each day, one of the five repertory groups was given the script based on that day's story. The following day meant rehearsal of the story for that first group and the launching of the story/text for the second repertory group. After one week, the full cycle was established: Each day meant introducing a new story (or revisiting an old favorite), and each day one group was ready to perform (see Table 3.2 for an overview of the weekly cycle).

During rehearsal, Laura and one additional researcher typically circulated in the room, both monitoring and working with the groups. Our field notes are written in long columns that cover only half the page,

TABLE 3.2

THE FIVE-GROUP DAILY ROUTINE FOR READERS THEATRE

Group	Monday	Tuesday	Wednesday	Thursday	Friday
1	Introduced to new story	Rehearse	Rehearse	Rehearse	Perform for class
2	Perform for class	Introduced to new story	Rehearse	Rehearse	Rehearse
3	Rehearse	Perform for class	Introduced to new story	Rehearse	Rehearse
4	Rehearse	Rehearse	Perform for class	Introduced to new story	Rehearse
5	Rehearse	Rehearse	Rehearse	Perform for class	Introduced to new story

leaving the open space alongside to allow for more analytic writing and asides (Emerson, Fretz, & Shaw, 1995). In these notebooks, however, the open space now contains lots of sketches and doodles—of words and ideas that students requested explanations for as they worked in their groups. Our field notes hold drawings of a porch swing, a barrel, a porcupine, a plow, a tarp, an eagle, and much less representational sketches—for concepts like scattered, battered, tinsel, and unwind.

The students rehearsed approximately 20 minutes each day (days 1–3), rotating scripts so that each student practiced each part as he or she readied for performance. On the day prior to performance (the fourth day of the rehearsal sequence), students decided on the parts they would play in the performance reading. On the fifth day, on stools or chairs and with an audience at their feet, holding their scripts tightly and in a way not to block their faces, the group performed the script for their peers and occasional invited guests. Each Readers Theatre troupe performance took the final 10–15 minutes of the language arts block. In the remaining minutes before lunch, the class was given the opportunity to respond to the script and performance.

Minilessons Focused on Character

As described earlier, it was during the introduction of the story, its reading, and the follow-up discussion that students were purposefully led into awareness of story characters. Laura's instruction explored many dimensions of character study—ranging from what the story characters wanted and needed, to how others saw those characters, to what characters revealed by their own talk and actions, to the ways in which characters changed. Almost daily, children talked about what made the characters compelling and complicated. Of course, not all characters were complex, and not all readers identified with all characters, but it was through character that the children and Laura made meanings together. In a carry-over to writing, students created their own characters, wrote descriptions, decided on characters' motivations, and wrote stories from different characters' points of view.

What We Learned

Although we hoped these fourth graders would find satisfaction and enjoyment in meeting others like themselves in books, for this investigation we also anticipated some additional gains: that children would produce increasingly fluid (fluent) interpretations, and that reading level, language proficiency, literary awareness, and character understanding might increase. In a pilot test of Readers Theatre during the previous spring in Laura's class, after only seven weeks students had made measurable gains in reading level (as determined from an informal reading inventory) as well as in their rate of reading unrehearsed material. We anticipated that by adding time, materials, and focused instruction to Readers Theatre, we could support reading gains.

Gains in Reading Level

Informal reading inventories were used to determine student reading levels in both English and Spanish for both classes at the beginning and end of the school year. The Flynt-Cooter Reading Inventory (Flynt & Cooter, 1998) was used to measure Spanish reading levels, and the Qualitative Reading Inventory (Leslie & Caldwell, 2000) was used to measure English reading levels. At the beginning of the school year, Spanish reading scores in both classes ranged from primer to fifth-grade level. After the Readers Theatre intervention, Spanish reading scores in Laura's class ranged from first- through ninth-grade level, but in Stephen's "comparison" classroom, the range was from first- to seventh-grade reading. The average gain in Spanish reading for Laura's students was 1.75 grades compared with the average gain of 0.5 of a grade level in the comparison class.

TABLE 3.3

FOURTH GRADERS' POSTTEST LEVELS IN ENGLISH AND SPANISH AS MEASURED BY INFORMAL READING INVENTORIES FOR READERS THEATRE AND COMPARISON GROUPS

		Level in English Reading		Level in Spanish Reading	
	Levels	Readers Theatre class	Comparison class	Readers Theatre class	Comparison class
Number of scores at each level	pp/P	1	4	1	1
	1st	2	4	2	4
	2nd	2	1	2	1
	3rd	5	4	1	
	4th	1	1	2	5
	5th	1	1	5	4
	6th			2	1
	7th+			2	1
	Total	12	15	17	17

At the beginning of the year, Laura's students' English reading scores on the Qualitative Reading Inventory ranged from preprimer to third grade, and Stephen's students ranged from preprimer to fourth grade. By year's end, English reading scores in Laura's class ranged from primer (one student) to grade 5, and the range in Stephen's class was from preprimer (one student) to grade 5. The average gain in English reading level for Laura's students, however, was 1.34 grades, while students in the comparison class gained 0.75 of a grade level in English (see Table 3.3). In addition, seven of the children in the comparison classroom made no measurable gain in English reading level, and nine made no gain in Spanish reading level—compared with Laura's class, in which only two students registered the same English and Spanish reading levels (one of these was the same child who showed no test score gain in either English or Spanish).

Gains in Rate

As mentioned earlier, reading rate was not the sole indictor of fluency. Certainly, effective oral interpretations are sometimes based on slowing rather than speeding the reading. Similarly, students were neither asked to "read with expression" or to "read faster" as they rehearsed for performance. Instead, they worked to let a deepened understanding of character seep through their voices to reveal the story world through which the character moved. We used our ears to judge increasing fluency across performances but also administered a pre- and posttest of reading rate based on words read per minute at each student's instructional level in both languages. At the outset, Laura's students had an average rate in Spanish reading of 82 words per minute (wpm), with a range of 46–136 wpm. Stephen's class averaged 87 wpm at the beginning of the year, with a range of 49–139 wpm. For English reading, Laura's students' initial rates ranged 51–104 wpm, with an average of 70 wpm. In Stephen's class, the pretest rate average was 77 wpm, with a range of 17–134.

At the end of the school year, when we again took reading rates on unrehearsed passages at the students' instructional levels, Laura's students averaged 102 wpm in Spanish (with a range of 54–134) and an average of 106 wpm in English (range of 73–134). In the comparison class, the average end-of-year rates were 92 wpm in Spanish (range of 57–135) and 97 wpm in English (range of 22–138).

To make sense of the changes in rate across the school year, we computed average gains in rate in the two classes. That is, we averaged the pre- and postscore differences for each student in the classes (see Figure 3.3). Students in Laura's room made an average gain of 46 wpm in English reading rate and 14 wpm in Spanish. In the comparison class, the students gained about 19 wpm in English and almost 5 wpm in

FIGURE 3.3

AVERAGE YEARLY GAIN IN RATE IN ENGLISH/SPANISH

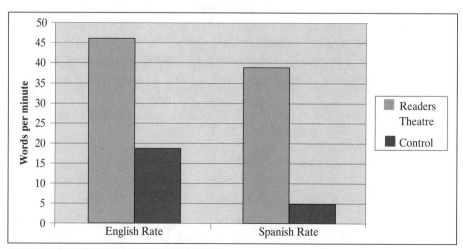

Spanish. These shifts can possibly be ascribed to the effect that practicing reading in a language has on the reading rate in that language. As four of Laura's groups practiced mostly in English, there was greater gain in English.

Changes in Character Awareness

At the beginning, much of the character talk seemed skin-deep and gender-bound (Julio: "I am brown, too, and I'm a boy like him."). Later, the depth to which characters were talked about became more thoughtful and supported (Larentina: "I have made mistakes like that and been afraid to say like him."). Possibly, though, the growth in character awareness had been scaffolded by Jorge's poems, with which the children continued to resonate: "Can we write?" the children asked Laura, and they did: poems in two languages, each on half of the page, just like Ms. Medina. José responded to "Los hombres no lloran/Men Don't Cry," a poem in which Jorge returns home to find his father with reddened eyes talking on the phone (see Figure 3.4). Jorge remembers being taught by his papá, "The only time a man can cry is when his mother dies." The poem ends with the uncertainty of the phone call and with the need for inference about Papá's weeping. José wanted to title his work "What Happened Next?" and he asked for help with getting started. His writing and drawing take the poem to his own world—in which the phone might be outdoors on a stand rather than in a living room—but which clearly illustrates his empathy with a grieving father character ("Your grandmother died, so I start crying with my dad"). It was only after reading stories and poems in two languages that children attempted this "biliterate" behavior—and, just as the writing revealed understanding of character, it also revealed important information about the students' levels of mastery of English and Spanish writing systems.

Field notes and tapes provided another view on children's shifting understanding of characters. We found children relating to characters, as with this example of talk about *Going Home* by Eve Bunting (1996):

C1:   I know, I know, Miss, me mama, she went to see...how do you say...?

C2:   Great, great grandfather.

C1:   ...over the little break. And she took a picture of my little brother. And my grandfather, he got tears in his eyes.

FIGURE 3.4

JOSE'S RESPONSE TO "LOS HOMBRES NO LLORAN [MEN DON'T CRY]"

Similarly, while reading *Friends From the Other Side* by Gloria Anzaldúa (1995), the students shared experiences with *la migra*:

Teacher: Why did the other woman yell *la migra* is coming?

C1:   It's the police.

Teacher: It's the police?

C2:   No.

Teacher: Ramón says no.

C3:   When they get the people who come over here.

C4:   The people who stand at the border...

C5:   ...that check for papers...

C1:   My uncle was drunk and Immigration found him two times and took him back.

C6:	Sometimes *la migra* go to places where a lot of Mexicans work. It happened to my cousin, but he had his papers.
C7:	Sometimes people don't tell the truth when they come and ask.
C1:	It's just like in the story.
C8:	My aunt went with someone else's papers. They put her in jail for weeks.
C4:	I'm going to use my cousin's papers when I go in March.
Teacher:	What do we know about Reitita?
C9:	She helped the boy.
C3:	She protected him in front of the other little boys.
C9:	When *la migra* came, she helped.

They identified, talked over, and disagreed about characters' traits and actions, as in *A Day's Work* by Eve Bunting (1994), a story in which a boy and his grandfather, hired as gardeners in the United States because the boy presented his Spanish-speaking grandfather as experienced, pull the flowers and leave the weeds:

C1:	That wasn't okay. The boy told a lie.
C2:	He didn't.
C1:	He did.
C2:	He knew about gardening. They're different flowers in Mexico and America.
Teacher:	Was that the problem?
C2:	Yes.
C1:	(picks up the book to verify and then reads) "I do not know gardening." That's a lie.
Teacher:	What does this tell you?
C1:	He's a liar.
C5:	A mean boy.
C6:	Mean, mean.
C7:	A little bit liar.
C8:	He lies a little bit.

C2:   Grandfather didn't know what he said.

C9:   He didn't knew.

C10:   Maybe he didn't understand what the man said.

C11:   He wanted that his grandfather had work so that's why he told the lie.

C2:   Just trying to help his grandfather.

C3:   Even though he couldn't...

It is important that they became responsible for supporting their analysis of character traits, as both the above discussion and this excerpt from a group talk about *My Name Is María Isabel* by Alma Flor Ada (1993) demonstrate:

C1:   Miata forgot the skirt on the bus.

C2:   They're not very patient.

Teacher: What do you mean?

C2:   She didn't want to wait for the phone to talk to Anna.

Some children began to show awareness of an author/illustrator behind the work who had made purposeful decisions about character, as the following discussion of *Nacho, Tito y Miguel* by Bobbi Salinas (1998) shows:

C1:   All have mustaches or whiskers!

C2:   They all have sombreros.

C3:   Same eyes.

C4:   Same mouth.

C5:   Same skin.

C6:   Tito's skin is different.

C7:   Tito has little spots.

C8:   Miguel has different skin. Darker.

C1:   If they're brothers, how come they don't have the same skin?

Teacher: Good question. Are you and Dulcé exactly the same shade? Did Bobbi Salinas do this on purpose?

C2:   He [sic] wanted the pigs to be different.

C9:   I think Miguel is darker because he worked a lot.

C6:   There's darker patterns of straw and adobe.

C1:   Dark, darker, darkest.

We also used an interview to gauge children's growth in character awareness. Both prior to the introduction of Readers Theatre and again at the end of the year, a researcher read aloud Cynthia Rylant's (1985) short story "Slower Than the Rest" to both classes. Published in a collection of short stories, this story is an allegorical tale of Leo, relegated to special education because he is "slower than the rest," and Leo's love for a turtle, Charlie, who is also slow. When Leo wins a prize for the best forest fire report (in which he explains that fires are unfair to slow creatures), Leo feels fast for the first time. Following the reading of the story, one researcher talked with each of the children individually about their notions of characters, their traits, their origins, and how they change. For example, each student was asked such open-ended questions as the following:

> Talk to me about Leo [main character in the story]. What is he like?
>
> Is Leo like you? How is he like you or how is he different from you?
>
> Does Leo change in the story? Why do you say that?

The interviews were audiotaped and scripted. The tapes were later transcribed and compared. Across the school year, children seemed to increase in their awareness of character—not only in ability to tell what a character is ("They are the one that are doing the story. They work in the story. They talk and do."), but also to name and discuss favorite characters (Pokèmon, Junie B. Jones) and to begin to describe character traits more deeply than physical features (From "I'm a boy and he's a boy," to "He's slow and I'm fast, but he feeled fast because he won."). By the end of the year of studying character, children seemed more aware that characters may change in stories ("They are people that maybe have problems and they solve them. Maybe at first they're sad and then they're happy."). Finally, the children seemed to understand that characters are created by authors in purposeful ways ("She put in a lot of details to make Charlie interesting.").

It is logical to assume that children learn what they are taught. Therefore, if their instruction focuses on character, they will take away more about character than a comparison class, and so it appears from an inspection of the interviews from both classes. Even so, Laura's students' insights about characters can be compared with a cross-grade study we conducted using the same instrument (Martinez et al., 2002); that is, Laura's fourth graders' map to their agemates and older children in their insights about characters.

Summary and Implications

We hoped that, given the opportunity to read and reread scripts developed from culturally relevant and appropriately leveled children's books (in English), intermediate-grade students would demonstrate increased fluency in English, as well as deepened understandings of literary language. This chapter has described the teaching procedures and plans as well as the results for these 9- through 11-year-old fourth graders who worked both to increase their fluency and to entertain their peers.

There are several implications to draw from the procedures and from the findings. First, this chapter didn't show the "underbelly" of introducing Readers Theatre into a classroom in which some children already had some issues with school and with reading. Our field notes and Laura's journal contain not only students' insightful commentaries on books, but they also are peppered with worries: "Jesse and Ricardo weren't sure of the characters' mistakes—that weeds had been left and plants pulled. It makes me wonder whether it would be better to review the structure—the plot—before focusing on character." There are observational notes about two children whose classroom lives were as often spent diving under desks as taking a seat: "Javier lands across desk, topples backwards, swats Oscar, puts feet on desk, reads annoyingly, shouts at others, lunges across desk, but...reads." Our notes also contain the challenging language and concepts we might have missed teaching, the cognates we tried to acknowledge and those that slipped, and our budding concern that, culturally, overly inflected or expressive oral interpretation is unacceptable—especially to boys. We noted some children's need for a microphone and bemoaned the unrelenting need for "more scripts."

Nevertheless, most children profited from rereading across the year in Laura's class. Unlike an earlier study in which we speculated that there may be a "window"—a range of reading levels—at which children would gain most from opportunities to read and reread, we found no particular pattern among these children. For example, one student whose initial reading level in English was preprimer was assessed at third-grade level in English by the end of the year. Still another child with the same initial preprimer score in English was reading only about a half grade better after a whole year of instruction. Even so, 9 of 11 students in Laura's room improved at least one grade level in English reading, and 14 of 17 made at least one grade level gain in Spanish. In the comparison class, 8 students made gains in English reading, and 7 did not. Similarly, 6 students made gains in Spanish reading, but 10 did not. If the classes could be construed as somewhat equivalent at the beginning of the year, then planned and purposeful rereading may be implicated in these differences.

Most important, however, is that the opportunities to read and reread were directed toward making socially constructed sense of carefully selected texts—stepping inside stories to see the world together. And lucky were those of us who were stepping in with these children. At the beginning of the year, as they peeled back the layers of Jorge's Anglo teacher, they could find no hidden prejudices. Just because Mrs. Roberts does not want Jorge to call her "teacher" because she tells him that the word *teacher* as he says it sounds like *T-shirt*, and just because Mrs. Roberts calls Jorge "George," is no indication that she is guilty of ignorance at best or prejudice at worst, according to Laura's students. Ana explained, "She wanted to help Jorge with his speaking, his pronunciation." Hector said, "Maybe he was new and she didn't know." Daisy said, "How does the teacher know Jorge's name if he didn't tell her already?" Even José excused her: "It's the first day of school." Somehow, this refusal to mistrust Mrs. Roberts with her faults comforted the Anglo teachers and researchers who were learning about learning from these students.

In the presence of good literature, good instruction, and thoughtful compadres, there was honest exchange, better insight, and deeper understanding. At the beginning of the year, the records showed that only one child in Laura's class had reached grade level in her home language, and no child had achieved it in the second language. Even so, their language and literacy curriculum (like that in all good classrooms) focused on inquiry, thinking, analyzing, speculating, explaining, supporting, and interpreting—the real basics of education—and they (like children everywhere) grew.

REFERENCES

Allington, R.L. (1983). Fluency: The neglected goal. *The Reading Teacher, 36,* 555–561.

Au, K.H. (1998). Social constructivism and the school literacy learning of students of diverse backgrounds. *Journal of Literacy Research, 20,* 297–319.

Bishop, R.S. (1992). Multicultural literature for children: Making informed choices. In V.J. Harris (Ed.), *Teaching multicultural literature in grades K–8* (pp. 37–53). Norwood, MA: Christopher-Gordon.

Cullinan, B.E., & Galda, L. (1998). *Literature and the child* (4th ed.). Fort Worth, TX: Harcourt Brace.

Dowhower, S.L. (1987). Effects of repeated readings on selected second grade transitional readers' fluency and comprehension. *Reading Research Quarterly, 22,* 389–406.

Dowhower, S.L. (1994). Repeated reading revisited: Research into practice. *Reading and Writing Quarterly, 22,* 389–406.

Droop, M., & Verhoeven, L. (1998). Background knowledge, linguistic complexity, and second-language reading comprehension. *Journal of Literacy Research, 30,* 253–271.

Emerson, R.M., Fretz, R.I., & Shaw, L.L. (1995). *Writing ethnographic field notes.* Chicago: University of Chicago Press.

Emery, D.W. (1996). Helping readers comprehend stories from the characters' perspectives. *The Reading Teacher, 49,* 534–541.

Flynt, E.S., & Cooter, R.B., Jr. (1998). *Flynt-Cooter Reading Inventory for the Classroom.* Columbus, OH: Merrill.

García, G.E. (2000). Bilingual children's reading. In M.L. Kamil, P.B. Mosenthal, P.D. Pearson, & R. Barr (Eds.), *Handbook of reading research* (Vol. 3, pp. 813–834). Mahwah, NJ: Erlbaum.

Guthrie, J.T., Van Meter, P., McCann, A.D., Wigfield, A., Bennett, L., Poundstone, C.C., et al. (1995). Growth in literacy engagement: Changes in motivations and strategies during concept-oriented reading instruction. *Reading Research Quarterly, 31,* 306–332.

Hancock, M.R. (1993). Exploring the meaning-making process through the content of literature response journals: A case study investigation. *Research in the Teaching of English, 27,* 335–368.

Harris, V.J. (1992). Preface. In V.J. Harris (Ed.), *Teaching multicultural literature in grades K–8* (pp. xv–xvii). Norwood, MA: Christopher-Gordon.

Hoffman, J.V. (1987). Rethinking the role of oral reading in basal instruction. *The Elementary School Journal, 87,* 367–374.

Jiménez, R.T., Garcia, G.E., Pearson, P.D. (1996). The reading strategies of bilingual Latina/o students who are successful English readers: Opportunities and obstacles. *Reading Research Quarterly, 31,* 90–112.

Koskinen, P.S., & Blum, I.H. (1986). Paired repeated reading: A classroom strategy for developing fluent reading. *The Reading Teacher, 40,* 70–75.

Langer, J.A. (1995). *Envisioning literature: Literary understanding and literature instruction.* New York: Teachers College Press; Newark, DE: International Reading Association.

Lehr, S.S. (1991). *The child's developing sense of theme: Responses to literature.* New York: Teachers College Press.

Leslie, L., & Caldwell, J. (2000). *Qualitative Reading Inventory* (3rd ed.). Boston: Allyn & Bacon.

Martinez, M., Keehn, S., Roser, N.L., Harmon, J., & O'Neal, S. (2002). An exploration of children's understanding of character in grades 1–8. In D.L. Schallert, C.M. Fairbanks, J. Worthy, B. Maloch, & J.V. Hoffman (Eds.), *51st yearbook of the National Reading Conference* (pp. 310–320). Oak Creek, WI: National Reading Conference.

Martinez, M., Roser, N.L., & Strecker, S. (1998/1999). "I never thought I could be a star": A Readers Theatre ticket to fluency. *The Reading Teacher, 52,* 326–334.

McGinley, W., & Kamberelis, G. (1996). Maniac Magee and Ragtime Tumpie: Children negotiating self and world through reading and writing. *Research in the Teaching of English, 30,* 75–113.

Moll, L.C. (1988). Key issues in teaching Latino students. *Language Arts, 65*(5), 465–472.

Moll, L.C. (1992). Funds of knowledge for teaching: A qualitative approach to connect households and classrooms. *Theory Into Practice, 3*(2), 132–141.

National Institute of Child Health and Human Development. (2000). *Report of the National Reading Panel. Teaching children to read: An evidence-based assessment of the scientific research literature on reading and its implications for reading instruction* (NIH Publication No. 00-4769). Washington, DC: U.S. Government Printing Office.

Rashotte, C., & Torgesen, J.K. (1985). Repeated reading and reading fluency in learning disabled children. *Reading Research Quarterly, 20,* 180–188.

Samuels, S.J. (1979). The method of repeated reading. *The Reading Teacher, 32,* 403–408.

Smith, E.B. (1995). Anchored in our literature: Students responding to African American literature. *Language Arts, 72,* 571–574.

Strecker, S., Roser, N.L., & Martinez, M.G. (1998). Toward understanding oral reading fluency. In T. Shanahan & F.V. Rodriguez-Brown (Eds.), *47th yearbook of the National Reading Conference* (pp. 295–310). Chicago: National Reading Conference.

Thornburg, D. (1993). Intergenerational literacy learning with bilingual families: A context for the analysis of social mediation of thought. *Journal of Reading Behavior, 25,* 321–352.

Wollman-Bonilla, J.E., & Werchadlo, B. (1995). Literature response journals in a first-grade classroom. *Language Arts, 72,* 562–570.

Worthy, J., & Broaddus, K. (2002). Fluency beyond the primary grades: From group performance to silent, independent reading. *The Reading Teacher, 55,* 334–343.

Yokota, J. (1993). Issues in selecting multicultural children's literature. *Language Arts, 70,* 156–167.

CHILDREN'S LITERATURE CITED

Anzaldúa, G. (1995). *Friends from the other side*. San Francisco: Children's Book Press.

Bunting, E. (1994). *A day's work*. New York: Clarion.

Bunting, E. (1996). *Going home*. New York: HarperCollins.

Flor Ada, A. (1993) *My name is María Isabel*. New York: Antheneum.

González, L. (1994). *The bossy gallito*. New York: Scholastic.

Medina, J. (1999). *My name is Jorge on both sides of the river*. Honesdale, PA: Boyds Mills Press.

Rylant, C. (1985) "Slower than the rest" in *Every living thing* (pp. 1–7). New York: Simon & Schuster.

Salinas, B. *Nacho, Tito and Miguel*. (1998). Albuquerque, NM: Pinata.

Soto, G. (1994). *The skirt*. New York, Yearling.

CHAPTER 4

Book Club in a Fourth-Grade Classroom: Issues of Ownership and Response

Torry H. Montes and Kathryn H. Au

Early in the school year, fourth-grade students in the first author's class conducted a Book Club discussion about *Sadako and the Thousand Paper Cranes* (Coerr, 1977):

Jenna:	I wouldn't tell the secret because it's my own secret and not theirs, and if I don't really want to tell them, then I don't really need to.
Brian:	Okay. Your turn, Megan.
Megan:	If I were Sadako I wouldn't tell the secret, unless it is important, then I would. But if I'm hurt or someone is hurt, then I wouldn't keep a secret.
Brian:	I'm going to share about my picture.
Megan:	Yeah, you can share about your picture.
Brian:	I'm going to share about my picture. They are standing at the finish line, the starting line, and then they are going to go around the track and then. My secret was I would keep my secret because I don't want people to think I am a loser.
Jenna:	And her secret was, she was going to keep her secret and her secret was that she was getting wheezy and stuff and she was going to fall over.
Megan:	I drew a picture of Sadako winning because it just caught (?) inside her head.
Brian:	Oh, okay. That's kind of interesting.
Jenna:	My picture is about her telling that the big race is today.
Brian:	Any questions about anyone's pictures?
Jenna:	No.

(October 15)

This transcript highlights two key issues to be addressed in this chapter. The first issue, made evident by the superficial nature of the discussion, is the students' lack of understanding of how to respond to literature, either through conversation or writing. The second issue, illustrated by the students' low level of engagement, is their lack of ownership of reading. Our aim is to discuss how teachers might improve students' ability to respond to literature and heighten students' ownership of reading.

As a fourth-grade teacher, Torry noticed that many of her students did not enjoy reading and struggled with both comprehension and decoding. She wanted to find a way to change their feelings about books and reading, to make reading come alive for her students. Torry found a solution in Book Club, a model of literature-based instruction developed by Raphael and her colleagues (Raphael et al., 1994; Raphael & McMahon, 1994; Raphael, Pardo, Highfield, & McMahon, 1997; see also chapter 5 of this book). In this chapter we describe how the teacher (Torry)—working with one other researcher (Kathy) and outside a collaborative network of teachers—implemented Book Club and the effects of this approach on her fourth-grade students in terms of (a) written response to literature, (b) literature discussions with peers, and (c) ownership of literacy. (We follow the convention of using *Book Club* with capital letters for the overall model and *book club* with lowercase letters for the small-group discussions.)

Ideas Underlying Book Club

Book Club builds on two major perspectives. The first perspective derives from the social constructivist views of the Russian psychologist Vygotsky (1934/1978), whose writings emphasize the social nature of language and learning. Vygotsky's work implies that students will become good readers when they interact with others in the context of meaningful, collaborative literacy activities. During these activities, learning is scaffolded by the teacher and other students. In the classroom, however, we often limit students' opportunities to explore literature through social interaction. Typical activities include teacher-led, whole-class discussion (in which students give brief, superficial answers) and individual reading and writing. Book Club seeks to reverse these typical patterns by making time for in-depth discussions of literature among students.

The second perspective is that of reader response theory, especially the work of Rosenblatt (1978). She proposes that readers move along a continuum of stances, with the aesthetic stance forming one end of the continuum and the efferent stance the other. When readers read from an aesthetic stance, they read for the sheer pleasure or experience of reading. When they read from an efferent stance, they read for the purpose of taking information from the text. Rosenblatt argues that, in the reading of literature, the aesthetic stance should be the more prominent. Yet it is common for students to read literature from an efferent stance in order to respond to set questions. Book Club reverses this pattern by providing time for students to read from an aesthetic stance, construct individual responses to literature, and share these responses with peers.

Reader response in Book Club takes two forms: written responses and book club discussions in small groups. Lehr and Thompson (2000) provide a framework for examining student responses. They describe these responses as having a range of complexity, from the literal response in which the student gives concrete answers to the interpretive response in which the student describes themes and makes generalizations in an abstract manner. In Book Club, students' responses should show this movement from superficial to deeper, interpretive responses in both writing and oral discussion.

Research suggests that students who participate in text discussions think at a higher level, apply problem-solving skills, and gain a deeper understanding of the text (Gambrell, 1996). The small discussion groups of the Book Club model allow the students to participate in genuine conversations about books, in contrast to classroom recitations in which they are quizzed by teachers. When first introduced to Book Club, students do not start out with genuine conversations (McMahon, 1997). This is not surprising because students have had many experiences with classroom recitation but few with open-ended literature discussions in which they set the agenda. They must learn to engage in such discussions.

Students who come to care about books will develop ownership of literacy. Au (1997) suggests that students who have ownership of literacy value reading and writing and use these processes for their own purposes, both in and outside school. According to Dudley-Marling and Searle (1995), ownership in a literacy setting reflects student independence, autonomy, and choice. Students in Book Club classrooms may have limited choice about the books they read when the teacher has selected certain books because of their theme, level of challenge, or relationship to the curriculum. However, students have independence, autonomy, and choice in terms of how they respond to the literature. They choose the form and content of their written responses, and they decide which ideas in the literature warrant group discussion. The Book Club model can promote students' ownership of literacy because of the responsibility students are given for directing their own reading and responses to literature, and because of the deep involvement with and appreciation for literature that result.

Book Club Components

Raphael et al. (1997) describe the Book Club model as having five components. The first component is the reading of high-quality literature that reflects important issues and real-life concerns of readers. These books allow readers to enter other worlds and make connections to their own lives.

The second component is writing in response to literature. Three types of responses may be explored: personal, creative, and critical. McMahon and Raphael (1997) describe personal responses as the first impressions that are evoked by the text, with an emphasis on feelings and personal connections. Creative responses stretch student thinking through the exploration of "what if?" types of speculation. Critical responses require analysis of the text, with students examining the author's craft and the effectiveness, purpose, and coherence of the text.

The third component is the small-group, student-directed book clubs, which center on genuine conversations about books. In book clubs, students are not grouped according to reading achievement levels. They use their written responses as the basis for entering into conversations about the literature.

Following the book clubs, the teacher leads the class in a community share, the fourth component. This is an opportunity for the teacher to bring the class together as a community of readers, a time when the book club groups can share their insights and learn from one another.

The fifth component is instruction, which may occur within the context of the previous four components or in separate lessons. The teacher is constantly modeling and providing minilessons for students.

Topics covered include discussion techniques, various responses to literature, literary elements, and conventions.

The literature covered in Torry's class had an Asia-Pacific focus with an emphasis on multicultural literature. This chapter focuses on students' interactions with three books: *Sadako and the Thousand Paper Cranes* (Coerr, 1977), *In the Year of the Boar and Jackie Robinson* (Lord, 1984), and *Call It Courage* (Sperry, 1940).

A Classroom in Hawaii

In this study, we wanted to learn what effects the Book Club model would have in a fourth-grade classroom in Hawaii with its multiethnic mix of students. Torry's school reflected the diversity of cultures found in Hawaii, comprising students of Hawaiian, Filipino, Japanese, and Caucasian ancestry. In Torry's classroom, 53% of the students were of Hawaiian ancestry. She provided language arts instruction to 24 students, including five struggling readers who received remedial (Title I) services, one English language learner, and three students in the enrichment program. At the beginning of the school year, most students were reading below grade level, with levels ranging from the second grade to seventh grade.

Procedures for Collecting Data

The students in Torry's classroom participated in Book Club for three 60-minute periods a week. Torry created six book clubs with four members each; students reading at a range of levels were included in each group. One group was audiotaped daily, on a rotating basis, and the audiotapes were transcribed. The fishbowl conversations were both audio- and videotaped, then transcribed. To gauge ownership of reading, Torry had her students complete a teacher-developed survey in which they noted reading preferences and whether they considered themselves to be readers. Early in the school year, Torry created a chart based on class discussions of what it means to be a reader. Information was added to this chart at the end of the school year to see if students had expanded their understanding of reading. Students maintained a reading portfolio in which they kept their best-written responses to literature. At the end of the school year, each book club group was interviewed.

The students talked about their experiences in Book Club and perceptions of themselves as readers.

Challenges to Implementation

Torry wanted to implement all five components of the Book Club model as described by Raphael et al. (1997). As she sought to introduce Book Club in her classroom, Torry immediately ran into two issues: First, students needed to learn how to write a response to the literature; second, they needed to develop the skills to have a genuine conversation about a book.

In dealing with the first issue, Torry found that she needed to move students along gradually. She found it best to start with the kind of written response students knew best: predict, retell, and wonder. She introduced other types of response during minilessons conducted throughout the year.

The nature of the text dictated to some extent the types of responses that it made sense to introduce to the students. *Sadako and the Thousand Paper Cranes* lent itself well to personal response. One of the first types of response Torry introduced asked the students to put themselves in the character's place. Students could respond personally, making a connection between themselves and Sadako. Most students knew someone who had become seriously ill. They could place themselves in Sadako's shoes and explore the implications of that situation. At this time, students could manage such personal and creative responses more successfully than critical ones.

An interesting turn of events occurred when Torry had the students write to depict the relationships among characters. The students began by drawing webs to show these relationships, but the webs quickly became complex and confusing. One student took his web and converted it to a matrix. This strategy caught on with the others, and soon many students were creating character matrices rather than webs. Later the students began to create webs and matrices analyzing the characters' actions, feelings, and attributes. In short, as the year went on, students took control of their written responses and even created new forms of responding.

Figure 4.1 presents the Reader's Journal Response List that Torry and her students developed. The 11 different types of responses are listed in the order in which they were introduced.

FIGURE 4.1

READER'S JOURNAL RESPONSE LIST

When I respond, I can...

1. Predict (before), validate (after), document (evidence from the story)

2. Retell/summarize

3. Wonder (question: why, how, what if)

4. Draw something from the reading that I feel is important (write a description of my picture)

5. Character web/matrix

    Character relationships
    Character analysis: description, feelings, attributes, actions

6. Favorite/least favorite part, because...

7. If I were the character..., because...

8. Me and the book: personal connections (link it back to the story)

9. If I were the author..., because...

10. Connections with other stories I have read

11. Create my own response type.

The second issue, helping students have genuine conversations about books, proved to be the greater challenge. In order for the book clubs to be successful, Torry knew that students needed a set of guidelines to follow. The students were familiar with TRIBES (Gibbs, 1995), a community-building curriculum, and so the TRIBES language of agreements was used to help define the behavioral expectations. Torry led a class discussion in which students came up with the following five agreements:

1. Follow the TRIBES agreements.

2. Listen to each other. Focus on the speaker.

3. Focus on real book conversations.

4. Come to Book Club prepared: reading and readers' journal response finished.

5. All members need to participate and share.

After the first day of Book Club, the class added a sixth agreement:

6. Book Clubs have the right to ask a member to sit out.

Because the students were unsure about how to begin talking in their book clubs, Torry led another discussion, which resulted in these five guidelines:

1. Talk about what you read.

2. Talk about any questions about the reading.

3. Share your reader's journal responses. What did you write? Why?

4. Any questions about the responses?

5. Decide on one idea or question to share with the class.

However, although the students themselves had generated this list, the guidelines were too vague to foster genuine conversations. A second set of guidelines was developed after the students had participated in a fishbowl activity:

What makes a good Book Club?

1. Good listeners and good speakers.

2. Good ideas and information.

3. All members should participate. Listening is okay.

4. Ask questions to invite the shy person to jump in.

5. If possible, don't interrupt.

6. Ask questions so others will share more information and ideas.

7. Ask questions if you don't understand something from the story or something someone is talking about.

8. Come to book club prepared to share ideas and ask questions. No yes/no answers, one-word answers, or obvious questions. Ask *why, how, what if* questions.

9. Use ideas that help the book club come up with/think of new ideas.

These guidelines proved more effective because the students had been in their own book clubs and were also able to observe another book club in action. These experiences allowed them to develop guidelines that were much more specific and addressed the problems they were actually encountering. One problem was that of members who were shy about sharing. The students used the expression "jump in" to encourage these reluctant members. They also focused on the idea that in a real conversation, the speakers do not always take turns.

Learning how to speak about books in a conversational setting became a major focus of instruction throughout the year. The techniques used to support this focus included videotaping and analyzing the discussion as a class, self- and group reflection, and the fishbowl approach (Scherer, 1977). Torry found that students gained the most from the fishbowl approach. In this approach, a small group of students sits in the center of the classroom and engages in a book club conversation, while the rest of the class observes. After the conversation is complete, the students discuss what went well and what could be improved. The following excerpt comes from a book club in a fishbowl discussing their conversation and the improvements they should make.

Jasmine:	I think we did well in our conversation. Because we all jumped in and we all had something to say.
Bryson:	We were all answering questions.
Tyra:	I think we did well in what we suggested and how—and the good comments we had and how we like stick together with one thing.
Teacher:	How did you feel when you started out with a prediction and they didn't pick it up? What did you think of that?
Tyra:	I thought the thing that I picked up was junk.
Teacher:	You thought your idea was junk or do you think it was junk that they didn't pick up on it?
Tyra:	I think it was junk that they didn't pick it up.
Teacher:	So it felt kind of funny?
Tyra:	Yeah.
Teacher:	So if someone has an idea, is it nice to pick up on that idea?
Jasmine:	Uh-huh.
Bryson:	So we should talk about people's good ideas and build on them.

(March 8)

These students knew that their book club was doing well, but they also knew that they could improve the quality of the conversation. Tyra did not like having her idea ignored. Bryson suggested that they should build on the ideas of others. This point was added as the last guideline.

After giving students several experiences with the fishbowl activity, Torry found that they were discussing books much more effectively. Prior to the fishbowl experiences, the student conversations were flat and tended to progress in a round-robin manner, as illustrated in the excerpt used at the beginning of this chapter.

After the fishbowl experiences, the student conversations were deeper and much more animated. Here is a description of a typical conversation that occurred during the reading of *Call It Courage*. One student brought up the idea of the war canoes. He felt that Mafatu should sail to the cannibals' island and destroy their canoes. The other students thought this was an exciting idea. They began to plan how Mafatu could leave the island, burn the canoes, and escape undetected. One student then pointed out that Mafatu should take a souvenir as proof of his bravery. He said that Mafatu had to have proof so that his father would know that he was courageous. As the conversation progressed, students were listening to each other, but their speech overlapped as they excitedly shared their ideas.

Results of Book Club Intervention

Written Responses to Literature

The students' efforts to make personal connections and explore themes are shown in their written responses to the first Book Club text, *Sadako and the Thousand Paper Cranes*. Although it was early in the year, some students wrote thoughtful responses. (Student responses are presented in unedited form.)

> Last Days Me and the Book
>
> This story relates by when they put the lantens outside in the streams for the spirits who died from the atom bomb to see the ones they loved the lantens are for when it's dark they can see. My great gand papa was in the warwar to he told me that it was a wrong thing that we'v done.
>
> (Tyra, November 3)

Tyra began by providing background knowledge, explaining her understanding of the Obon festival, in which the Japanese remember loved ones who have passed away. Tyra and her family had attended the festival before, and she knew the belief that lanterns help to guide the spirits of the loved ones. Next, Tyra made a personal connection by relating what her great-grandfather had told her about the impact of war.

Other students' responses did not reflect this level of thoughtfulness.

I would keep the secret because pepel mite thint im a luser

(Brian, October 15)

Brian dealt with the issue of whether Sadako should keep her illness a secret. If people knew her secret, Sadako would be off the running team and thus a loser. Brian's response suggests that he was more concerned about what others might think than about the gravity of Sadako's illness. His response does not demonstrate the sensitivity or depth of understanding seen in Tyra's writing.

These early responses show that the students were attempting to make personal connections and explain their understanding of themes such as peace and death. However, they needed to make the connections more clear and deliberate by including details from the text. Tyra supported her ideas with some details from the text, but most other students did not. In addition, the students did not expand on their ideas.

The last book read was *Call It Courage*, the story of Mafatu, a young boy who is afraid of the ocean. He leaves his home to find a new island, and he must survive against great odds. The students' written responses to the story demonstrate considerable growth. Survival, courage, and overcoming fear are predominant themes in this story, and the story encourages students to explore what they might have done in similar situations. Early in the year, as seen above, students tended to give brief, one-part responses. By the end of the year, the responses were in three parts: predict/wonder, thinking response, and drawing and summary caption of an important event.

Figure 4.2 is an example of a three-part student response. By the end of the year, Louisa was comfortable responding in a variety of ways. She utilized a number of different types of responses. In the left column of her work, Louisa made intertextual connections highlighting her understanding of the underlying themes of each text. In the right column, she examined the literary technique of foreshadowing and then used this tool to make the accurate prediction that is illustrated at the bottom of the page: "I predict that Mafatu will fight a shark to show courage."

FIGURE 4.2

LOUISA'S THREE-PART RESPONSE

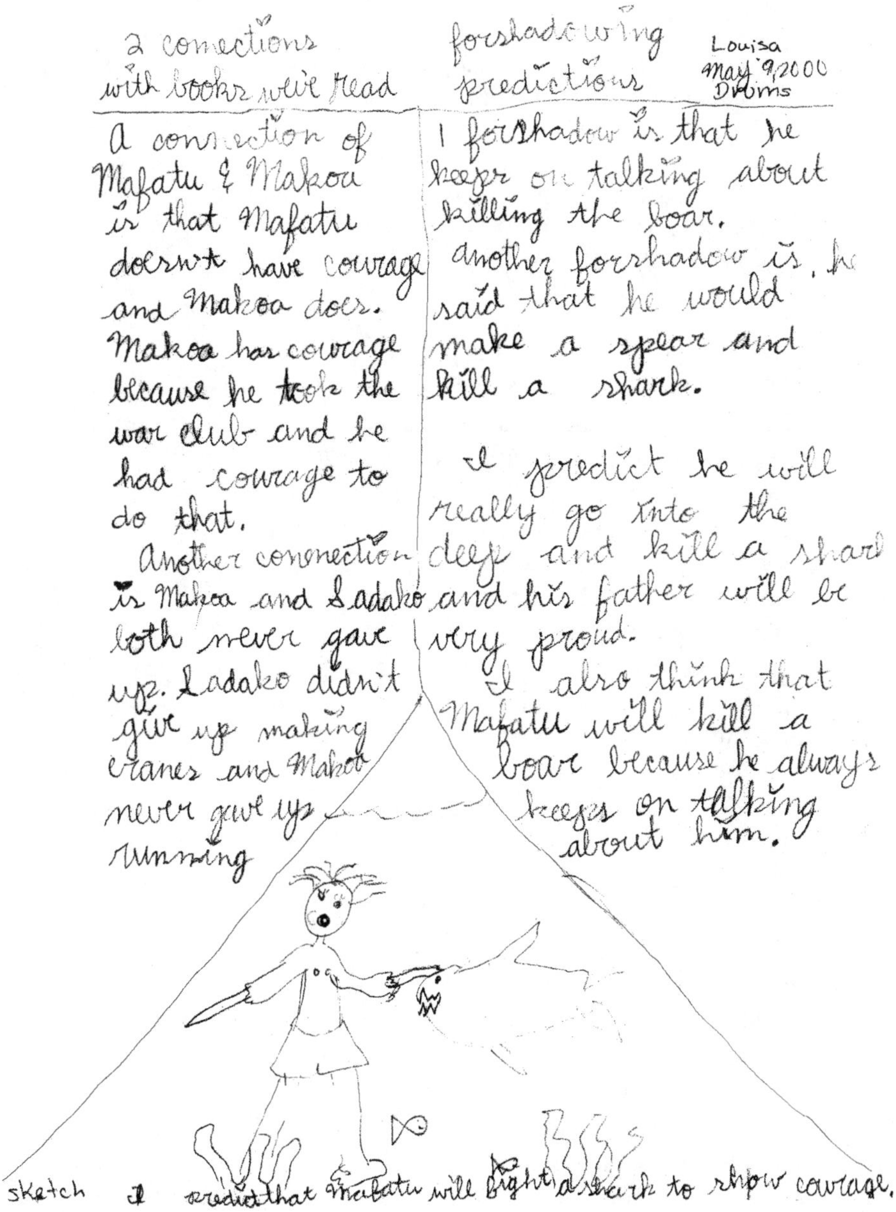

2 connections
with books we've read

forshadowing
predictions

Louisa
May 9,2000
Drums

A connection of
Mafatu & Makoa
is that Mafatu
doesn't have courage
and Makoa does.
Makoa has courage
because he took the
war club and he
had courage to
do that.
    Another connection
is Makoa and Sadako
both never gave
up. Sadako didn't
give up making
cranes and Makoa
never gave up
running

I forshadow is that he
keeps on talking about
killing the boar.
Another forshadow is, he
said that he would
make a spear and
kill a shark.

    I predict he will
really go into the
deep and kill a shark
and his father will be
very proud.
    I also think that
Mafatu will kill a
boar because he always
keeps on talking
about him.

sketch   I predict that Mafatu will fight a shark to show courage.

Other students were able to write complex responses by the end of the school year. Due to length, only a portion of Kaleo's responses is presented.

> I wonder why Mafatu decided to go on the canoe when he was still scared. If I were Mafatu then I would not go on the canoe if I was scared because I wouldn't let Kana get over it.
>
> (Kaleo, April 24)

> Mafatu killed the Ma'o (shark). Mafatu killed the Ma'o because he loved Uri and he saved Uri from getting killed. I wouldn't do it because I would not want to go troght so much bad things happening to me. I would just stay afraid.
>
> (Kaleo, May 10)

In these responses, Kaleo was able to put himself in the story, to make judgments, and to suggest plausible changes. Kaleo understood the power of love. He stated why Mafatu risked his life for Uri. He made an inference about Mafatu's actions and went on to explain that he would have lacked the courage to perform the same act. Kaleo described how he felt about Mafatu's actions and how he would react in a similar situation. He seemed to be having an internal dialogue about his own fears and values.

These later responses show that the overall quality and depth of the students' understanding had improved. Lehr and Thompson (2000) suggest that we should expect students over time to move from literal to interpretive responses. This is exactly what occurred in Torry's classroom. The early responses were literal. Later, as students gained experiences with Book Club, they were able to respond in an interpretive manner.

Book Club Conversations

Earlier, we mentioned studies showing that students do not automatically know how to participate in thoughtful book club conversations and noted that this same difficulty was evident in Torry's classroom at the beginning of the school year. We saw this difficulty in the discussion of Sadako presented in the introduction, in which students shared their responses in a round-robin manner. As with the written responses from early in the year, the students' book club discussions remained at the literal level and did not draw deeply from ideas in the text.

These problems continued with the next book, *In the Year of the Boar and Jackie Robinson*. This story is based on the author's experiences as a young Chinese girl immigrating to the United States in the 1950s. The main character, Shirley, must learn a new language and make friends in a new school and country. Baseball and Jackie Robinson are symbolic of the many new concepts she must grasp and come to appreciate. This story lacked the strong themes of *Sadako* and *Call It Courage*. As a result, the students focused on many surface-level events and issues. However, they were able to identify racism in the United States as one issue raised by the text.

In a change from earlier in the year, the students demonstrated that they could listen and respond to one another's comments. Still, Torry felt that the discussions lacked depth. The students were not using the book clubs as an opportunity to explore the issues and gain a deeper understanding of the stories. In order to improve the quality of the conversations, Torry organized a number of fishbowl sessions. The following transcript is taken from one of the fishbowls held at this time:

Jasmine: I predict that they might go to a baseball game.

Bryson: Maybe. (Bryson is sitting back, as if keeping his distance from the group.)

Jasmine: The clues are she is learning about Jackie Robinson and she learned about colored people.

Tyra: Colored people?

Bryson: Do you think she would be good at baseball or, in other words, stick ball?

Tyra: No, she keeps on closing her eyes when she tries to hit the ball.

Jasmine: But she is good at running.

Bryson: Do you think someone will buy her a ticket to go to a baseball game?

Jasmine: Probably Mabel.

Tyra: Yeah.

Jasmine: Or her dad.

Tyra: To make her more happy.

Jasmine: Uh-huh.

(March 8)

Jasmine made an inference about what might happen to Shirley, and she tried to back up her inference with details from the story. Tyra picked up on the theme of racism, but Bryson changed the course of the conversation. Together, Bryson, Tyra, and Jasmine built an understanding of Shirley and baseball. Bryson acted as the more knowledgeable one, raising questions to draw Tyra and Jasmine into the conversation. This was a role he played throughout the discussion. Later, Tyra returned to the issue of racism:

Tyra: What did you say on top the movie?

Jasmine: Oh yeah. I was watching this movie where they were following, this lady tell this girl to follow people with colored skin, because they think people with colored skin steal a lot.

Tyra: Steal a lot? You mean like dark people? (She points to her arm.)

Jasmine: Uh-huh.

Bryson: African Americans.

Tyra: Like Martin Luther King? (Jasmine is looking around uncomfortably.)

Jasmine: Umm, I wonder why they think that?

Tyra: I know. It is just colored skin.

Bryson: Yeah, no one is different.

Tyra: Yeah, I know.

Jasmine: Everyone is mostly the same.

Bryson: Not from the outside, but the inside is same.

Jasmine: Everyone has feelings.

(March 8)

The students sought to gain a better understanding of racism and how people of color were treated. They were trying to come to terms with a moral issue, and they worked as a group to build a common understanding of this issue. (It should be noted that racism did not come up in any of the students' written responses.) Previously, the students had had difficulty making intertextual connections, both to other books and to movies. Jasmine's comment about a movie provided the first evidence that students were able to make this type of link.

These second-semester connections showed terrific growth on the part of the students. After several fishbowl experiences, students were more focused on the issues and having conversations that led to a deeper level of thinking and understanding for each book club member. The written responses at this time also showed growth, and the students were bringing these ideas to the book clubs and using them as starting points for the conversations.

This growth continued. The ideas the students discussed in *Call It Courage* were very complex. Their conversations showed that they were using critical thinking skills to gain a deeper understanding of the story. In addition, they continued to use the written responses to begin thinking about the important points they would discuss with their book clubs.

The following response and transcript excerpt occurred during students' reading of the first chapter of *Call It Courage*. Brian wrote,

> I predict heys going to brack the canoe and hes going to flot to an island and fing bons and mack a knife and cill the god. I wonder if he is going to face a storm on the way?

> (April 24)

Brian included a drawing of the canoe breaking apart in a storm. It was this written response that provided the starting point for most of the following conversation:

Kaleo: Well, I think, that the mother said that they were going to die when they were in the canoe.

Brian: And happened to die on another island maybe. Happened to survive to another island.

Kaleo: And, what do you think, Puanani?

Puanani: I don't know.

Brian: Oh, I have a wonder, I mean a prediction. I predict that, umm, he said that it was storm season, and then he's also going out on the water and then it's also rough, so I'm predicting that a wave or something's going to break the canoe.

Kaleo: Good question. Umm, Puanani? Would you like to say something?

Puanani: No.

Brian:	What do you think?
Kaleo:	I predict that if Mafatu does, the canoe does break ---, he will be saved by his --- mother's spirit.
Brian:	--- Or the God will take him off to another island.
Brian:	--- By his mother's spirit and then a big fish or something will save him, like a whale or a whale shark.
Megan:	I wonder, I wonder like he's going to face the storm and his canoe breaks and a there's a shark that's going to attack him and he is going to kill the shark (referring to the front cover).
Brian:	Wait, he's going to float to an island and then he's going to like find bones there and then going to sharpen a bone into a knife and then he's going to go into the water and then the shark's going to try to kill him, but he's going to kill the shark, by stabbing it in his head.
Kaleo:	I wonder if he, when he is going to be back from the canoe, or if he lives or dies?
Brian:	If he lives or dies?
Kaleo:	I hope he lives.
Brian:	He could die on the canoe, 'cause then he could run out of water. He could run out of food.
Kaleo:	He could die --- of the shark.
Brian:	Or he could live of the shark, but we don't know that yet. So ---
Kaleo:	And he could, I think he, when his father dies, after he's proven he has a stout heart, when his father dies, he'll take his father's place as the chief.
Brian:	Yeah, but when he comes back, the father's going to tell them, this is my son and his name is brave heart or something. And he's going to, the father's going to die in a war and he is going to survive and he's going to like take his father's place as the chief.

(April 24)

The dashes in the excerpt indicate overlapping speech; the students spoke in a rapid and animated fashion throughout this discussion. Brian and Kaleo built a complex inference about what would happen to

Mafatu. Brian led this interaction—using clues from the story, his previous experiences with and understanding of the adventure/survival genre, and his own experiences sailing with his father—to build a sophisticated and accurate prediction. The students continued to construct a prediction, building on one another's ideas. Kaleo got wrapped up in Brian's prediction and added to it. Together, they were building a foundation for understanding the rest of the book. Later in this conversation, Megan posed another scenario. She brought up the idea of a shark attacking and killing Mafatu. The group toyed with this idea. Then Brian seemed to realize that if Mafatu died, the story would be over. He posed another scenario, and the discussion took off again. A notable feature of this conversation is that the students had only read a portion of the first chapter, yet they were able to apply prior knowledge to create an accurate and complex prediction.

The conversations from *Call It Courage* show that the students had learned how to talk about books in genuine, meaningful conversations. They were skillfully applying higher order thinking skills. They probed the ideas from the story, made complex inferences based on multiple levels of evidence and experience, and evaluated the growth of the character.

Understanding of Reading and Ownership

Torry knew from experience that her fourth-grade students tended to have a superficial understanding of what it means to be a reader. She believed her students would not develop ownership until they had gained a broader understanding of reading. As mentioned earlier, Torry conducted a whole-class discussion in September centered on the question, What is a reader? The initial responses students gave are shown in Figure 4.3. In May, at the end of the school year, students addressed the question again. The responses shown in italics were added at this time.

Early in the year, students' answers clustered in four areas: reads for meaning, time, attitude, and choice of books. The students understood that meaning is important, that readers understand what they read, and that they have strategies to help them when reading is difficult. They stated that readers read frequently and that they do so for enjoyment. They spoke of how readers have a purpose for choosing a book, whether for enjoyment or learning. The students did not understand that readers connect with the texts they read. They did not understand that readers respond to the text along a continuum of feelings.

FIGURE 4.3

STUDENT THOUGHTS ON WHAT MAKES A GOOD READER

Choice of Books
- reads a variety of genres
- chooses interesting subjects and authors
- reads for different reasons
  enjoyment
  to learn
  assignments
- *reads books/authors/series he or she likes*
- *writes about new things*
- *travels everywhere in the mind*
- *sees new people, places, and things*

Time
- reads daily
- reads in his or her free time
- reads a variety of materials
- takes the time to understand
- goes to the library and bookstores
- buys books from book orders
- *rereads favorite books/ stories*
- *reads whenever he or she can*
- *frequently goes to library and bookstore and orders- books*

Talk
- *talks about books*
- *fishbowls*
- *compares books to life*
- *feelings*
- *changes to story*
- *messages/learnings*
- *summarizes*

Attitude
- absolutely, positively loves to read
- loves books, words, and authors
- has feelings for stories
- gets sucked into books, cannot stop reading
- has a good attitude about reading
- shares books and stories with others
  gives book talks
  shares feelings
  reads to others
  helps others read
- *great imagination*
- *jumps into the book— imagines the story as it happens*
- *cares for books*
- *has humor or happiness or sadness from story*
- *respects and appreciates characters and different cultures*

Reads for Meaning
- takes the time to understand what he or she reads
- reads to his or her best ability
- makes sense of what he or she reads
- reads to learn
- understands vocabulary
  big vocabulary
  sparkling jewels
  uses dictionary to learn new words
- writes and reads his or her writing
- uses exciting words
- uses sentences and paragraphs to understand words
- understands and uses a variety of story parts
- *Reads to*
  connect
  think
  feel

Response
- *webs*
  story
  character
- *draw*
  characters
  retell
- *share personal experiences (me and the book)*
- *favorite/least favorite parts*
- *author's message*
- *author's/character's shoes*
- *connections*
  personal
  other books
- *predict and wonder*
- *feelings*
- *story map*
- *character matrix*
- *author—publishes books and stories*

The students understood that good readers enjoy reading, but they did not understand why. They also did not understand that there are a variety of ways to respond to and talk about literature.

By May, students' understanding of the original concepts had deepened. Two new categories were added: response and talk. Through their book clubs, students had discovered that talking about books was an important part of being a reader. Although they linked talk to attitude and the idea that readers share books with others, they felt talk needed to be a category of its own. They stated that readers respond to texts in a variety of ways, listing the types of responses they had learned to write in their reader response journals. They made the connection between reading and writing: authors publish books and readers are often authors. The students had made a huge leap forward in understanding the purposes for reading and writing.

The depth of student ownership also can be verified by examining the book club conversations. Early in the year, the conversations were stilted, only addressing the assigned written responses. Students concentrated simply on reading their written responses rather than listening and responding to others. As the students became more skilled at talking about books, they began to take control of the conversations. With appropriate support, they were able to expand the conversations to include questions and concepts they wanted to pursue. They were making autonomous decisions about the topics and flow of the conversation and now owned these discussions.

In addition to the issues of autonomy and control, ownership also can be seen in the students' willingness to participate fully. Again, differences are readily apparent in comparisons of the early and later book club conversations. Initially the students were hesitant to share their ideas. They read from their written responses verbatim, carefully taking turns. They did not collaborate to construct new understandings of the literature. Later conversations reflected a greater willingness to build on one another's thinking. The students were jumping in, sharing ideas, adding to the ideas of others, and occasionally contradicting or correcting a peer. The students became very skillful at talking about books in meaningful and authentic ways. The self-consciousness and hesitancy evident earlier had disappeared. They were in control, participating fully and willingly, making their own choices about the topics of conversation. They showed ownership of the book club discussions.

The final piece of the issue of ownership is self-perception. The students were asked about their perceptions of themselves as readers before Book Club was implemented and after a year's experience with this model. When asked if they considered themselves readers prior to Book Club, 60% of the students responded "no" or "maybe." When asked about their perceptions of themselves after having participated in Book Club, 85% of the students answered that they considered themselves readers. Of the 15% who did not feel they were readers, one student still answered "maybe" to the question. By the end of the year, the majority of students saw themselves as readers who had ownership of literacy.

Conclusion

In conclusion, we offer both caveats and practical advice to teachers interested in trying Book Club in their classrooms. First, the caveats. Highly structured, packaged reading programs have been very popular in many schools. One caveat is that making the switch from such a program to Book Club will not be easy. Teachers making the change will want to be sure that they have a good source of professional and moral support, such as a teacher network or university course. Another caveat has to do with the availability of multiple copies of the right literature. Many schools do not have the collections of trade books needed to support Book Club, and it may take teachers a number of years to accumulate enough copies of the titles needed. A final caveat is that teachers must have patience with the process of change. They need to be patient with themselves and the trial-and-error process that inevitably comes with implementing a dynamic new instructional approach requiring high levels of professional knowledge and judgment. They need to be patient with their students because students will be struggling to learn a way of reading and responding that is largely new.

Now for the practical advice. First, teachers will want to be certain to select books with themes worthy of discussion. Many wonderful books are available, but not all of these books lend themselves to the probing discussions we want to see in book clubs. For example, *Sadako and the Thousand Paper Cranes* and *Call It Courage* proved to be better choices than *In the Year of the Boar and Jackie Robinson*. Although students enjoyed reading this last book, they found fewer issues meriting deep discussion.

Second, teachers should start slowly. It helps if students are all reading the same book, especially at the beginning of the year. This makes it easier for the teacher to establish routines, monitor the students' reading, and promote sharing among the book club groups. As teachers become more accomplished and confident in managing the Book Club classroom, they may wish to offer students a choice of two, three, or even four different books within the same theme. In this way, teachers can better meet the needs of students with different interests and different levels of reading achievement.

Third, teachers will need to give students a great deal of guidance in conducting book club discussions. In Torry's classroom, more instructional time had to be devoted to teaching students discussion skills than to anything else. The fishbowl technique proved valuable in providing students with models of what to do and what not to do. Once discussion skills were in place, book club conversations blossomed, along with students' thinking and ownership. At this point, management of book clubs ceased to be a problem. Because the students could direct their own conversations, the teacher did not have to keep jumping from group to group. Instead, she could closely monitor and observe the discussions evolving in the various groups.

Fourth, teachers must be clear about the relationships between written responses and book club discussions. In the beginning, Torry worried a great deal about the poor quality of the students' written responses. Although the written responses improved as the year went on, they did not exhibit the deep thinking that occurred in the book clubs. After a time, Torry had the insight that the written responses did not need to be wonderfully polished to serve as starting points for discussion. The students used the written responses simply as a place to begin formulating ideas, and they did not have the ability to express their ideas in writing as well as in conversation. Time was a factor, too. With only 10 to 15 minutes to draft their responses, the students did not have time to polish their ideas.

In this classroom, the written responses served as preparation for the book club discussions, not as an end in themselves. It was during the book club discussions that the students had both the time and support to do their best thinking. As Vygotsky's theory suggests, social interaction—in this instance, discussion with peers—played a key role in promoting students' thinking as readers. The students could scaffold each other's thinking. They gained the ability to make inferences, solve problems for the character, respond on a personal level, and make judgments. They used this time to understand their lives, see themselves as citizens of the world, and gain insights about the human condition.

Finally, teachers must learn to trust their students. This recommendation may pose the greatest challenge to teachers accustomed to directing students' every move. Successful Book Club teachers prepare students and then turn responsibility over to them, and they recognize that students must occasionally be allowed to struggle and make mistakes as part of the learning process. As the students in this study became more adept at discussing books, they became more confident as readers. They discussed ideas that were important and meaningful to them. The book club conversations belonged to the students, and the teacher did not dictate their topics. Slowly but surely the students' attitudes changed, as they came to understand their own motivations, purposes, strategies, and choices as readers. When they took control of and responsibility for the book club discussions, they moved closer to ownership of their own literacy and literacy learning.

After a year of Book Club, Torry saw striking changes in the students. Overall, the Book Club model proved effective in improving both the students' abilities as readers and their attitudes toward reading. Their written responses to literature demonstrated a deeper level of understanding and thought. Their conversations evolved from round-robin reading of their written responses to free-flowing discussions of the characters, events, and themes in the literature. They had a better understanding of what it means to be a reader and developed ownership of literacy. This model gave back to the students the joy and excitement that can be experienced while reading.

Ultimately, we must strive to help students develop ownership of literacy. Ownership serves at once as the goal of learning and the driving force for further learning. As a result of Book Club, the students in this classroom began to take full ownership over their own reading processes. Many of the students became readers in the truest sense of the word, in the sense that they valued and enjoyed reading as a worthwhile pursuit.

> Before we were in Book Club I hated reading. I was reading little books like Franklin and stuff. Now I am reading long books like Harry Potter. Now I am a reader.
>
> —*Brian, a former struggling reader*

REFERENCES

Au, K.H. (1997). Ownership, literacy achievement, and students of diverse cultural backgrounds. In J.T. Guthrie & A. Wigfield (Eds.), *Reading engagement:*

Motivating readers through integrated instruction (pp. 168–182). Newark, DE: International Reading Association.

Dudley-Marling, C., & Searle, D. (Eds.). (1995). *Who owns learning? Questions of autonomy, choice, and control.* Portsmouth, NH: Heinemann.

Gambrell, L.B. (1996). What research reveals about discussion. In L.B. Gambrell & J.F. Almasi (Eds.), *Lively discussions! Fostering engaged reading* (pp. 25–38). Newark, DE: International Reading Association.

Gibbs, J. (1995). *TRIBES: A new way of learning and being together.* Sausalito, CA: CenterSource Systems.

Lehr, S., & Thompson, D.L. (2000). The dynamic nature of response: Children's reading and responding to *Maniac McGee* and *The Friendship. The Reading Teacher, 53,* 480–493.

McMahon, S.I. (1997). Book clubs: Contexts for students to lead their own discussions. In S.I. McMahon & T.E. Raphael (Eds.), *The book club connection: Literacy learning and classroom talk* (pp. 89–118). New York: Teachers College Press; Newark, DE: International Reading Association.

McMahon, S.I., & Raphael, T.E. (Eds.) (1997). *The book club connection: Literacy learning and classroom talk.* New York: Teachers College Press; Newark, DE: International Reading Association.

Raphael, T.E., & McMahon, S.I. (1994). Book Club: An alternative framework for reading instruction. *The Reading Teacher, 48,* 102–116.

Raphael, T.E., McMahon, S.I., Goatley, V.J., Bentley, J.L., Boyd, F.B., Pardo, L.S., et al. (1994). Literature and discussion in the reading program. *Language Arts, 69,* 54–61.

Raphael, T.E., Pardo, L., Highfield, K., & McMahon, S.I. (1997). *Book club: A literature-based curriculum.* Littleton, MA: Small Planet Communications.

Rosenblatt, L. (1978). *The reader, the text, the poem: The transactional theory of the literary work.* Carbondale, IL: Southern Illinois University Press.

Vygotsky, L.S. (1978). *Mind in society: The development of higher psychological processes* (M. Cole, V. John-Steiner, S. Scribner, & E. Souberman, Eds. and Trans.). Cambridge, MA: Harvard University Press. (Original work published 1934)

CHILDREN'S LITERATURE CITED

Coerr, E. (1977). *Sadako and the thousand paper cranes.* South Holland, IL: Yearling.

Lord, B.B. (1984). *In the year of the boar and Jackie Robinson.* New York: Harper Trophy.

Sperry, A. (1940). *Call it courage.* New York: Macmillan.

CHAPTER 5

Constructing Curriculum for Differentiated Instruction: Inquiry in the Teachers' Learning Collaborative

Taffy E. Raphael, Susan Florio-Ruane, Marcella J. Kehus,
MariAnne George, Nina Levorn Hasty, and Kathy Highfield

Amy, Karen, Nina, MariAnne, and Kathy, members of the Teachers' Learning Collaborative (TLC), are meeting in the conference room at Rose Pioneer Elementary School in a suburban town in southeastern Michigan, USA. They have come from various places—from cities, other suburbs, and the class-room down the hall. They also come from different classroom settings—different grades and different kinds and levels of resources for teaching. Despite their differences, the five have been talking at length about guided reading—what it is, the contexts in which they have each embedded guided reading, and how a guided reading lesson flows. Moreover, they are thinking aloud, with examples from their own practice, about what guided reading is, what it is for, and how to use it as a tool for pupil learning.

Amy, who teaches third grade, leads the guided reading discussion by de-scribing her three-day instructional cycle of guided reading in which, while the rest of her class participates in self-selected reading, she calls each group over to a carpeted area at the back of her classroom for guided reading instruction. Amy describes for the TLC her focus on comprehension and fluency with each guided reading group. MariAnne, also a third-grade teacher, describes a similar three-day rotation of guided reading, with a similar focus in her small-group instruction. However, while she works with guided reading groups at a small table in the back of the room, the rest of the class engages in a writer's workshop. Karen then shares her format for guided reading. She meets with

Adapted from Raphael, T.E., Florio-Ruane, S., Kehus, M.J., George, M., Hasty, N.L., & Highfield, K. (2001). Thinking for ourselves: Literacy learning in a diverse teacher inquiry net-work. *The Reading Teacher, 54*, 596–607. This chapter reproduces much of the text of that article and includes an update based on activities that have transpired in the Teachers' Learning Collaborative since we wrote the article.

one group per day for a longer period of time and focuses on instruction in the strategies and skills outlined in her basal series. Nina ends this round of sharing by describing guided reading with her first-grade students, emphasizing—as did MariAnne and Amy—comprehension and fluency.

Listening to her colleagues, Karen comments on her focus on skill instruction in the reading groups, a focus that contrasts sharply with the small-group instruction described by the others present. She speculates that perhaps she is "not doing guided reading at all." Rather, she is, perhaps, reproducing in her own practice a style of literacy education by means of direct instruction in tracked reading groups that she experienced as a pupil.

Hearing others' descriptions of their teaching, Karen begins to think about her own practice, comparing and contrasting it with other pedagogies shared in the group. She begins to inquire into (a) the nature of guided reading (its forms and functions) and (b) her own practice. Karen asks pointed questions as she works to understand guided reading and how she might change the focus of her interactions with her students in the future. In this way, Karen sows the seeds of inquiry and possible reform in her own classroom and also invites further engagement by the other teachers in their diverse images of the somewhat elusive practice of guided reading. *(Adapted by Kathy Highfield from field notes of participant observation in the Teachers' Learning Collaborative)*

Between 1996 and 2000, members of the Michigan Teachers' Learning Collaborative (TLC) Network explored a common problem of practice—how to re-engage struggling readers in meaningful school literacy. A diverse group (representing a range of years of experience, diverse ethnicities, and a variety of school contexts from rural and suburban to inner-city), the teachers in TLC came to know each other as professionals over a sustained period of time. In this way, TLC is atypical of professional development groups. Members of TLC represented diverse school districts, grade levels, and background knowledge—and they had an opportunity to tackle self-directed learning over a several-year period.

TLC was composed of three teacher study groups. One group, the Literary Circle, began meeting in 1996 with the express purpose of experiencing book club activities: reading, writing, and talking about books with a substantive thematic focus. The Literary Circle chose to read books that had strong themes related to culture, learning, and the immigrant experience. A second group, the Book Club *Plus* Study group, met from 1998 to 2001. Members were interested in drawing on what they had learned from their experiences in teacher book clubs (e.g., Literary Circle, graduate course–based book clubs) to develop a literacy curriculum designed to reengage struggling readers. The third group, the Literacy Circle Study Group, was a school-based group engaged in teacher book clubs using professional texts, including but not limited to texts about Book Club. They met from 1999 to 2001. Together, members of the three groups formed the network that became TLC.

What bound the three teacher study groups together as a network was a common problem of practice and a commitment to learning by means of dialogue and inquiry. The TLC Network was supported in part by the Center for the Improvement of Early Reading Achievement (CIERA) and in part by the Walgreen Teachers in Residence Program at the University of Michigan. However, the Network primarily was supported by individuals' voluntary commitment of time and energy to something in which they believe. Members of each Network "node" met approximately once or twice a month within their study groups, and the Network met together as an entire group once or twice a semester.

In the research on TLC for this chapter, we attempted to document the learning of participating teachers. We viewed the inquiries undertaken by TLC as a form of innovative professional development. We used participant observation, interview, and analysis of oral and written discourse to track teacher development over time and in context. This was an important part of a wider study in which CIERA researchers were concerned with the relation among teacher development, classroom instruction, and the re-engagement of struggling young readers and writers in TLC members' classrooms (see Florio-Ruane, Raphael, Highfield, & Berne, 2002, for a description of this research).

Although participants in TLC learned about many aspects of literacy instruction, the focus of this chapter is differentiated instruction. We describe teachers' collaboration to design and field-test a curriculum framework for literacy instruction and assessment to accelerate the literacy learning of struggling readers and to meet the diverse needs of literacy learners. We begin with a focus on how we developed as a professional community and on the role TLC served in our focus on re-engaging our struggling readers. We then describe the curriculum framework we developed and the assessment system created to align with our instruction and document our students' progress. We end with a discussion of the importance of our teachers' finding a voice in the curriculum reform efforts that affect our professional activities in literacy education.

Linking Study Groups Through Common Grounds

We believe that inquiry is central to the work of teaching, that it requires community, and that communities of practice can take myriad forms. We live and work many miles from one another, along traffic-choked freeways throughout southeastern Michigan. We give up Saturdays and evenings to keep in touch about our work, and we have had to become computer literate to communicate with one another by means of e-mail. What holds a group such as ours together? It is the common ground of a problem of practice with which we all struggle in our respective teaching contexts: How can we re-engage low-achieving readers?

We come to this question as experienced teachers who have often felt frustrated and isolated in our work. Too often, we have identified struggling readers and worried that our very interventions to support their learning of skills and strategies have, in fact, derailed them from literacy. While they spend most of their time in drill and practice, our more able readers seem to move quickly beyond grade-level expectations, engage in reading and writing, and talk about text in motivating and empowering ways. Thus, without intending to do so, we sometimes find that we have set up classrooms in which the rich get richer and the poor get poorer. How can we create learning communities in classrooms in which the skills and strategies we diligently teach are practiced by all our students in powerful, engaging ways? In TLC we have an opportunity to ask and answer this question in studies in our own classrooms and in conversation with one another. Some members of TLC teach in Title I schools where there are many programs and pressures to raise literacy achievement. Some work in more affluent school districts and have greater autonomy to create individual programs, yet they still are accountable for students' learning and their performance on high-stakes achievement tests. In each case, we find that it is easy to lose our way as we try to construct coherent, meaningful literacy experiences for all our students. Figure 5.1 illustrates an example from one of our school districts of the forces that influence the teaching of literacy in one of our member's classrooms.

Describing this figure at the annual International Reading Association Research Awards Address, Nina Hasty, one of the authors of this chapter, said the following:

> The circles in this diagram illustrate the various groups with a stake in literacy instruction in my district, and many people have had a voice in

FIGURE 5.1

INFLUENCES ON TEACHING AND TEACHER LEARNING

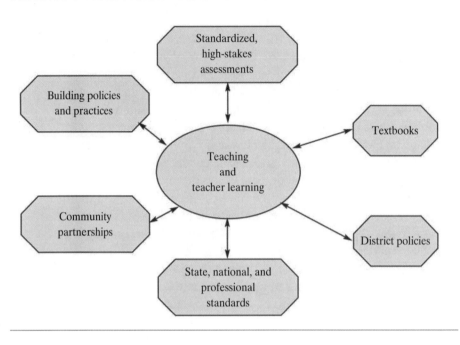

these—publishers, administrators, curriculum specialists, politicians, university professors. Notice that the teacher is at the center of this diagram. I am in the center in terms of my direct work with children and my accountability, but it is hard for me to have a voice about my own practice outside the confines of my room. In a group such as TLC, I use my own voice to learn with other teachers so that I can improve literacy education for youngsters. In inquiring into the factors that shape my practice, I am discovering that the curriculum is not the reading series. It is not the MEAP [Michigan Educational Assessment Program] test or my district's exit skills for promotion to the next grade. The literacy curriculum is about spoken and written language. The curriculum is an ongoing conversation with and among my students.

This conversation, as Bruner (1986) has taught us, is iterative—moving back and forth as it, metaphorically, folds back on itself and gets more complex as we learn. As such, it frames what we read, write, say, and hear in the process of learning literacy. In the learning conversation in Nina's classroom, she and her students talk and wonder together about how language works, what written language is used for, how authors use different kinds of text to convey ideas, how to make sense of their lives through reading and writing, and how their lives are "storied."

Why We Need One Another

To understand how our community of practice worked to explore problems of practice, it is useful, we believe, to understand the history of our TLC Network's development. All the members of the Network were interested in re-engaging low achievers through authentic interactions with literature, and most of us were particularly intrigued by the idea of having our students participate in book clubs, using and adapting the Book Club program (Raphael, Pardo, & Highfield, 2002) for our classrooms. But, we realized that two things stood in our way: (1) few of us had any experiences participating in book clubs with friends or colleagues, and (2) we wanted Book Club to be more than just an enrichment activity for already successful decoders.

In their role as teacher educators, two authors of this chapter were particularly concerned with the problem of teachers being asked to teach in dialogic ways without having experienced this kind of teaching themselves, and with the related problem of lack of experience with sustained inquiry. Teacher education students and practicing teachers rarely have the opportunity to experience sustained exploration of a complex idea, let alone to do so through dialogic practices, yet these are experiences schools expect teachers, especially those in the intermediate grades, to be able to create in their own classrooms. TLC provided a context for teachers to engage in dialogue and sustained inquiry around a complex idea, to parallel the kind of experiences in which they would engage their own students and embed appropriate instruction. One such complex idea that we have found to be particularly challenging as adult learners is that of culture— especially as it is manifest in classrooms throughout the United States and as it affects literacy teaching and learning.

In the beginning of what became TLC, Susan Florio-Ruane adapted the Book Club instructional framework developed by Raphael and her colleagues to teachers' learning about culture. Book Club had been developed to support intermediate- and middle-grade students'

skill and strategy development in the areas of comprehension and interpretation of text. Susan modified Book Club to apply to adults, developing the cultural theme in a master's-level course she then taught. In
this initial Book Club course, participants (including some of the authors of this chapter) read, wrote, and spoke about culture in response
to autobiographical literature emphasizing the immigrant experience.
In addition, we thought about our own development as literacy learners
and as members of a culturally diverse society, as other teachers taking the course developed vignettes revealing their own autobiographies
as literacy learners. Course members remained together, meeting
monthly, to form the Literary Circle study group. Our ongoing teaching
and research finds that because culture is so hard for us to talk about,
sustained reading and conversation engaging multiple texts are needed
repeatedly to explore the concept. Thus, conversation can be a powerful
way to learn about *complex concepts in indeterminate domains* (Spiro,
Coulson, Feltovich, & Anderson, 1988; Spiro, Feltovich, Jacobson, &
Coulson, 1992).

There is a family resemblance between teachers' learning about a
complex construct such as culture and the kind of curriculum conversations we want to see—and to support—through our students' reading,
writing, and talking about text. Children's conceptions of culture, both in
their own lives and as a key part of learning to contribute to a democratic society, are like our own—remarkably, but not surprisingly,
impoverished. Learning about democratic values—currently listed as
one of the primary national goals within U.S. national and state social
studies standards—requires not only the expository knowledge that typically is transmitted through textbooks but also the important experiences that stem from engaging with that process. Thus, a second "node"
in the TLC Network was formed through the creation of the Book Club
Plus Study Group, focused on extending what we had learned through
the course and Literary Circle to developing meaningful literacy curriculum for diverse learners.

The "Our Storied Lives" Curriculum

Being a literate individual is more demanding today than ever before,
and the challenge to educators is greater today than ever before. Not
just the "college track" but "every school in America will ensure that all
students learn to use their minds well" (National Education Goals

Panel, 1995, p. 11). U.S. political leaders have established as a national priority the goal that all students leave third grade able to read. However, in addition to decoding print, all children need to engage in the higher order thinking associated with literacy, a demand that continues to grow as students move through intermediate and middle school grade levels. To this end, the members of the TLC Network recognize that as literacy teachers we have dual—and what have sometimes been characterized as competing—obligations. The members of the Book Club *Plus* Study Group took the lead in curriculum development, moving from our own learning experiences to creating curriculum to engage and re-engage young readers. This curriculum work involved identifying important contexts for instruction and developing important thematic content to provide a substantive focus to study within the new curriculum.

On the one hand, we are obligated to make sure all students have decoding skills sufficient to read independently. Thus, it is vital for all students to have sufficient practice using reading materials that are at their instructional level. On the other hand, it is a crucial goal to make sure that students learn to *think* as readers and writers. Students must, therefore, also have access to age-appropriate material that challenges their thinking and fosters thoughtful talk and writing about text. We cannot choose between these two obligations, nor must we view them as being in opposition. Good literacy education must involve both.

As things currently stand, low-achieving readers may conceivably go through school never engaging with challenging texts appropriate for their age level, texts that require higher order thinking and interpretation skills such as those laid out in our national agenda as being most desirable. Moreover, these struggling readers do not have the opportunity to talk with peers about such materials and the ideas they contain. Further, in such circumstances the classroom becomes stratified. It is difficult in that setting, if not impossible, for low-achieving readers to join in, or for the teacher to create a functioning community of learners, with such a wide diversity of needs and abilities present in any classroom. TLC identified this problem as being at the core of the reengagement of struggling readers. From 1997 through 2001, the teacher-researchers in TLC designed, taught, and evaluated the Book Club *Plus* curricular framework aimed at solving this problem.

Book Club *Plus*

In Book Club *Plus*, we created a design based in thematic units that enable us to take advantage of two contexts for reading, writing, and talk about text: Literacy Block and Book Club (see Figure 5.2). Each is an extended period of time in the school day within which important activities take place, each serving a different purpose in students' learning.

In Literacy Block, activities related to the skills and strategies of reading and writing are taught and practiced. They may include writers' workshops, practice activities to foster word-level decoding skills, reading (or listening to) books individually or in peer groups, and so forth. However, one important feature of Literacy Block is guided reading, or teacher-led discussion around specific skills, strategies, and words to be taught. Students learn these within the guided reading groups using texts at their instructional level. These texts are all thematically linked to the unit in which the entire class participates and to the books that are discussed in weekly book clubs.

In Book Club, heterogeneous student-led book clubs are where students apply the strategies they have been taught by discussing compelling, age-appropriate literature. Access to the literature discussed in the book clubs can involve a variety of routes: independent reading, buddy reading, listening or viewing centers, and teacher read-alouds.

FIGURE 5.2

INSTRUCTIONAL CONTEXTS OF BOOK CLUB *PLUS*

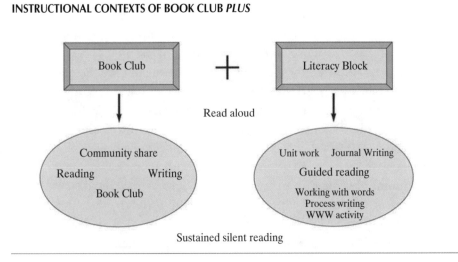

What is crucial is not that every child read every Book Club book independently, but that all children have access to these challenging, age-appropriate books and all students write and speak in response to them. As they respond to the texts and to one another, students learn to link texts to examine complex ideas.

Just as culture was a core theme of the TLC members' reading, writing, and talk about books, it became one of the complex ideas we explored to anchor our year-long curricular theme, Our Storied Lives. Students address this theme in three six- to eight-week units: Stories of Self, Family Stories, and Stories of Culture. This progression of units allows us to begin with a focus on the self, a concept that fits with curricular materials across grade levels, and it contextualizes the self within the broader areas of family, community, and society.

Each unit within the Our Storied Lives framework draws from a set of books that allows the particular focus to be developed fully. Focus development occurs through the Book Club book, the guided reading books and/or stories, the teacher read-aloud, shared reading books that are often the basis for minilessons during Writers' Workshop, and the classroom library, which often serves students' sustained silent reading. Further, each unit includes a culminating project requiring students to apply and integrate language arts skills and strategies along with the overarching theme. Teachers alternated students' Book Club activities (two or three days per week) with the guided reading and independent unit work of Literacy Block (two or three days per week).

Table 5.1 lists the books we used when teaching the Family Stories unit. We featured the work of Patricia Polacco, a prolific Michigan author who bases her writings on her own life, highlighting relationships among family members, cultural heritage, and family stories. In describing this unit we make reference to students' work in the classroom of MariAnne George, one of the authors of this chapter.

Each unit involved reading, writing, and talking about the thematically organized books, in contexts that included a teacher read-aloud, guided reading, shared reading, writers' workshop, and Book Club. For example, in the Stories of Self unit, an early writing project involved creating timelines of students' lives, with a key event from each year represented by a combination of an artifact or set of artifacts and text. Students used their timelines as sources for ideas about writing, such as a family story in which they are a main character. The culminating project that students in MariAnne's third-grade classroom

TABLE 5.1

FAMILY STORIES TEXTS

Context	Books Used in Grade 3
Book Club Book	*Chicken Sunday*
Guided Reading	Above grade level: *Meteor!*
	At grade level: *Some Birthday!*
	Below grade level: *My Rotten Red-Headed Older Brother*
Read-Alouds	*Babushka's Doll*
(also used as models	*The Keeping Quilt*
for process writing	*Thank You, Mr. Falker*
activities)	*The Bee Tree*
	Boat Ride With Lillian Two Blossom
	Picnic at Mudsock Meadow
	Appelemando's Dreams
	Pink and Say
	Thundercake
	Tikvah Means Hope
	Firetalking (Polacco autobiography)
Viewing	*Dream Keeper*

created involved oral retellings of family stories based on artifacts they valued. For example, Nathan's great-grandfather had come from Ireland. When it came time to share his family story, Nathan brought a pickle barrel he and his father had made and shared a story he had learned by interviewing his grandfather. As Nathan tells it, his great-grandfather had to leave Ireland rather suddenly and in secret, so he stowed away inside a pickle barrel and escaped on a boat. Hearing about the interactions Nathan had with his father and grandfather bring home the importance of such assignments, and the family story content highlights one of the many histories of how the United States was built.

The variety of artifacts students brought to this task reflected what they had learned from reading picture books such as William Joyce's (1997) *The World of William Joyce Scrapbook* and from hearing autobiographies of Roald Dahl (1984), Gary Paulsen (1998), Jean Craighead George (1996), and others. Moreover, students were informed by their continually developing reading, writing, and discussion skills as well as their knowledge of culture and of how lives are presented and represented. These family stories are so deeply rooted in the students' cultural heritage that it was a natural transition to the third unit in the theme, Stories of Culture.

The students learned what an artifact was and, in so doing, discovered culture in material aspects of everyday life. They saw how these matter—not just as festivals or tokens of ethnic identity—but as receptacles of collected and collective meaning, signals of the shared activities and understandings within social groups. Writing and oral language are artifacts of culture by this definition, as are such objects as pickle barrels.

In MariAnne's third grade, students learned about themselves and each other and about their relationship to other family members and their cultural heritage. In Marcella's eighth-grade class, students used different books but a similar thematic focus and instructional framework to explore more complex issues of identity, conformity, and social responsibility.

MariAnne's ongoing teacher research examines whether and how this curriculum supports students' learning to make intertextual connections—across texts, between the texts and students' own lives, and across the contexts of writing, reading, and discussion—to understand a complex concept (Hartman, 1991). At least two decades of research document the importance of background knowledge for text understanding, and important sources for such knowledge include other texts students read, as well as the "texts" of their own lived experiences (Anderson, Hiebert, Scott, & Wilkinson, 1985). MariAnne chose to study the role of students' intertextual connections in meeting the diverse needs of students for many reasons, with one of the most important being how such connections impact students' response to literature, their text comprehension, and the interpretations they make.

Two examples illustrate the intertextual connections students make and why we teach so that students come to value such connections. In the first example, we highlight how Mrs. George's students used text-to-text connections as they responded to books within the Family Stories unit. In the second, a connection from text to life helped one of her second language learners find a way to talk about his own feelings of frustration in dealing with living in a new country.

The first example is taken from an entry MariAnne made in her teacher researcher log, dated February 12. Following a read-aloud, she was eavesdropping on her students as they talked during snack time. In her log, she wrote,

> Today I was absolutely thrilled at the discussion that took place after
> my read aloud of Patricia Polacco's book *Thundercake*. As I finished,
> Megan raised her hand and said, "That story is a lot like *Chicken Coop
> Monster* because Melissa's Grandpa helped her get over her fears like
> Patricia Polacco's grandmother did." Josh added, "Only it was her
> Babushka [grandmother] instead of her grandfather like in *Chicken
> Coop Monster*." Chelsea then chimed in, "It was kinda like that but the
> opposite in Tomie dePaola's book *First One Foot and Then the Other
> [Now One Foot, Now the Other]* because Tomie helped his grandpa get
> over his fears.

The children's intertextual connections began by noting that the
role of the grandparents in each of two stories was quite similar, helping their grandchild overcome a specific fear. They contrasted the two
on the basis of gender. Chelsea's contribution was even more sophisticated, making a connection at the level of characters' agency in the
story and highlighting that the two generations' roles were reversed in
dePaola's story, in which a child helps his grandfather overcome a fear.
Their comments were spontaneous, rather than orchestrated by the
teacher, the connections showed depth, and the fact that they occurred
during snack time suggests that the students had internalized what
they had been taught about both text interpretation and conversation.

When the unit drew to a close, the teacher led a whole-class discussion in which she asked students to think about the big ideas or
themes that reflected commonalties across their texts. Hands shot up,
and one of the first themes to be identified was "facing your fears."
We took this as evidence that conversations outside the formal context
of Book Club and Literacy Block were as important to students' meaning making as those orchestrated within.

In the second example, the text of *Molly's Pilgrim* (Cohen, 1983)
helps a second language learner develop the language to talk about his
often-frustrating school experiences. Johann, an ESL student from
Germany, joined the class in February, speaking little English, though
able to read at about a second-grade level. *Molly's Pilgrim* was a Book
Club selection that was part of the Stories of Culture unit. Johann was
"buddied" with a more proficient reader during the silent reading portion of Book Club. From MariAnne's teacher research log, we read,

> After reading the assigned chapters, the children moved into written
> response time in their literature logs. However, instead of writing,
> Johann put his head down on his desk. I walked over and sat with him
> trying to help him think of an idea to put down on paper. After a few

probing questions, Johann responded "I didn't like the song 'Jolly Molly.'" "Why?" I asked. "The girls laugh at her." He then tried to explain to me that's how he felt at times because he was new and not from America. This exchange represented a breakthrough for us, since until this point I had not been able to engage Johann in writing or talking about text. The feelings he shared with Molly, the main character of the story, made the writing and talk meaningful. Johann wrote his two sentences (with my support) and was later able to share this with his Book Club group.

If, as Gavelek and Raphael (1996) have argued, learning is a complex, iterative process of social engagement, reflection, and transformation, then Book Club seems to foster learning about self, others, and text. The multiple texts students and teacher can reference include the published books they discuss, the writing they do in response, the oral stories they hear, and the stories they dare to tell one another. These intertextual connections make a fabric within which literature can be understood and the conventions of reading and writing practiced to powerful ends. Thus, in our network's research, we focus on these connections and hope to understand better the role of curricular frameworks in teaching and teacher thinking, and the effectiveness of a framework like Book Club *Plus* for re-engaging struggling readers.

Assessment Research in Book Club *Plus*

It should be clear by now that our "problem of practice" of trying to re-engage struggling readers is an enormous one. Attempting to solve it opened the door to many associated and interesting problems from literature selection, to supporting materials, to classroom organization, to meeting the needs of all learners, to what was perhaps the most challenging—figuring out how to assess learning. With all the goals we were trying to accomplish, we engaged in *collaborative inquiry* to work out the details of the curriculum, teaching, and instruction. Even in one of our most hierarchically organized school districts, in which teachers must use a particular textbook series for reading instruction, our members felt bold enough to work "outside the box," appropriating and transforming the units to make Book Club *Plus* come to life in our classrooms, *putting our voices in the center of the conversation*.

The much harder task for us involved assessment in two major facets:

1. student learning in Book Club *Plus* to evaluate whether our framework was effective in supporting learning

2. finding ways to document student learning in terms that were useful within our classrooms' related communities and responsive to the standards to which we are all accountable

We looked around and learned from others, especially from Au (Au, Carroll, & Scheu, 1995) and Valencia (1999), and their teacher research colleagues in Hawaii and Washington, respectively. We began to think that both we and our students might be able to put our own voices in the center of the assessment conversation. Thus, on one summer weekend, a small group of us got together in a cabin in northern Michigan to generate the following "I Can" statements:

Reading
I can retell a story in my own words.
I can make meaning when I read a variety of texts.
I can make connections between my own life and what I am reading.
I can make connections within and between texts.
I can figure out a theme from my reading.

Writing
I can write to communicate my ideas.
I can use writing for different purposes and audiences.
I can show "me" in my writing.

Discussion
I can contribute to a good book club discussion:
  • I can stay on topic when I talk.
  • I can share my feelings and ideas.
  • I can respect others' ideas and opinions.
  • I can build on others' ideas.
  • I can bring others into the discussion.

Evaluation
I can show and/or tell what I learned and how I learned it.

Culture
I can use artifacts to describe
  • my own cultural heritage,
  • others' cultures, and
  • similarities and differences across cultures.
I can define culture and how cultures change.

We used these "I Can" statements to create an assessment system for Book Club *Plus* guided by national, state, and district standards but tailored to the goals and commitments of our curriculum framework. For the first time, these "I Can" statements pushed us to say in our own words what was important to teach, learn, and assess within Book Club *Plus*.

Perhaps tackling assessment is the strongest example of our efforts to think for ourselves as teachers of literacy. The "I Can" statements can be thought of as an artifact constructed within the TLC community of practice. As such, they stand in stark contrast to many of the assessments the teachers were required by their schools, districts, or state to undertake. They were devised in ways cognizant of other yardsticks against which teachers and students would be measured, but they were framed in terms that made sense within the TLC teachers' classrooms and Book Club *Plus* curriculum. To develop these statements, we moved from the formal statements of official documents from national, state, and district standards to language we could use with our students. For example, one standard in our Michigan English Language Arts Framework says, "Students can engage in extended conversations with teachers and/or peers about subject matter in a way that builds an improved and shared understanding of ideas and topics."

Our own wording for that standard highlights specific ways our students could be expected to contribute to a good discussion. Thus, the "I Can" for this discussion goal begins with the general statement, "I can contribute to a good book club discussion," and then is broken down into much more specific indicators of what the student knows, can do, and, with the teacher, can accumulate evidence for having learned:

I can stay on topic when I talk.

I can share my feelings and ideas.

I can respect others' ideas and opinions.

I can build on others' ideas.

I can bring others into the discussion.

These "I Can" statements provided the foundation from which grade-level benchmarks and subsequent rubrics could be developed. These rubrics and benchmarks became the foundation of our assessment system, providing the framework for student self-evaluation, teacher evaluation, and portfolios that together provide evidence of learning. We aimed to make our language clear and simple for our students.

Ironically, once we had made these "I Can" statements for each of the standards, we found that we had also created language much preferred by our parents, administrators, and colleagues. Thus, the "I Can" statements gave us a common language to discuss our work both in going public with our colleagues and as we continue our research on student learning in Book Club *Plus*.

The "I Can" statements are divided into five related areas of learning: reading, writing, discussion, evaluation, and content knowledge (in our examples, the content knowledge was "culture," but this content focus varies depending on the focus of a particular unit or set of units). The first four areas cut across grade levels, differentiated only at the benchmark level, but the content goals often varied. In the unit MariAnne taught and researched, the focus was on culture. In Marcella's eighth-grade classroom, the focus was on social responsibility. Just as we worked collaboratively to define these "I Can" statements, so, too, did we want our students to feel a similar sense of ownership within our classrooms. To that end, we each turned to our students—from Nina's second graders to MariAnne's third graders to Marcella's eighth graders—to identify the benchmarks that defined what we mean by "success" in a given area. Marcella's eighth-grade classroom is illustrative. After a series of student-led discussions, the eighth graders built from the "I Can" statements about discussion to create a set of criteria for a good discussion:

- Voice own opinions
- Back up opinion with facts
- Have good eye contact
- Not overuse *like*
- Ask good questions
- Not jump around topics
- Make connections
- Be polite
- Speak clearly
- Promote (and tolerate) some disagreements
- Be open to everyone talking

These criteria, in turn, became the rubric for assessing students' progress, both as a self-evaluation and from teacher observations. We did similar activities with students' writing, reading, and content learning. We feel confident that such a sweeping assessment model meets the needs of all stakeholders in communicating about student achievement.

Our overall assessment system, reflected in Figure 5.3, flows from the "I Can" statements. It is designed to track student learning in these five areas in a variety of ways—from the work samples collected in portfolios, to standardized tests of reading and language arts, to running records and teacher observations, to pre- and postevaluations of

FIGURE 5.3

ASSESSMENT SYSTEM

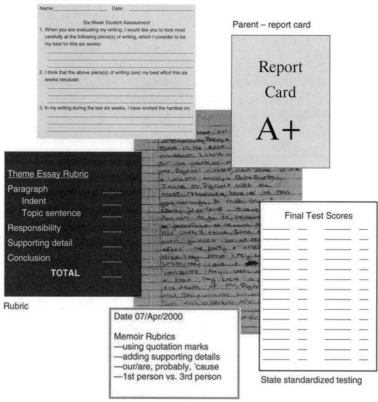

student-led book club discussions. Along with this assessment, we present one summative essay related to our reading theme to illustrate how we are able to assess at various levels and for different audiences or stakeholders. For this piece of writing, we began with a student's self-evaluation that informed both student and teacher as to how this student was performing in relation to his or her own learning goals. For our own teaching purposes, we also kept anecdotal notes to inform our teaching. This piece of writing would also be evaluated more formally using a rubric based on "I Can" statements and our negotiated benchmarks; such a rubric serves to inform multiple audiences, primarily the students and parents, as to how the work matches our criteria of success in the given area. This same rubric could also be translated into a number or letter grade for district report cards, communicating the achievements of students at many different levels of literacy learning for local school and district accountability. Last, in the broadest sense, the work could be evaluated according to state or national standards, such as giving holistic scores to students' writing indicating their levels of proficiency.

Building on the generative nature of the "I Can" statements for students, we are also beginning to develop "I Can" statements for ourselves. Few studies in education have tried to link changes in teachers' knowledge with changes in students' knowledge. This means that we do not know well what makes for optimum teacher education in the service of literacy learning for all students. As we look at our roles as leaders in our profession and participants in the preparation of the next generation of teachers, we hope to devise "I Can" statements for teacher learning that are powerfully connected to the learning of students. We believe this is important because we are coming to find that the teacher learning must be differentiated, meaning that the teacher learning needed to teach literacy well is, like literacy learning itself, complex and multifaceted.

Thinking and Speaking for Ourselves

In this chapter, we have drawn from the Michigan Teachers' Learning Collaborative to illustrate the potential of teacher research for informing our field, as well as to demonstrate a particular model within which such research can be accomplished. Teachers worked with their peers as well as with university-based researchers and teacher educators to investigate complex problems of both theory and practice. Our focus stemmed from our concern about struggling readers across grade levels. Specifically, we wanted to create meaningful and rich literacy experiences for these students—experiences that stimulated their higher order and critical thinking while still maintaining a place for instruction in basic skills in language conventions.

Through conversation in professional study groups, we became convinced that we needed a new, or at least a substantially modified, curriculum. In TLC, we met in book clubs and study groups for experience in conversation-based learning, emphasizing critical thinking, and working within a community of learners to solve a problem. We took from our experiences as readers, writers, and thinkers insights for our own teaching. That led us to the design, teaching, and assessment of the Our Storied Lives curriculum and to studying how our struggling readers both experienced and learned from that curriculum.

We have also begun to "go public" with our ideas through both informal and formal presentations. In doing this, we introduce our ideas to members of a broader professional community who, in turn, further *our* thinking by their response to our work. The contexts in which teachers work today tend to be isolated from other professionals. They are embedded within a hierarchical system in which the teachers' day-to-day activities are governed by external forces: administrative mandates, parental requests, and, somewhat unique to today's climate, legislative directives. Missing from the lives of teachers is the opportunity to articulate and investigate with others the means for improving our practice and the learning of those with whom we work. Study groups provide an activity setting in which these voices and views can be expressed as part of learning.

From psychological perspectives, teacher study groups are illustrative of the power of a learning community. For the past two decades, many literacy educators have drawn from the work of Ann Brown (Brown & Campione, 1990; Lave, 1990; Lave & Wenger, 1991; Palincsar & Brown, 1984; Rogoff, 1990) and others to detail the ways in which Vygotsky's (1934/1978) theory of learning plays out in discourse practices. Vygotsky's basic tenet is that learning is a social phenomenon. Individuals learn, but that learning begins, and is based in, social activity or the social plane. This social plane is reflected in the public and shared discourse of the teacher study group as ideas are appropriated and transformed.

Sociolinguists such as Swales (1991) and Gee (1992) have helped us to understand the importance of this public discourse. Knowledge of the language practices within a discourse community provides access to that community and defines who the community members are. Language is a key factor in the development of educators' identities— as professionals, as educators, as literacy educators, and as teacher researchers. Understanding the importance of the discourse community helps us create opportunities for access and opportunities to harness the power of conversation to move beyond the immediate setting and to effect important changes in practice.

In our collaborative research, we found that out of a dialogue among our diverse participants, we constructed knowledge that might otherwise have eluded us if we had conducted either traditional university-based research or innovative school-based practitioner research in isolation. Rather than define practitioner research as being alternative to or in opposition to university-based research on teaching, we hope to have argued persuasively for a model of "learning community" (Schwab, 1975), or negotiated knowledge and meaning within a diverse group with common concerns. Thus, although we are not naive about the historical privileging of academic research in which teachers serve as "subjects" or "informants," we are also not sanguine about such work. We underscore teacher research as another powerful but—like university-driven research—also limited genre for the study of education.

In organizing our group explicitly to work against the traditional isolation of teacher from teacher, university from classroom, novice from experienced educator, we hope to craft a new professional community with a new discourse for the understanding and improvement of practice to meet the diverse needs of all learners through differentiated instruction. From the content of our teaching, to our authorship of the curriculum, to our commitment to supporting diverse learners, to our reflections on the experience to date, TLC Network participants reflect the power of dialogic models of professional development.

REFERENCES

Anderson, R.C., Hiebert, E.H., Scott, J.A., & Wilkinson, I.A.G. (1985). *Becoming a nation of readers: The report of the Commission on Reading*. Washington, DC: U.S. Department of Education.

Au, K.H., Carroll, J.H., & Scheu, J.R. (1995). *Balanced literacy instruction: A teacher's resource book*. Norwood, MA: Christopher-Gordon.

Brown, A.L., & Campione, J.C. (1990). Communities of learning and thinking, or a context by any other name. In D. Kuhn (Ed.), *Developmental perspectives on teaching and learning thinking skills* (Vol. 21, pp. 108–126). Farmington, CT: Karger.

Bruner, J. (1986). *Actual minds, possible worlds*. Cambridge, MA: Harvard University Press.

Florio-Ruane, S., Raphael, T.E., Highfield, K., & Berne, J. (2002, November). *Re-engaging struggling young readers and writers by means of innovative professional development*. Paper presented at Improving Reading Achievement Through Professional Development conference. Washington DC: Rutgers University, The Carnegie Corporation of New York and The Laboratory for Student Success (LSS).

Gavelek, J.R., & Raphael, T.E. (1996). Changing talk about text: New roles for teachers and students. *Language Arts*, *73*, 182–192.

Gee, J.P. (1992). *The social mind: Language, ideology, and social practice*. New York: Bergin & Garvey.

Hartman, D. (1991). The intertextual link of readers using multiple passages: A postmodern/semiotic/cognitive view of meaning making. In J. Zutell & S. McCormick (Eds.), *Learner factors/teacher factors: Issues in literacy research* (40th yearbook of the National Reading Conference, pp. 616–636). Chicago: National Reading Conference.

Lave, J. (1990). The culture of acquisition and the practice of understanding. In J.W. Stigler, R.A. Shweder, & G. Herdt (Eds.), *Cultural psychology* (pp. 309–327). Cambridge, UK: Cambridge University Press.

Lave, J., & Wenger, E. (1991). *Situated learning: Legitimate peripheral participation*. Cambridge, UK: Cambridge University Press.

National Education Goals Panel. (1995). *The national education goals report: Building a nation of learners, 1995*. Washington, DC: U.S. Government Printing Office.

Palincsar, A.S., & Brown, A.L. (1984). Reciprocal teaching of comprehension-fostering and comprehension-monitoring activities. *Cognition and Instruction*, *1*, 117–175.

Raphael, T.E., Pardo, L.S., & Highfield, K. (2002). *Book Club: A literature-based curriculum* (2nd ed.). Littleton, MA: Small Planet Communications.

Rogoff, B. (1990). *Apprenticeship in thinking: Cognitive development in social context*. Oxford, UK: Oxford University Press.

Schwab, J.J. (1975). On learning community: Education and the state. *The Center Magazine*, *8*(3), 30–44.

Spiro, R.J., Coulson, R.L., Feltovich, P.J., & Anderson, D.K. (1988). Cognitive flexibility theory: Advanced knowledge acquisition in ill-structures domains. In *10th annual conference of the Cognitive Science Society* (pp. 375–383). Hillsdale, NJ: Erlbaum.

Spiro, R.J., Feltovich, P.J., Jacobson, M.J., & Coulson, R.L. (1992). Knowledge representation, content specification, and the development of skill in situation-specific knowledge assembly: Some constructivist issues as they relate to Cognitive Flexibility Theory and hypertext. In T.M. Duffy & D.J. Jonassen

(Eds.), *Constructivism and the technology of instruction: A conversation* (pp. 57–75). Hillsdale, NJ: Erlbaum.

Swales, J.M. (1991). *Genre analysis: English in academic and research settings.* Cambridge, UK: Cambridge University Press.

Valencia, S. (1999). *Literacy portfolios in action.* Fort Worth, TX: Harcourt College.

Vygotsky, L.S. (1978). *Mind in society: The development of higher psychological processes* (M. Cole, V. John-Steiner, S. Scribner, & E. Souberman, Eds. and Trans.). Cambridge, MA: Harvard University Press. (Original work published 1934)

CHILDREN'S BOOKS CITED

Cohen, B. (1983). *Molly's pilgrim.* New York: Morrow.

Dahl, R. (1984). *Boy: Tales of a childhood.* New York: Puffin.

dePaola, T. (1998). *Now one foot, now the other.* New York: Putnam.

George, J.C. (1996). *The tarantula in my purse and 172 other wild pets.* New York: HarperCollins.

Joyce, W. (1997). *The world of William Joyce scrapbook.* New York: HarperCollins.

McKissack, P. (1992). Chicken Coop Monster. In *The dark thirty: Southern tales of the supernatural* (pp. 111–122). New York: Scholastic.

Paulsen, G. (1998). *My life in dog years.* New York: Delacorte.

Polacco, P. (1989). *Boat ride with Lillian Two Blossom.* New York: Philomel.

Polacco, P. (1990). *Thundercake.* New York: Putnam.

Polacco, P. (1991). *Appelemando's dreams.* New York: Philomel.

Polacco, P. (1991). *Some birthday!* New York: Simon & Schuster.

Polacco, P. (1992). *Chicken Sunday.* New York: Philomel.

Polacco, P. (1992). *Picnic at Mudsock Meadow.* New York: Putnam.

Polacco, P. (1993). *The bee tree.* New York: Philomel.

Polacco, P. (1994). *Babushka's doll.* New York: Simon & Schuster.

Polacco, P. (1994). *Firetalking.* Katonah, NY: Richard C. Owen.

Polacco, P. (1994). *The keeping quilt.* New York: Simon & Schuster.

Polacco, P. (1994). *My rotten red-headed older brother.* New York: Aladdin.

Polacco, P. (1994). *Pink and Say.* New York: Philomel.

Polacco, P. (1994). *Tikvah means hope.* New York: Yearling.

Polacco, P. (1996). *Dream Keeper.* New York: Philomel

Polacco, P. (1998). *Thank you Mr. Falker.* New York: Philomel.

Polacco, P. (1999). *Meteor!* New York: Philomel.

CHAPTER 6

Establishing Instructional Congruence Across Learning Settings: One Path to Success for Struggling Third-Grade Readers

Rachel L. McCormack, Jeanne R. Paratore, and Kristina Farrell Dahlene

When the third-grade teachers at South Elementary School agreed to let their struggling readers go "down the hall" with the reading specialist during their scheduled reading block, they did so with a great amount of trepidation. They knew that their most vulnerable students would participate in the reading specialist's intervention—and they trusted her—but it left them with many questions: What would the students be missing while they were out of the classroom? How would the students feel when they got back to the classroom? What happened to our school's full inclusion model?

Three months into the intervention program, the third-grade teachers not only began to make comments on the noticeable progress their students were making, but they began to ask a very different question: "What do you do down there, anyway?" This is the story of what we did and our (intended and unintended) results.

During recent years, substantial attention has been directed toward intervention programs for children who struggle to learn to read in the first and second grades. Several approaches to early intervention have met with positive results (e.g., Foorman, Francis, Shaywitz, Shaywitz, & Fletcher, 1997; Hiebert, 1983; Pinnell, 1985; Santa & Hoien, 1999; Taylor, Strait, & Medo, 1994) indicating that when difficulty in learning to read is addressed early and intensively, widespread failure can be prevented for many children. However, despite the success of these early intervention efforts, there is evidence that a considerable number of children continue to experience difficulty in reading beyond second grade. For example, at the national level in the United States, results from the 2000 National Assessment of Educational Progress (Donahue, Finnegan, Lutkus, Allen, & Campbell, 2001) indicate that only 63% of fourth-grade students achieved at or above the basic level of achievement. At the state level, as well, large-scale testing typically indicates that large numbers of children are achieving below grade level in reading.

In the state of Massachusetts, where the work presented in this chapter was implemented, a report issued by the Massachusetts Department of Education (2000) indicated that at the fourth-grade level, 13% of all students who took the state assessment the previous spring achieved failing grades in English language arts. Disaggregation of results underscored the unevenness of achievement for particular types of learners: 7% of regular education learners, 39% of students with identified special learning needs, and 43% of students acquiring English as a second language made failing scores. These results do not include the students who did not take the test at all, which included approximately 13% of the children identified with special education needs and more than 40% of the children identified as English language learners.

The consequences of not learning to read at a level commensurate with one's peers are substantial. As described by Stanovich (2000), differences in reading ability enable differential support of further vocabulary, knowledge, and cognitive structures outside school. These bootstrapped knowledge bases then create further individual differences that are made manifest in differential performance as children grapple with subsequent in-school content and skills.

The negative consequences of failure in reading may extend well beyond the areas of an individual child's cognition and intellect. In recent years, both federal and state policymakers raised the stakes for schools and children even higher by tying evidence of grade-level achievement to funding for institutions and promotion and graduation for individuals. At the national level, the No Child Left Behind Act of 2001 (see U.S. Department of Education, 2002) includes a stipulation that federal funding be reduced in states that fail to demonstrate results in academic achievement. At the state level, consequences vary widely from state to state and district to district. In Massachusetts, individual children often face grade retention in the early grades, and in the later grades, beginning in 2003, failure to achieve the standard on the state's comprehensive assessment will prohibit the awarding of a high school diploma. In school districts in which high percentages of children test below grade level, takeover by state educational officials has been threatened as a possible sanction.

It was in this climate that this chapter's study evolved. At the time that we planned and implemented the study, one of the authors, Rachel McCormack, was one of two reading specialists in a local school. Along with her colleague, she was charged with the responsibility to help classroom teachers bring every child to grade-level performance in reading. Although previous efforts at reading intervention in first and second grades had been judged to be relatively successful, a locally developed literacy performance assessment administered at the beginning of grade 3 indicated that several children continued to struggle in reading. As we began to plan an instructional program for these children, we confronted two apparently conflicting research findings. Juel (1988, 1990) reported that children do best when they are taught with materials at their instructional levels (that is, 90% or better accuracy in word identification) and most poorly when materials are at their frustration level (below 90% accuracy in word identification). This finding has led many teachers to continue the traditional practice of differentiating children's reading instruction by changing the text in which they read.

Although differentiation allows children to read words in the text with relative ease, there is evidence that suggests it may have an unexpected consequence: Easier texts may bar access to concepts and ideas otherwise acquired by reading grade-appropriate texts. As a result, when such texts represent the only or even the primary material read by students routinely in classrooms, these children may develop what Fielding and Roller (1992) refer to as "knowledge handicaps" (p. 680). That is, the lack of exposure to grade-level concepts, vocabulary, and syntax may prevent children from acquiring information that contributes to their development of language, comprehension, and writing.

We sought an instructional intervention that would allow us to reconcile these apparently conflicting findings, one that would provide children access to grade-appropriate language, ideas, and concepts and, at the same time, help them to improve their ability to read unknown words and, therefore, to advance toward independence in reading. We drew from evidence that children would need explicit, systematic, and intensive instruction in word-study strategies (Adams, 1990, 1998; Ehri, 1997; Torgesen, Wagner, & Roshotte, 1997). We also drew from evidence that instructional strategies such as preteaching of vocabulary (Beck & McKeown, 1991), discussion of background knowledge

(Pearson & Fielding, 1991), and repeated readings (Dowhower, 1987; O'Shea, Sindelar, & O'Shea, 1985; Rasinski, 1990; Samuels, 1979; Sindelar, Monda, & O'Shea, 1990) would allow children to read and reread text that might otherwise prove too difficult, and we considered the importance of explicit instruction in reading comprehension for readers of all levels of achievement (Anderson, Chinn, Waggoner, & Nguyen, 1997; Pearson & Fielding, 1991; Pressley, 1997; Raphael, 1997).

As we clarified the intervention plan, we also refined our research focus, and we ended up with a single question to investigate: When children enter third grade reading substantially below grade level, what are the effects of grouping children homogeneously for part of their literacy instruction and providing instruction using grade-level text in combination with explicit, systematic, and intensive instruction in both word and comprehension strategies? In the sections that follow, we describe the context in which we implemented our work, the procedures we followed, and the results we achieved.

The Context

South Elementary School is a suburban school of approximately 650 students in kindergarten through fifth grade. Most of the children are of European American descent, and most of the families are of middle-class socioeconomic status. Rachel had been a classroom teacher at South Elementary for more than 20 years and, during the year of the study, was one of two reading specialists in the school.

Identifying Children in Need of Extra Help

At the beginning of the school year, the second- and third-grade teachers, reading specialists, and special education teachers worked cooperatively to identify children who were likely to benefit from additional help in reading. To do so, they relied on three primary sources of evidence: (1) a locally developed reading performance assessment, administered by the reading specialists to all third graders at the beginning of the school year; (2) the California Achievement Test (CAT-5), administered to all children in the school district at the end of grade 2; and (3) second- and third-grade teachers' observations and impressions of the children.

The reading performance assessment was designed by the reading specialists and administered individually to all 108 third graders during the first three weeks of the school year. The assessment included two measures: an oral reading of a 255-word fable selected from the district-adopted published anthology for third grade, and an oral retelling immediately thereafter. The oral reading was recorded and evaluated using the running record procedures outlined by Clay (1993). The retelling was recorded and analyzed using the standards established by Morrow (1983). Reading specialists also kept anecdotal records detailing any additional observations they had of the children's reading behaviors.

During the three-week period in which the individual assessments were taking place, classroom teachers recorded their own observations about their students' classroom reading behaviors. When they had questions and concerns about particular students, they consulted with a student's second-grade teacher to inquire about the previous year's experiences and progress in reading. In addition, they collected and examined the results of the CAT-5, administered at the end of second grade, for more information about children's reading behaviors.

At the end of the third week of school, with all tests administered and all information gathered on each child, the classroom teachers and the reading specialists met. As some of the children had been previously identified as having special learning needs, the special education teachers also participated in the review meeting. The team sought to identify children who would be likely to benefit from a special intervention in reading, based on the following criteria: they scored in the bottom quartile on the CAT-5; classroom observations during either second or third grade indicated that they were having difficulty reading grade-level texts in either reading or content areas; and, on the Reading Performance Assessment, they achieved a score below 90% on the running record and a score of 3 or less on the oral retelling. Based on a review and discussion of the evidence, the team identified 12 general education and 6 special education students they believed would benefit from extra help in reading.

Planning and Implementing the Intervention

The intervention plan was based on a flexible-grouping model (Paratore, 1991, 2000) developed initially for use with children in general education classrooms. In the original iteration of the model, all students have access to the same grade-appropriate text, and the teacher is expected to differentiate instruction by forming small, needs-based groups in which children are provided with instruction and practice in the particular skills and strategies they need to successfully read and respond to the text.

During our visits to classrooms, we had observed that in many cases when teachers implemented the model as it was originally designed, they did not always effectively differentiate instruction for children who were experiencing substantial difficulty in reading. Often, teachers were observed engaged in whole-class instruction for long periods of time, and even in classrooms where teachers formed small needs-based groups, we observed that teaching methods often did not include the types or intensity of decoding or comprehension instruction that could be expected to advance the lowest performing students toward greater independence in reading. As a result, some children received insufficient support and often failed to make appreciable gains, perhaps not because they lacked the ability to make progress, but rather because they lacked appropriate and effective instruction. In many instances, they seemed to spend more time listening and responding to text than actually reading it.

In planning the intervention for the 18 identified children, we held onto the basic tenets of the original grouping model—that access to grade-appropriate text was important for the development of vocabulary and concepts that influenced both comprehension and composition and also was important if all children were to have full access to the classroom literacy community. However, we deviated from the initial model by choosing to deliver instruction outside the classroom within a group of relatively homogeneous students. As the content of the instruction was largely similar to that which was occurring in the classroom, we called the group a "pull-aside" rather than a "pull-out" group. In the "pull-aside" model, the children would read the same text as their higher performing classroom peers; however, their instruction would be "beefed up" with more systematic and intensive instruction in word-study strategies, increased opportunities for repeated readings to build fluency, and more explicit and systematic instruction in comprehension monitoring strategies.

In order to carry out our plan, we needed the cooperation of the third-grade teachers and the special educators. This meant careful planning and a great deal of compromising. For example, all third-grade teachers had to agree to teach reading using the same literature at the same time, as the students would be pulled from four different classrooms. They also had to agree to keep the pacing of instruction consistent—and that meant that the reading specialist had to keep a brisk pace. Finally, they had to agree that when the students returned to the classroom each day, they would be reintegrated into ongoing literacy instruction and be full participants in the classroom literacy community. In the case of the special education teachers, they had to agree to permit the reading specialist to take responsibility for teaching reading to children who had been identified as having special learning needs. This was a significant programmatic departure in this school, where up to this point, any child identified as needing special education services received instruction in reading from the special education teacher.

Clearly, this was a daunting proposition for the teachers involved. It meant that classroom teachers would give up some of their autonomy in choosing what their students would read and when they would read it. It also meant that lessons could not be executed on the fly. Strict adherence to the plan was necessary if the programs offered in the two separate settings were to remain cohesive. With this ideal in mind, the intervention began.

Beginning during the first week in October, the students were provided with the intervention in pull-aside instruction four days per week in one of two groups. The groups were formed on the basis of the classroom teachers' preference: two had volunteered to send their students during the first hour and teach reading in the classroom during that time. The other two teachers delayed teaching reading until the second hour of the day, when they would send their students to the group. In each group there was a combination of general education and special education students.

A typical session included the following activities. Before reading, students reviewed and practiced retelling what they had read the previous day. The students' inability to recall and retell information had been a major consideration when selecting them for the group, and so this task received substantial emphasis. Next, the students were introduced to new vocabulary essential to the comprehension of the day's focal selection. Sight words were introduced, practiced, and added to the classroom word wall. Decodable words were introduced and practiced using appropriate word-making strategies and activities (Cunningham, 1995). Following word study, children browsed through the selection and previewed text and illustrations, shared predictions, and posed questions.

Next, the reading specialist read the text aloud while students followed along in their own copies of the book. As she read, the reading specialist used think-alouds to model comprehension-monitoring strategies such as self-questioning, visualizing, and summarizing. After the read-aloud, the children shared their reactions, returned to and discussed their predictions, and attempted to answer any questions they themselves had posed. Following the discussion, students read the selection with a peer using a variety of oral reading strategies, including echo reading, choral reading, Readers Theatre, and buddy reading.

After peer reading, students reread a selected passage to the reading teacher, individually or in pairs. They ended the reading hour by self-selecting books to read independently or in pairs. When they returned to their classrooms, they rejoined the classroom literacy community. Along with their classroom peers, they recorded their responses to the focal selection in their reading journals, and then all children were given additional time to read self-selected books.

Monitoring Progress

We monitored the children's progress at three different intervals. First, as noted previously, almost every day students reread at least one page of text to the reading specialist; these rereadings were used to determine whether or not instructional strategies were effective in helping the students to read difficult text on their own. Instruction was redirected or refined as necessary based on children's oral reading performances. Second, approximately every three weeks, a running record of each student's oral reading was taken using "transition text"—that is, the same text they were reading, but a chapter or selection not read previously. These assessments were used to determine whether or not children were learning to apply the strategies they were using routinely in familiar text when reading unfamiliar text. Lessons after these assessments were partly devoted to doing a retrospective miscue analysis (Goodman & Marek, 1996) of common errors seen in the assessment. Sentences or excerpts were recorded on an easel, and the teacher and students discussed ways in which the students might self-correct while reading on their own, using strategies to help them decode the unfamiliar words. Third, in January, after approximately 12 weeks in the intervention program, the Reading Performance Assessment was readministered to each of the 12 general education students. The purpose of readministering the assessment at this point was to determine if any of the students had made enough progress to be discharged from the intervention program. As weekly assessments had indicated that the special education students continued to require substantial support to read grade-level text, they were not included in the readministration of the performance assessment.

Mid-Year Results

The results of the Reading Performance Assessment indicated that after the first 12 weeks of instruction, 6 of the 12 general education students had achieved grade-level norms, all surpassing 90% accuracy in word-reading and all exceeding a score of 7 on the retelling measure. Their classroom teachers also observed improvement in the students' reading performance on classroom tasks. Teachers noted that the students were able to read the science and social studies texts with relative ease and that they displayed more independence in literacy tasks in general. On the basis of this information, these six students were discharged from the intervention group and joined the classroom literacy community full time.

As for the other six students, although each achieved higher scores on the performance assessment, some even achieving at the grade-level benchmark, the children were not perceived by their classroom teachers to be experiencing the same level of success on routine classroom literacy tasks. As a result, the reading specialist and the classroom teachers were not confident that the gains they made would be maintained without continued support, and they decided to keep them in the intervention program.

As the group was now substantially smaller in size, third-grade teachers were asked if they had observed that any children in their classroom reading groups were struggling. All had one or more students whom they believed would benefit from joining the intervention groups, and each of those students was added to one of the two groups. The groups now comprised six original general education students, six new general education students, and six original special education students. Instruction then continued as was described previously.

End-of-Year Results

For the purposes of this study, we analyzed the results of the original group of 12 general education students and the 6 special education students who entered the intervention project in September. Recall that at the end of second grade, all 12 general education students had scored in the bottom quartile on the CAT-5. The mean percentile ranking achieved by the group was 21.5. At the end of third grade, the school district replaced the CAT-5 with the Iowa Test of Basic Skills (ITBS). Although the tests are not directly comparable, they are similar in format and in the types of literacy tasks assessed. In addition, each test represents children in relation to national norms. On the ITBS, one child advanced to the second quartile, nine advanced to the third quartile, and two remained in the bottom quartile. The mean percentile ranking achieved by the group of 12 was 31.5.

On the locally developed Literacy Performance Assessment administered in September, the 12 general education children achieved a word-reading accuracy score of 86% and a comprehension score of 3.7. In June, the word-reading accuracy score increased to 97% and the comprehension scored increased to 9.4. In both September and June, children were tested on passages that were grade-appropriate.

In the case of the six children with special learning needs, the changes in literacy performance were dramatic. In the September administration of the Reading Performance Assessment, the children with special learning needs experienced substantial difficulty. No student was able to complete the reading of the fable and, in five cases, it was discontinued after 125 words. One student made no attempt to read it at all, stating, "I stink at reading." When the accuracy score for the 125-word abbreviated passage was calculated, the mean score was 72%. As students read a short passage from the fable, they were not asked to complete the retelling task. The June administration yielded dramatic gains for all six students. Each completed both the oral reading and the retelling. The mean word-reading accuracy score was 93.8%; the mean comprehension score was 9.6. The validity of these scores is supported by the students' performance on the Qualitative Reading Inventory II (Leslie & Caldwell, 1995). On the third-grade-level reading passage, five of the students performed at the instructional level in both word reading accuracy and comprehension.

We also wondered how children perceived the pull-aside program; at the start, classroom teachers had expressed concern that children would feel singled out and "stigmatized" by inclusion in the program. Happily, this was not the case. Teachers reported that the students looked forward to going to the intervention groups and that they had not heard any negative comments about being pulled out of the classroom. In fact, as it turned out, some seemed to perceive participation as a special privilege. In one instance, two girls burst into tears when their teacher quietly explained to them that the groups were being redesigned and there was a chance that they would remain in the classroom for reading instruction. In another case, a parent encountered in the lobby of the school at dismissal time explained that her daughter, the twin sister of a boy in one of the intervention groups, had lamented at a recent family dinner, "My teacher says I'm a good reader, and I got 100% on my last two reading tests, and I *still* can't get into Mrs. McCormack's reading group!"

Unintended Results: Emergence of Another Research Setting

We were pleased with the results, and we were eager to share them with our colleagues and our students. After doing so during one class session, one of our graduate students, a Title I teacher in a local school, decided to implement the intervention model with her own students and to gather evidence of the outcomes. In this section, we tell about her experience.

Kristina's Intervention

Kristina Dahlene, one of the authors of this chapter, is a Title I teacher in a large urban setting. Centrally located in this setting is the Parker School, comprising 504 students in prekindergarten to sixth grade. Most of the students in this school system are economically poor, with 78% eligible for free or reduced-price lunches. Forty-five percent are children of color, primarily African American or Latino, and 25% speak English as a second language. On state testing, this school district scored within the cluster of five lowest performing districts in the state, despite the school's and district's commitment to high literacy achievement for all students.

Kristina worked closely with two third-grade teachers. In both classrooms, she was responsible for the students on individual educational plans (IEPs), but she also taught others (i.e., non-IEP students) in the classroom who were low-performing readers. Typically, the instruction she provided to the struggling readers was substantially different from that given to their more able peers. She used reading materials of a lower reading level than those used by the classroom teacher, and most of her instructional time was focused on decontextualized word-study activities. The children she worked with were either pulled to a table in the back of the classroom or to an office space outside the classroom.

Kristina convinced one of the third-grade classroom teachers with whom she worked, Mrs. Caron, to allow her to try an intervention similar to the one described in this chapter. She planned to use the district-adopted published anthology as the core text, the same text that the classroom teacher used with all the students. As a team, Kristina and Mrs. Caron planned their lessons so that all the students would be receiving instruction in reading using the same text and the same pacing. They also agreed to keep detailed lesson plans to help each other stay on track and to administer periodic running records and end-of-year performance assessments on all students to document progress.

Reading instruction followed a predictable format each day. Using Paratore's (1991, 2000) flexible grouping model, all students gathered for prereading activities. Then, Kristina pulled aside the lowest performing readers to spend more time in systematic phonics instruction, to guide students through repeated readings of the selection after her initial read-aloud, and to engage the students in discussion. Mrs. Caron, meanwhile, worked with the more able readers. They read and reread the text alone and with partners, and then they completed an assigned comprehension task with partners. The students then met with Mrs. Caron to discuss the selection and their cooperative learning activities and to participate in direct instruction of a focal decoding or comprehension strategy. Then, both groups reconvened for shared writing, group discussions of the selection, or individual responses in response journals. In addition, each day Kristina and Mrs. Caron provided ample opportunities for all students, including the lowest performing students, to read other selections at their independent levels to practice the strategies taught in their groups.

The Outcomes

Before Kristina and Mrs. Caron began their work together, they administered the performance assessment to every child in the class. The 9 lowest performing students (out of a total of 24) achieved a mean word-reading accuracy score of 81% and a mean comprehension score of 3. In May, after a year of instruction in the intervention group, those same students achieved a mean word-reading accuracy score of 94% and a mean comprehension score of 8. In both administrations of the test, the level of text difficulty was grade-appropriate.

In addition to student outcomes, this implementation also yielded teacher outcomes. Kristina commented that planning for this group of students was more rewarding and meaningful than for the other groups with whom she worked. Her observations of the children's actions and interactions in the classroom convinced her that they had a greater sense of belonging and connectedness to their peers. She attributed this to the fact that they were reading the same literature and engaging in the same literature-related activities.

She also believed that the repeated readings of selections of the text were effective in helping the students to build fluency and gain confidence in their reading. The periodic performance assessments confirmed her belief. The students with whom she worked made steady progress in word-reading accuracy and comprehension on grade-level text. Moreover, she understood that the frequent opportunities that the students had to read easier text gave them the practice and responsibility to decode unknown words and gain fluency.

Mrs. Caron, a seasoned teacher, was equally pleased with the effectiveness of the intervention. She noted that struggling readers became more fluent, more engaged during sustained silent reading, and generally more confident about reading. With one year of the intervention behind her, she made rigorous plans to continue the intervention the next year with Kristina.

What Have We Learned?

We began our work with a single question in mind: When children enter third grade reading substantially below grade level, what are the effects of grouping children homogeneously for part of their literacy instruction and providing instruction using grade-level text in combination with explicit, systematic, and intensive instruction in both word and comprehension strategies? At the start, our work was motivated primarily by three factors, mentioned earlier and recapped here. First, despite early intervention and effective classroom teaching in first and second grades, many children continue to struggle in reading. Second, failing to learn to read in the early grades has long-term cognitive and intellectual consequences for children, leading many of them to school failure. Third, in the increasingly politically charged educational climate, the consequences for reading failure are compounded by threats of retention, denial of high school graduation, and reduced funding to schools and communities.

During the months of implementation, we became aware of a new and growing practice—one that further increased our interest in the outcomes of the work that we had underway. As we talked with teachers and visited classrooms in our regions, we found that teachers were increasingly returning to the grouping practices of the past. That is, under the guise of a practice called "guided reading," teachers were grouping children by ability and were meeting with five and six different groups each day, groups formed on the basis of the books children could read with relative ease. With few exceptions, these groups represented most, at times all, of what children read.

As we considered this practice, we understood the teachers' motivation. We, too, were concerned with the evidence that the shift away from ability grouping that took place during the 1980s and 1990s led many teachers to abandon grouping altogether and instruct children in whole-class settings. We, too, were concerned with the evidence that for many children, the reading lesson had become, in fact, a listening lesson—a time when complex text was read aloud to them and when they were invited to discuss and write, but rarely to read. This practice, of course, might be effective in building language and comprehension, but unless a teacher was going to follow a child into adulthood, without independence in reading, eventually the learning would stop. So, although we understood teachers' motivation and shared their concerns, we had an additional concern—that children *cannot learn what they are not taught.* That is, failure to teach children to read high-level vocabulary, concepts, and ideas will likely deny them an equal opportunity to acquire the knowledge they will need to continue to develop their cognitive and intellectual abilities, to succeed in comprehending complex language and ideas, and to become proficient at writing and sharing complex language and ideas. As the pendulum began to swing one more time back toward the practices of the past, our work took on even greater meaning for us.

So, how do we make sense of our evidence? First, the fact that children achieved high levels of performance on text that was judged to be "too difficult" for them reminded us that reading difficulty does not reside in the text alone, but that text difficulty interacts with the linguistic characteristics of the text and the actions of the teacher. Years-old research in schema theory (Anderson & Pearson, 1984), vocabulary knowledge (Beck & McKeown, 1991; Beck, Perfetti, & McKeown, 1982), text structure (Meyer & Rice, 1984), and motivation theory (Wigfield & Asher, 1984) taught us that using readability formulas without attention to the ways and the contexts in which children are taught often leads us astray in choosing appropriate text for children to read. Our work reaffirmed the need to pay attention to this earlier research. Systematic and routine use of time-honored strategies including preteaching vocabulary, building background knowledge, reading aloud to diminish text difficulty, engaging children in rereadings, and guiding retellings with graphic organizers paid off in making difficult text accessible to children and thereby allowing them to *read*, not just listen to, high-level text.

Second, we were reminded that meeting individual needs does not mean creating different tracks, nor does adhering to a common text mean "one size fits all." Again, this was not a new finding, but, in an educational climate of extreme pendulum swings, it is one that may need to be reaffirmed. Evidence tells us that tracking often has negative consequences for students, placing them on pathways that lead them to different destinations (Barr & Dreeben, 1983; Braddock & Dawkins, 1993; Collins, 1971; Oakes, 1985; Slavin, 1987; Wilcox, 1982). In reading instruction, the use of ability grouping typically means that some children read easy text, while others read more difficult text. When this constitutes all or even most of what happens routinely in classrooms, children often have very different instructional experiences (Allington, 1983; Hiebert, 1983). As a consequence, children may end up in very different places, in relation to both the levels of reading proficiency they achieve and the types of future opportunities they have (Allington, 1991, 1994; Mehan, Villanueva, Hubbard, & Lintz, 1996). On the other hand, teaching to the whole class leads to similarly negative findings, resulting in lower rates of achievement for both higher and lower performing readers (Lou, Spence, Poulsen, Chambers, & d'Apollonia, 1996). But there is a middle ground between tracking by ability and whole-class instruction. In the instructional model that we studied, we recognized children's learning differences and grouped the children accordingly, so that we could meet their particular needs. But we kept them on the same track as their higher performing peers in two ways. We instructed them using the same curriculum as their grade-level peers, and their classroom teachers made certain that when these children returned to their classrooms each day, they were fully integrated into the classroom literacy curriculum. In short, we differentiated instruction, but not curriculum. The payoff for our students was improved reading fluency, which advanced them toward independence in reading, and improved reading comprehension, which holds the potential for supporting their continued achievement not only in reading but also in schooling in general.

Third, we were reminded that in school contexts in which teachers take a collegial and cooperative stance, seemingly difficult and complex instructional arrangements can be implemented effectively. In our work, we saw this play out in two very different settings. In each, an instructional specialist won the cooperation of grade-level colleagues, who agreed to adhere to a particular time to teach reading, to consistent instructional pacing, and to particular assessment practices. It is important to note that these were not settings in which teachers were given additional planning time in order to carry out the special program; rather, teachers used the time already available, often catching each other "on the fly" to plan, in order to continue to offer a coordinated and cohesive program for the children for whom they were responsible.

Fourth, we were reminded of the remarkable power of good instruction. What we believe is important in our results is the fact that we did not formulate a new, creative, or special approach to teach struggling readers. Rather, we took instructional practices that have been well documented as effective, combined them into what we believed to be a balanced approach, and implemented them in a systematic and intensive way. We were heartened by the progress of all the children, but we were especially encouraged by the substantial progress of the six children with special learning needs. Although the data are far too limited to allow us to generalize beyond this classroom, the children's progress and performance raised questions for us about the wisdom of the common practice of offering children with special learning needs instructional programs that are substantially different from those provided to their classroom peers. Once again, this is not a new finding. Allington and McGill-Franzen (1989) for example, questioned the effectiveness of what they termed "different programs" but "indifferent instruction" (p. 75) for children identified as special education learners. Yet, many years later, such practices persist, with seemingly little momentum in achieving large-scale programmatic change.

As we reflect on what we did and what we learned, and as we attempt to sort out the circumstances that allowed these teachers to make a difference in the literate lives of the children they taught, we find a long list of contributing factors. We have distilled the list to three that we believe were critical in explaining children's success. First, the instructional model itself brought together much of what we have learned about the effective teaching of reading, and, by so doing, it offered children explicit and systematic instruction in both word-study and comprehension strategies and opportunities to practice the strategies they were learning in high-level texts. Second, although the instructional model framed one hour of literacy instruction, it was only part of what teachers and children did. In addition to the one-hour literacy lesson, when children returned to the classroom, they not only joined a context in which their peers shared the same texts and activities but they also had daily opportunities to read and talk about books they selected to read on their own, books as easy or difficult as they chose. In addition, they read across the content areas with and without instruction from the teacher. Third, the children were taught by teachers who were knowledgeable about the teaching of reading, effective classroom managers, and enthusiastic about their roles as teachers—motivated enough to ask the reading specialist, when they observed how well children were doing, "What do you do down there, anyway?!" In short, the children were taught by teachers who liked teaching and who were constantly seeking to become better teachers. We suspect that each of these factors was equal in importance to the success we observed, and that if any one of the factors were to be taken away, the success we observed would likely be taken with it.

REFERENCES

Adams, M. (1998). The three-cueing system. In J. Osborn & F. Lehr (Eds.), *Literacy for all: Issues in teaching and learning* (pp. 73–99). New York: Guilford.

Adams, M.J. (1990). *Beginning to read: Thinking and learning about print*. Cambridge, MA: MIT Press.

Allington, R.L. (1983). The reading instruction provided readers of differing reading ability. *The Elementary School Journal, 83*, 548–559.

Allington, R.L. (1991). The legacy of slow it down and make it more concrete. In J. Zutell & S. McCormick (Eds.), *Learner factors/teacher factors: Issues in literacy research and instruction* (40th yearbook of the National Reading Conference, pp. 19–30). Chicago: National Reading Conference.

Allington, R.L. (1994). Content coverage and contextual reading in reading groups. *Journal of Reading Behavior, 16*, 85–96.

Allington, R.L., & McGill-Franzen, A. (1989). Different programs, indifferent instruction. In D.L. Kerzner & A. Gartner (Eds.), *Beyond separate education: Quality education for all* (pp. 75–98). Baltimore: Paul Brookes.

Anderson, R.C., Chinn, C., Waggoner, M., & Nguyen, K. (1997). Intellectually stimulating story discussions. In J. Osborn & F. Lehr (Eds.), *Literacy for all: Issues in teaching and learning* (pp. 170–188). New York: Guilford.

Anderson, R.C., & Pearson, P.D. (1984). A schema-theoretic view of basic processes in reading. In P.D. Pearson, R. Barr, M.L. Kamil, & P. Mosenthal (Eds.), *Handbook of reading research* (pp. 255–294). New York: Longman.

Barr, R., & Dreeben, R. (1983). *How schools work*. Chicago: University of Chicago Press.

Beck, I., & McKeown, M.G. (1991). Conditions of vocabulary acquisition. In R. Barr, M.L. Kamil, P.B. Mosenthal, & P.D. Pearson (Eds.), *Handbook of reading research* (Vol. 2, pp. 789–814). White Plains, NY: Longman.

Beck, I., Perfetti, C.A., & McKeown, M.G. (1982). The effects of long-term vocabulary instruction on lexical access and reading comprehension. *Journal of Educational Psychology, 74*, 506–521.

Braddock, J.H. II, & Dawkins, M.P. (1993). Ability grouping, aspirations, and attainments: Evidence from the National Educational Longitudinal Study of 1988. *Journal of Negro Education, 62*, 324–336.

Clay, M.M. (1993). *An observation survey of early literacy achievement*. Portsmouth, NH: Heinemann.

Collins, R. (1971). Functional and conflict theories of educational stratification. *American Sociological Review, 36*, 1002–1019.

Cunningham, P. (1995). *Phonics they use: Words for reading and writing*. New York: HarperCollins.

Donahue, P.L., Finnegan, R.J., Lutkus, A.D., Allen, N.L., & Campbell, J.R. (2001). *The nation's reading report card: Reading 2000*. Washington, DC: U.S. Department of Education, Office of Educational Research and Improvement, National Center for Education Statistics.

Dowhower, S.L. (1987). Effect of repeated reading on second-grade transitional readers' fluency and comprehension. *Reading Research Quarterly, 22*, 389–406.

Ehri, L.C. (1997). Sight word learning in normal readers and dyslexics. In B.A. Blachman (Ed.), *Foundations in reading acquisition and dyslexia: Implications for early intervention* (pp. 163–190). Mahwah, NJ: Erlbaum.

Fielding, L., & Roller, C. (1992). Making difficult books accessible and easy books acceptable. *The Reading Teacher, 45*, 678–685.

Foorman, B.F., Francis, D.J., Shaywitz, S.E., Shaywitz, B.A., & Fletcher, J.M. (1997). The case for early reading intervention. In B. Blachman (Ed.), *Foundations of reading acquisition and dyslexia: Implications for early intervention* (pp. 243–265). Mahwah, NJ: Erlbaum.

Goodman, Y.M., & Marek, A. (1996). *Retrospective miscue analysis*. Katonah, NY: Richard C. Owen.

Hiebert, E.H. (1983). An examination of ability grouping for reading instruction. *Reading Research Quarterly, 18*, 231–255.

Juel, C. (1988). Learning to read and write: A longitudinal study of fifty-four children from first through fourth grade. *Journal of Educational Psychology, 80*, 437–447.

Juel, C. (1990). Effects of reading group assignment on reading development in first and second grade. *Journal of Reading Behavior, 22,* 233–254.

Leslie, L, & Caldwell, J. (1995). *Qualitative Reading Inventory-II.* Glenview, IL: HarperCollins.

Lou, Y., Spence, P.C., Poulsen, C., Chambers, B., & d'Apollonia, S. (1996). Within-class grouping: A meta-analysis. *Review of Educational Research, 66,* 423–458.

Massachusetts Department of Education. (2000, November). *Spring 2000 MCAS Tests: Report of state results.* Malden, MA: Author.

Mehan, H., Villanueva, I., Hubbard, L., & Lintz, A. (1996). *Constructing school success: The consequences of untracking low-achieving students.* New York: Cambridge University Press.

Meyer, B.J., & Rice, E. (1984). The structure of text. In P.D. Pearson, R. Barr, M.L. Kamil, & P. Mosenthal (Eds.), *Handbook of reading research* (pp. 319–352). New York: Longman.

Morrow, L.M. (1983). Using story retelling to develop comprehension. In K.D. Muth (Ed.), *Children's comprehension of text: Research into practice.* Newark, DE: International Reading Association.

Oakes, J. (1985). *Keeping track: How schools structure inequality.* New Haven, CT: Yale University Press.

O'Shea, L.J., Sindelar, P.T., & O'Shea, D.J. (1985). The effects of repeated readings and attentional cues on reading fluency and comprehension. *Journal of Reading Behavior, 17,* 129–141.

Paratore, J.R. (1991). *Flexible grouping: Why and how?* Needham, MA: Silver Burdett Ginn.

Paratore, J.R. (2000). Grouping for instruction in literacy: What we've learned about what's working and what's not. *The California Reader, 33*(4), 2–10.

Pearson, P.D., & Fielding, L. (1991). Comprehension instruction. In R. Barr, M.L. Kamil, P.B. Mosenthal, & P.D. Pearson (Eds.), *Handbook of reading research* (Vol. 2, pp. 815–860). White Plains, NY: Longman.

Pinnell, G.S. (1985). Helping teachers help children at risk: Insights from the Reading Recovery program. *Peabody Journal of Education, 62,* 70–85.

Pressley, M. (1997). Comprehension strategies instruction. In J. Osborn & F. Lehr (Eds.), *Literacy for all: Issues in teaching and learning* (pp. 113–133). New York: Guilford.

Raphael, T. (1997). Balanced instruction and the role of classroom discourse. In J. Osborn & F. Lehr (Eds.), *Literacy for all: Issues in teaching and learning* (pp. 134–169). New York: Guilford.

Rasinski, T.V. (1990). Effects of repeated reading and listening-while-reading on reading fluency. *Journal of Educational Research, 83,* 147–150.

Samuels, S.J. (1979). The method of repeated readings. *The Reading Teacher, 32,* 403–408.

Santa, C.M., & Hoien, T. (1999). An assessment of early steps: A program for early intervention of reading problems. *Reading Research Quarterly, 34,* 54–79.

Sindelar, P.T., Monda, L.E., & O'Shea, L.J. (1990). Effects of repeated readings on instructional and mastery-level readers. *Journal of Educational Research, 83*, 220–226.

Slavin, R.E. (1987). *Ability grouping and student achievement in elementary school: A best evidence synthesis*. Baltimore: Center for Research on Elementary and Secondary Schools, Johns Hopkins University.

Stanovich, K.E. (2000). *Progress in understanding reading: Scientific foundations and new frontiers*. New York: Guilford.

Taylor, B.M., Strait, J., & Medo, M.A. (1994). Early intervention in reading: Supplemental instruction for groups of low-achieving students provided by first-grade teachers. In E.H. Hiebert & B.M. Taylor (Eds.), *Getting reading right from the start: Effective early literacy interventions* (pp. 107–122). Boston: Allyn & Bacon.

Torgesen, J.K., Wagner, R.K., & Roshotte, C.A. (1997). Approaches to the prevention and remediation of phonologically based reading disabilities. In B.A. Blachman (Ed.), *Foundations of reading acquisition and dyslexia: Implications for early intervention* (pp. 287–304). Mahwah, NJ: Erlbaum.

U.S. Department of Education. (2002). *The No Child Left Behind Act of 2001. Executive summary*. Available: http://www.ed.gov/offices/OESE/esea/exec-summ.html

Wigfield, A., & Asher, S.R. (1984). Social and motivational influences on reading. In P.D. Pearson, R. Barr, M.L. Kamil, & P. Mosenthal (Eds.), *Handbook of reading research* (pp. 423–452). New York: Longman.

Wilcox, K. (1982). Differential socialization in the classroom: Implications for educational opportunity. In G. Spindler & L. Spindler (Eds.), *Doing the ethnography of schooling: Educational anthropology in action* (pp. 268–309). New York: Harcourt Brace.

CHAPTER 7

Tailoring a Middle School Language Arts Class to Meet the Needs of Struggling Readers

Irene W. Gaskins, Eleanor Wiley Gensemer, and Linda M. Six

It is the first full day of school. The bell has rung. Nine gangly seventh graders (five girls and four boys) straggle into their language arts classroom. None looks too thrilled to be here. These nine students are new to the middle school and have a history of underachievement in reading. They are all bright young people who, despite one or more years of attendance at Benchmark (a school for struggling readers), demonstrate a wide variety of difficulties in reading and writing, as well as in completing other school assignments. Their language arts teacher, Eleanor Gensemer, is already familiar to them. For each of them, she has been either his or her 6th-grade science teacher or summer reading tutor.

Waiting until students are settled and noticing that the homework box contains few papers, Eleanor briefly and matter-of-factly reminds students about several class routines discussed the previous week during orientation meetings, including where to put nightly reading summaries and what these summaries should include. As the observer, Irene Gaskins, listens, she is thinking that writing reading summaries should be old hat for these students. During their previous years at Benchmark, both fiction and nonfiction summary writing was explicitly taught and scaffolded; then, after much in-class support, chapter summaries were regularly assigned as nightly homework. These students have been writing summaries for a year or more—but today, for reasons only they know, just a few summaries find their way into the homework box. The physical act of writing is certainly not the problem, for all nine students have access to computers and brought superb keyboarding skills with them to the middle school, a product of daily practice during their elementary years. After her brief comments about summaries, Eleanor launches into her lesson.

"Our objective today is to begin a discussion about the book you read over the summer, *Bearstone* by Will Hobbs [1989]. Now is your opportunity to clear up any questions you have before we begin to write book reviews later today. Does anyone have questions or observations?"

A few students volunteer "safe" comments, such as "I didn't like the ending," but the discussion quickly flounders. Next, Eleanor asks, "What questions do you still have that were not answered by the book? What do you still want to know?" The discussion is superficial. Only four students have participated thus far. Eleanor shows some pictures related to *Bearstone*, as well as a map of the book's setting, each time attempting to generate discussion about *Bearstone*. Still, five students say nothing. Eleanor reads aloud specific lines from *Bearstone* to focus students' attention on key elements of the novel and to elicit their interpretations. Irene wrote in her notes that day,

> Great that Andy [all students have been given pseudonyms] is participating, but his questions and comments are ones that could be made without reading the book. James seems in a trance, yet we know that when there is a hands-on problem to be solved (e.g., difficulty retrieving a computer file), he will be the first to offer help. Sonya is analyzing and reanalyzing her fingers. She has a history of lacking confidence and being afraid to take risks until she is absolutely sure the teacher will not allow her to look bad.

Irene hears Eleanor ask, "Anything else you'd like to talk about in preparation for writing your book reviews?" There is silence. Each student seems unwilling to reveal anything he or she does not understand about the novel.

What could be scarier for an adolescent than having peers find out that, for you, reading a fourth-grade-level novel is overwhelming? Although all nine students seem to be feeling apprehensive, overwhelmed, or both, each handles his or her feelings differently. The reasons for feeling overwhelmed by the novel undoubtedly vary. Some students may have allocated so much attention to decoding that there was little attention left for understanding. Some may have spread the reading over several months, forgetting between readings what they had read and refusing to use the aids that were suggested, such as an audiotape or parent read-aloud. For others, the seeming immensity of reading an entire novel on their own made it easy to put off even opening the book. Such scenarios are repeated daily in middle schools throughout the United States.

The Foundation for Successful Teaching and Learning

During the previous summer, Eleanor Gensemer (a language arts teacher), Linda Six (a middle school supervisor), and Irene Gaskins (the school's principal) had reviewed the research to find guidelines for revising and adapting the seventh-grade middle school language arts program for these nine students who seemed most at risk. Our goal was to ensure success for every student. Upon completing our review, we integrated a pedagogical framework (summarized in Figure 7.1) proposed by Jackson and Davis (2000) in the book *Turning Points 2000: Educating Adolescents in the 21st Century* with research-based instructional recommendations particular to young adolescent struggling readers (see Figure 7.2).

FIGURE 7.1

TURNING POINTS 2000 FRAMEWORK FOR ENSURING SUCCESS FOR EVERY STUDENT

Curriculum
1. Ground the curriculum in rigorous and public academic standards, stating what students should know and be able to do.
2. Anchor the standards both in the concerns of adolescents and in how students learn best.
3. Organize the standards around concepts and principles.
4. Use a mix of assessment methods that allows students to demonstrate what they know and what they can do.

Instruction
1. Use methods that allow each student to achieve the standards and to become a lifelong learner.
2. Mesh instruction with students' needs, interests, and learning styles.
3. Include in each class students with diverse needs, achievement levels, interests, and learning styles.
4. Differentiate instruction to take advantage of diversity and how students learn best.

Staff Development
1. Choose teachers who are expert at teaching young adolescents.
2. Engage teachers in ongoing professional development.
3. Provide mentors and induction processes for new teachers.

Organization
1. Organize relationships for learning by dividing staff and students into teams.
2. Pay attention to the nature and quality of interactions among teachers and students, concentrating efforts on achieving high standards for teaching and learning.
3. Attend to critical elements of team success—size, composition, planning time, and continuity.

Leadership
1. Base decisions about appropriate programming for each student on input from the adults who know students best and on data drawn from various sources.
2. Make decisions democratically based on a relentless focus on attaining success for every student.
3. Design a "living" school improvement plan to guide change.

Environment
1. Provide a caring, safe, and healthy learning environment.
2. Foster positive intergroup relationships.

Parents—Develop communication and collaboration with parents to monitor and support students' academic progress.

FIGURE 7.2

SUMMARY OF RESEARCH RECOMMENDATIONS SPECIFIC TO YOUNG ADOLESCENT STRUGGLING READERS

Intensity: Success for struggling readers is related to low student-teacher ratios, amount of time devoted to reading and writing, and the professional expertise of the teacher (Allington, 2001; Pearson, 1999).

Support: Learning is embedded in social relationships, especially for adolescents (Lee & Smith, 1999). Thus, social support (i.e., positive, caring personal relationships with people who can help students do well) must be regularly available (Beane & Brodhagen, 2001; Darling-Hammond, 1997; Noddings, 1992).

Motivation: A key ingredient for success is motivation (Pressley, 2001). Undergirding motivation are the basic needs for competence, affiliation, and autonomy (Deci, 1995). Competence results when students are taught in a way and at a level that leads to success. Affiliation comes from satisfying relationships with teachers and peers. Autonomy, especially for adolescents, means having choices.

Management: Success is most likely when students spend a high percentage of time on task and involved in meaningful tasks (e.g., every-pupil-response activities); expectations are clear (e.g., via rubrics); materials are organized; and routines are well established (Cotton, 2001; Schmoker, 1996).

Interaction: Learning to work well with others is an important life skill (Csikszentmihalyi & Schneider, 2000). Successful interactions are fostered by explicitly teaching the interpersonal skills students need to communicate effectively, give feedback, share decision making, arrive at compromises, and support one another in solving everyday problems. Students profit from interacting with others about texts and tasks in teacher-led discussions and student collaborative groups (Strauss & Irvin, 2001).

Variety: Success is more likely in classrooms that feature a wide variety of methods and interesting materials (Langer et al., 2000), many levels and types of text (Allington, 2001), and opportunities to apply ideas, as well as to view ideas from a variety of perspectives (Darling-Hammond, 1997).

Explicitness: Success is enhanced by instruction that is explicit and systematic (National Institute of Child Health and Human Development, 2000). Teachers should explicitly explain the what, why, when, and how of cognitive and metacognitive strategies for the different levels of thinking students need for completing interesting and challenging tasks. Teachers should also model and scaffold the application of these strategies to authentic tasks (Gaskins et al., 1993; Langer et al., 2000; Pressley et al., 1992).

Knowledge: Knowledge, including beliefs and experiences, affects understanding (Alexander & Jetton, 2000). Teachers should anticipate gaps in students' knowledge that may impair understanding and should make provisions for filling those gaps, focusing on major concepts, principles, and processes (Csikszentmihalyi & Schneider, 2000). Students gain self-knowledge by regularly self-assessing how their performances relate to the presence or absence of self-regulated and strategic efforts (Rycik & Irvin, 2001).

Practice: Students who read the most are the students who become the most successful readers (Anderson, Wilson, & Fielding, 1988). Voluminous reading, including repeated, choral, or echo reading, in a wide variety of texts supports reading fluency and progress in reading (Allington, 2001).

Duration: Instruction for struggling readers must be long term (Allington, 2001; Pressley, 1998). Short-term interventions can get students on track, but struggling readers need something more to stay on track. They need instruction in how to take control of factors or personal characteristics that contributed to their reading and performance difficulties in the first place (Gaskins, 1998; Murphy, 1996).

The results of our integration of the framework with the recommendations are in Table 7.1. The categories on the horizontal axis of the table derive from the proposals of Jackson and Davis (2000), and the categories on the vertical axis are drawn from our literature review specific to young adolescent struggling readers. Note that the instructional points from the recommendations for adolescents (see preceding list) have been organized into four categories: intensity, support, motivation, and knowledge. These four categories are further elaborated in the following section of this chapter. When teachers expertly combine and weave the features of these categories into the pedagogical framework, the result is good teaching.

TABLE 7.1.

A PROGRAM FOR YOUNG ADOLESCENT STRUGGLING READERS

	Curriculum	*Instruction*	*Staff Development*	*Organization*	*Leadership*	*Environment*	*Parents*
INTENSITY	Concepts and principles Strategies Self	Presence of "academic press"	Teacher expertise	Low student-teacher ratio	Schoolwide academic thrust	Seriousness about learning	Support for student preparation
Management	Meaningful tasks	Time on task	Learning management techniques	Scheduling planning time	Protecting academic time	Consistent routines	Making academics a priority
Variety	Many materials and levels	Using many methods to meet needs	Learning many methods	Arranging materials by topic and level	No one method for all students	Diversity embraced	Supporting easy reading
Practice	Materials at appropriate levels	Voluminous reading	Discussing what is worth practice	Scheduling much time for literacy	Supporting practice for students	Posters supporting practice	Supporting practice
Long-Term	Conceptually appropriate instruction	Appropriate level	Discussing why long-term is necessary	Small groups	Support over years	Nurturing progress	Supporting time needs
SUPPORT	Relationships	Staff mentor for each student	Staff team meetings Mentors for staff	Working in professional teams	Team decision making	Pervasive atmosphere of caring	Communication
Interaction	Authentic tasks for collaboration and discussion	Teaching how to discuss and collaborate	Learning how to foster discussion and collaboration	Planning time for students to discuss and collaborate	Knowing and interacting with each student	Positive group relationships	Collaboration

(continued)

TABLE 7.1 (continued)

A PROGRAM FOR YOUNG ADOLESCENT STRUGGLING READERS

	Curriculum	Instruction	Staff Development	Organization	Leadership	Environment	Parents
MOTIVATION	Interests Needs	Teaching to student interests	Studying motivation theories	Organizing for competence, affiliation, autonomy	Fostering motivational influences	Discovering and nurturing interests	Supporting school and teachers
Competence	Teaching to multiple intelligences	Teaching to learning style	Learning how to scaffold	Reporting progress, not comparisons	Supporting success for all	Charting progress	Reinforcing progress
Affiliation	Relationships	Teaching necessary skills	Learning about relationships	Time for collaboration	Knowing students	Positive group relationships	Supporting teachers
Autonomy	Choice and decisions	Providing choices	Learning about autonomy	Allowing some choice	Allowing students to make decisions	Recognizing good choices	Supporting student choices
KNOWLEDGE	Standards Concepts and principles Strategies Self	Teaching different levels of thinking and habits of the mind	Learning the how of concepts, principles, strategies, self	Organizing knowledge across grades and around important concepts, principles	Developing school improvement plan with staff	Posting concepts, principles, strategies, and self-assessment	Valuing concepts, principles, processes, self-assessment
Explicit	Rubrics for tasks	Explaining, modeling, and scaffolding	Learning how to teach explicitly	Organizing teaching of strategies across grades	Supporting explicit teaching	Charts to tell how to do tasks	Supporting use of rubrics
Self-Regulation	Control Self-assessment	Teaching how to take control and self-assess	Learning about self-regulation	Using self-assessment to evaluate	Using self-assessment as one form of evaluation	Using charts with thinking dispositions	Supporting self-evaluation

Intensity

The intensity of a program for struggling readers is a key factor in determining the program's success. Intensity is grounded in the professional expertise of the teacher, a low student-teacher ratio, and a considerable portion of time devoted to reading and writing (Allington, 2001; Pearson, 1999). Intensity also includes academic press—a schoolwide thrust toward serious academics over a period of years (Lee & Smith, 1999). Where there is academic press, there are expectations that students will work on intellectually challenging tasks, come to class prepared, and complete assignments. Intensity is enhanced by well-managed classrooms in which students spend a high percentage of time on task, gaining essential understandings from a variety of levels and types of text and applying these understandings to meaningful tasks. A high percentage of time on-task is crucial because extensive practice is necessary for achieving competence (Anderson & Schunn, 2000). Additional features of well-managed classrooms include clear expectations, organized materials, well-established routines, and choice. A program for struggling readers that is known for its intensity does more than get students on track. It is a long-term program that helps students stay on track.

Support

A second key factor is support. Lee and Smith's (1999) findings from their large study conducted in Chicago, Illinois, regarding instruction for young adolescents confirms this view. They found that success is most probable when academic press occurs in the context of social support. Social support, in turn, exists when there is an environment characterized by caring relationships and connectedness with people who can help students do well (Jackson & Davis, 2000; Lee & Smith, 1999; Noddings, 1992; Roeser, Eccles, & Sameroff, 2000).

Having social support as a goal acknowledges both that cognitive development is embedded in the context of social relationships and that affiliation is one cornerstone of motivation. At its most effective, social support is regularly available, is aligned with the aims of the classroom, and is focused on learning. In schools where there is social support, a high value is placed both on collaborative teams of staff who share responsibility for children (Pianta, 1999) and on staff-student and student-student interactions. Staff foster student interactions by explicitly teaching the interpersonal skills students need to develop satisfactory relationships and to participate successfully in discussions and student collaborative groups.

Motivation

Teachers increase the likelihood of student motivation by helping students meet their basic needs for competence, affiliation, and autonomy (Deci, 1995). Competence is facilitated by explicitly teaching and scaffolding the use of cognitive and metacognitive strategies that students need to meet academic goals (Langer, Close, Angelis, & Preller, 2000). Affiliation is achieved through meaningful relationships with staff and peers. Autonomy results when students are given choices and opportunities for decision making. Motivation is further enhanced when students are given opportunities to apply the essential understandings and processes they are learning to topics and tasks that interest them (Jackson & Davis, 2000).

Knowledge

Understanding is an important goal of schools. The understandings students construct are related to background knowledge, including beliefs, experiences, and procedural knowledge (Alexander & Jetton, 2000); to appropriate application of strategy knowledge; and to knowledge of self. Strategy knowledge includes an awareness of when and how to use cognitive strategies (Shepard, 2000), as well as strategies for self-regulation, including taking charge of dispositions/habits of mind. Self-regulation has to do with students' self-generated thoughts, feelings, and actions as they relate to their ability to control the factors or conditions affecting achievement of their learning goals (Dembo & Eaton, 2000). Csikszentmihalyi and Schneider (2000), basing their work on a U.S. longitudinal study of how adolescents develop attitudes and acquire skills, outlined dispositions associated with competence that should be targets for self-regulation: self-discipline, internal locus of control, responsibility, persistence, strategic hard work, concentrated involvement, optimism, curiosity, enjoyment of a challenge, and ability to work with others. Teachers who foster knowledge of self and self-regulation among their students communicate to both parents and students that no one has more control over success than the student himself or herself.

Developing strategies and dispositions that lead to competence is facilitated by a student's ability to self-assess how well he or she is presently employing appropriate strategies and dispositions to achieve his or her learning goals. Self-assessment can take many forms, including reflective journals; projects and demonstrations that require applications of knowledge, strategies, and dispositions; collections of student work as part of portfolios; peer feedback; and student-teacher conferences. Whatever the means, assessment should be part of the learning process (Shepard, 2000). Self-assessment is facilitated when students have a clear understanding of the criteria for a specific task, so that they can evaluate their work in the same way that teachers will. Rubrics are helpful, especially when given to students at the time a task is assigned. The goal of both teacher-initiated assessment and self-assessment is to guide students in taking the next steps in learning.

The Students, the Middle School, and Language Arts

The Students

The language arts class introduced in the opening vignette was composed of nine seventh-grade students who, despite high average potential (Full Scale WISC III mean = 114), had a history that suggested they were the most at risk of the students entering Benchmark's middle school, composed of 65 students. At the beginning of seventh grade, the instructional reading levels for the nine students were two to four years below grade level. Based on the past year's progress reports, it appeared that the reasons for their struggles varied widely, yet the results were the same—nine very discouraged young people. According to their former teachers, some of the students appeared unmotivated. Others were reported to struggle with decoding. Still others struggled with comprehension. In addition, it appeared that these students' difficulties in school were aggravated by faulty belief systems. Students seemed not to have consistently experienced enough success to believe that strategic effort would result in success, and they tended to believe they were not smart. Generally, they were unwilling to take risks and were reluctant to take responsibility for their actions. All were well-behaved, genuinely nice young people. Our goal was to change their faulty beliefs and to help them recognize their potential as learners.

The Middle School

Benchmark is a grade 1–8 school that offers a full academic curriculum (see Gaskins, 1998, for a full description of the school). In the middle school (grades 7 and 8), two daily class periods (totaling 2 hours, 10 minutes) are devoted to reading and writing. These classes, as is true of all Benchmark Middle School classes, are designed to meet the criteria for intensity described earlier. The seventh-grade program begins students on the road to achieving the middle school's goal of developing self-regulated learners, thinkers, and problem solvers who recognize in any learning situation what they can do for themselves, what they need help to do, where to get the help, and what to do with the help.

Each day teachers assign authentic tasks that engage students in reading and writing many pages of text. Students are explicitly taught the strategies they need to read, understand, and write about these texts, and they are encouraged to collaborate with others to construct understanding and to solve problems. In addition, each evening at home, students apply comprehension strategies in order to complete assignments in content area textbooks, as well as to read materials they choose from the classroom library. Students are expected to arrive at school each day with written notes, reading summaries, and other homework completed.

In middle school classes, instructional methods vary according to what works best for each student. For example, to complete reading assignments, some students follow along in their books as they listen to an audiotaped version of the text, while other students read without the aid of tapes. To collect notes to use in discussions and in writing chapter summaries, some students use sticky notes as they read to highlight important ideas they want to share or include in their summaries. Other students use a teacher-designed note-taking form or develop concept maps. Some students find it helpful to rehearse their ideas about what they read with a partner or a teacher before they take part in a discussion or write a summary. The goal is that students learn to identify what works for them.

Relationships and social support are important components of the middle school program. A high priority is placed on building trusting relationships between staff and students. Trusting relationships enable teachers to be direct and open with students about their successes and their failures, and to help students set goals, including goals to overcome roadblocks. Much attention is given to establishing a community in which students feel safe taking risks and each student has a trusted adult mentor with whom to share problems, questions, concerns, and victories. Groups of four or five students meet with their mentors during a daily 30-minute mentor period. Both individually and in a mentor group or language arts group, students are taught the skills they need to work well with others. Mentors and teachers talk regularly with students about their learning styles and suggest ways for students to change, or to cope with, maladaptive styles that interfere with their achieving the competence they desire (Gaskins, 1998). To facilitate the development of motivated students, teachers make a point to know their students' interests and to choose topics and materials based on these interests. The overarching goal of mentors and teachers is to help students fulfill their needs for competence, affiliation, and autonomy, thus creating motivated students who know how to achieve.

Another important aspect of the middle school is the team approach. Teams of teachers meet weekly by grade level to discuss students, curriculum, and instruction and to make decisions about students. In addition, the entire middle school meets weekly to discuss items of interest to all middle school staff and to discuss ways to coordinate strategies and instruction from one grade level to the next, as well as how to help students apply and adapt concepts, principles, and strategies learned in one subject to other areas of the curriculum. A team approach enables teachers to understand the developmental progression of the middle school program and provides opportunities for staff to have input into decisions concerning their shared students.

Table 7.1 (see pages 141–142) outlines the key ingredients of the middle school program with respect to curriculum, instruction, staff development, organization, leadership, environment, and parent collaboration. For each of those categories, the program is developed to provide intensity, support, motivation, and knowledge. Due to space limitations, though, only the language arts curriculum and instruction for the nine struggling readers will be discussed in this chapter.

Language Arts

The focus during language arts teaching in the school is on three kinds of knowledge: knowledge about text (story elements, themes, the genre of literature under study, and the author's craft); knowledge about strategies (to decode, unlock word meanings, comprehend, and write); and knowledge of self. Emphasis is on different levels of thinking and the habits of the mind that enhance learning. Rubrics for written responses are given to students as a means of scaffolding their performance and as a way for students to self-assess how they are performing. Prior to giving an assignment, the teacher explains the what, why, when, and how of the cognitive and metacognitive strategies students will need to complete the assignment (Gaskins & Elliot, 1991). After explaining the strategy or group of strategies, the teacher models how to implement the strategy or strategies, then scaffolds students' application of strategies to accomplish the task. The focus is always on how students can take control of their own learning, thinking, and problem solving.

The language arts curriculum for our struggling readers is not a watered-down curriculum, but rather one that students find interesting and conceptually challenging. Students complete reading and writing tasks using a variety of high-interest materials, written on a variety of levels. Meaningful tasks are designed for developing word knowledge, fluency, comprehension, and writing, the areas of primary academic need for these students. Each day the two language arts periods are divided into four parts to feature instruction specific to each of these needs, while at the same time weaving through the specific featured instruction practice that addresses the other three needs. Several examples follow.

The Language Arts Program in Action

Fluency

It is the second full day of school. Eleanor asks students to define fluency. Every hand is in the air. Students suggest definitions, and others add to those definitions. The students' consensus definition is "Comfortable, accurate reading that flows." Next, students are asked to select one of the teen magazines at the front of the room and, from that magazine, to choose a short (about 50 words) article. Students quickly select one of the magazines and return to their seats. Eleanor reminds them that, as they read, they are not to skip any words, because reading the correct words is important to understanding. She reviews strategies that the students might use if they encounter a word they cannot decode.

Students read their articles silently. Most appear to complete the task in a very short time, but a few become stuck on unknown words and solicit help. Andy asks Irene (the observer) for help with the word *informative*. She asks him, "What is the first thing you do when you come to a word that you don't recognize?" Andy answers, "Look for familiar spelling patterns." Irene asks, "What is the first pattern?" He responds, "*i-n*." Thus, she guides Andy through the word, and he reads, "*In--for--ma--tive*; *informative*." Andy becomes stuck on another word—*supplement*—and Irene hears Eleanor guide him through the word chunk by chunk. Again, Andy is able to decode the word.

Partners are assigned, and Irene works with Sonya. Students read approximately 50 words of the article aloud to their partners. Sonya misreads six words. Each time she becomes stuck on one of these words, she claims that she thought she could read the word when she practiced the passage silently. For each word, Irene scaffolds Sonya's decoding. When students complete three oral readings of their 50-word passages, they assess their progress by filling in a Fluency Self-Report form that asks,

> Did your reading of the article improve from the first to the third reading? What made it better?

> What vocabulary did you need help with or did you need to stop to decode? What is your goal for becoming more fluent?

The fluency partner fills out a form that asks,

> Did your partner's reading of the article improve? What made it better?

> What suggestions can you make to help him or her improve in the future?

Sonya completes her assessment sheet and states her goal as, "To be aware of unknown words when I am reading silently and either decode them or ask for help." Eleanor asks students to share what they learned from the partner-reading experience.

Each day, in the weeks that follow, students participate in partner reading. Together the class develops strategies for fluency:

> Read through the article to recognize the words.

> Read through the article and take notes to understand the meaning.

> Practice for appropriate pacing and prosody.

The most exciting happening of the first several weeks of school is that partnerships are established with two classes of third graders. Students in Eleanor's class will practice reading materials related to the third-grade social studies curriculum. When they become fluent, they will read and discuss the materials with a "buddy" in a third-grade class. As a result of their responsibility to help younger students, we see an increased investment in reading words correctly and fluently, at least when preparing texts for their third-grade buddies.

By the end of October, we have changed our procedure for partner reading. Now each day all students read the same passage, a passage related to what our third-grade buddies are studying. First, the teacher reads the passage aloud, as students follow along in their copies, then, while Eleanor meets with a reading group of four or five students, the other students practice the text they are preparing for their third-grade buddies.

After silently practicing the passage from an easy-reading book about glaciers, students individually and orally read and discuss the passage with Irene. She finds that most of the students can read the words correctly, but they can't tell what they learned about glaciers. Most read with such poor phrasing that what they read does not make sense. They discuss the ideas in the text, and students practice using the punctuation and sense of the text to guide their intonation. Irene reminds each student that they will not only be reading the text about glaciers to their third-grade buddies but they also will be responsible for explaining anything in the text that the third-graders ask about glaciers. Each seems to return to his or her seat determined to make sense of what they read about glaciers.

Comprehension/Writing

In addition to conducting a class in which students' needs for competence, affiliation, and choice are met, Eleanor manages the class so that students spend a high percentage of time on-task. To accomplish this she often employs writing, both as a tool to enhance understanding and as an every-pupil-response (EPR) activity to keep all students involved in the lesson, as illustrated in the following example.

On the fourth full day of class, Eleanor begins class by asking students to write a definition of *reading* on their "think pads" (stapled-together scraps of paper). "What do you think reading is?" she asks. After every student has written a definition, students share their responses. "Words aren't spoken, but you get information." "The author expresses him/herself and you have to understand the author's message." "Something about construction." Eleanor reminds students that in recent days the concepts "active involvement," "background knowledge," and even "transaction between author and reader" have been mentioned in their definitions. There is more discussion, and, at Andy's suggestion, students write definitions in their notebooks in their own words, "so we know we understand it."

Next, Eleanor engages students in a discussion of the story read the previous day in *More Chills: 12 More Chilling Tales and Exciting Adventures* (Goodman, 1997). On the previous day a note-taking sheet was introduced, and Eleanor modeled how to complete it. The note-taking sheet contains four labeled boxes where notes are to be written:

1. SETTING—Where, When
2. CHARACTERS—Description, Traits/Goals, Actions
3. PLOT—Problem, Attempts to Solve Problem, Resolution
4. THEME/MOOD

All the story elements on the note-taking sheet are familiar to students, having been explicitly taught, modeled, and scaffolded in earlier grades. The goal today is to discuss the notes students wrote as they read the story and, as a group, to decide which notes will be helpful in writing a one-paragraph literature response. With notes in hand, all but two students respond to Eleanor's questions about the story problem, character traits, and how the resolution of the problem is related to character traits. There is tremendous disparity in their responses, suggesting confusion.

When a student makes a particularly perceptive comment about a character trait, Eleanor supports the group in finding the action in the text that illustrates the trait. As a result of rereading portions of the text, students begin to realize that there is a story within a story. Eleanor asks students to locate and share the part of the story that is a made-up story within the story. Throughout the discussion, Eleanor's comments are supportive: "The author is pretty tricky; I know I had to do some rereading to keep things straight." "I'm pleased that you are all being so flexible in helping one another straighten out what happened in this story." "By realizing that the story didn't make sense and taking action to seek clarification, you did what good readers do."

Once students seem to understand the story, Eleanor again solicits character traits and how they play a role in the resolution of the story problem. Notes are written on the chalkboard. Next, Eleanor guides students in writing a one-paragraph literature response. The lesson is concluded by Eleanor asking, "What strategies did you learn that you can use when you are confused?" Sally says, "Ask questions." Holly suggests, "Reread." Eleanor has been gifted in garnering peer support for her students. All had difficulty understanding the story and discovered that, by admitting what they did not understand and by supporting one another, they ended up feeling not only competent, but they developed a sense of belonging and being of value to the group. The lesson had taken 1 hour, 20 minutes, with all nine students actively involved for the greater part of the time. During the afternoon period, students read for a total of 35 minutes, first with partners to develop fluency, then silently in *More Chills*. Constructing meaning was the paramount goal.

Word Knowledge

One of the most common maladaptive styles our students exhibit is impulsively skipping unknown words. Thus, one of our goals is to provide students with decoding strategies, guided practice, and a sense of accomplishment so that they feel competent about decoding words that they might otherwise skip.

It is October 24. Students enter the classroom, and, on the table, at the place where each one sits, there is the usual Words of the Day sheet. Today there are three words from the story students will read in class: *particular*, *chronologically*, and *judgments*. Eleanor is absent, and Irene (usually the observer) is teaching this 12-minute segment of language arts. Students have become accustomed to the routine of coming into the classroom and immediately going to work on the Words of the Day. Irene reminds them that not only can we use patterns in the words that we know to decode unknown words but we can also look for meaning-based patterns we know, and these will provide clues to the definitions of words. After a few minutes of decoding on their own, students are assigned to work in pairs and to explain to their partners how they decoded each word and how they determined the meaning. George and Adair complain that they shouldn't have to "do" words every day because they learned "this stuff" in elementary school. Andy asserts that it is faster to look words up in the dictionary than it is to notice patterns and think of known words that have the same meaning patterns. Irene gives her "Psych 101" response: Students who have been actively engaged in Word Detective lessons (Gaskins, 2000) over the years have a vast store of patterns to which new words can be attached. Our brains are pattern seekers. They notice patterns and connect new words with familiar patterns to known words with the same patterns. That makes it easier to remember new words. In addition, we know that our brains remember better the more time we spend on task, being persistent, and practicing decoding and reading words.

Irene backs up her claims by briefly discussing the research about academic press (Lee & Smith, 1999). Every eye is on her as she talks. Middle school students are fascinated with information about how the brain works. She concludes, "It is not by chance that the two students in this class who spend the most time on task during seatwork and group instruction are also the students who are presently making the most progress." Sonya and Gigi beam! Students spend a few minutes discussing the three new words with their partners, then Irene asks for a volunteer to pick one word and tell how he or she would explain to someone how to decode the word. Andy responds by telling how to decode *particular*:

> I counted the vowels that I thought would represent sounds. There are four, so I knew there were four spelling patterns and four chunks. I divided the word into chunks and used key words with the same spelling patterns (*car, tic, flu, car*). The word is *par-tic-u-lar*, *particular*.

Irene asks, "Does anyone notice a familiar base word in *particular*?" Someone says *part* but cannot relate the meaning base to the probable meaning of *particular*. Irene uses the word in a sentence, and students conclude that the word means "a part different from others." She points out a list of words on the chalkboard (*apartheid*, *apartment*, *bipartisan*, *compartment*, *partial*, *partition*, *particle*), pronounces the words, and asks students what similarities they notice among the words. Students eagerly engage in a discussion of what they consider to be sophisticated words.

The remaining two words are discussed in a similar manner. Irene asks, "Which word do you think has a Greek base and why?" Gigi, a student of Greek ancestry, proudly explains, "It is *chronologically* because I remember that when *c-h* represents the /k/ sound, the word usually has a Greek origin and may be a science word." Irene tells students that *chrono* is a Greek base that means time, thus *chronological* means "arranged in order of time." She writes *chronic*, *chronicle*, and *chronometer* on the chalkboard. She says each word in a sentence, and students seem to enjoy the challenge of defining the words. At the end of the word lesson, George comments, "I like learning about big words." Adair chimes in, "Why can't we always do just big words, like we did today?" Our adolescent struggling readers have responded enthusiastically to success with tasks that they view as challenging and age-appropriate.

Conclusions and New Beginnings

It was an intense year of learning for our nine struggling readers. One of the highlights for them was reading and discussing text with their third-grade buddies. Students also enjoyed what came to be called Linguistics 101—lessons about how our language works, particularly with respect to decoding and meaning patterns in words. Explicit instruction also took place in how to construct understanding and to write paragraph responses to literature, then in how to combine paragraphs into effective essays. Finally, students were taught how to synthesize information from various sources into reports and essays.

Throughout the year, social support was at the heart of the academic program. Student-teacher and student-student interactions were caring, connected, and collaborative. Students became increasingly motivated as they became more competent, felt they were contributing members of the group, and stretched their wings to make better school-related choices and decisions. The most valuable knowledge students gained during the year was probably about themselves. They began to understand the characteristics about themselves that most impacted school success, and they used this knowledge to become more effective learners, thinkers, and problem solvers.

Acting on what they know about themselves has been the key to each of these students' successes a year later in eighth grade. As second-year middle school students, our nine students no longer need to be grouped together as special students who require more than the average amount of support. Four of the nine are now in a fast-paced language arts class in which they are learning to critically analyze literature and write thematic essays. The other five were assigned to a language arts class that is not as fast-paced but is equally challenging in content and writing expectations. All nine students are more confident and better able to explain in detail what they need to do as learners, thinkers, and problem solvers to make the most of their academic experiences. This is quite a change from last year, when all nine students believed they would fail before they had even tried and were anxiety-ridden with each new activity. These students continue to need the adults in their lives to praise them when their self-assessments are accurate and to guide them in identifying the role they play in their successes. Their newfound confidence is fragile but growing stronger with each success.

What can we learn from the instruction of these struggling readers that is applicable to other classrooms? From our experience, we believe that middle-grade struggling readers gain tremendous benefit from *explicit* instruction in fluency, comprehension, written expression, and word knowledge, especially if this instruction is accompanied by teacher modeling and scaffolding. Such instruction seems to work best if there are ample opportunities for practice and feedback and if the classroom setting provides social support for meeting students' needs for competence, affiliation, and choice. In addition, students seem to profit from classroom structures and management that allow them to spend a high percentage of time on task and involved in a variety of meaningful activities and interactions. Students also seem to profit from guided opportunities to self-assess their approach to school tasks and to acquire, understand, and use knowledge about themselves to overcome roadblocks to learning. For some struggling readers, one or two years of the type of instruction described in this chapter may not be enough. These instructional conditions need to be long-term, continuing until the skills, strategies, and habits of mind necessary for school success have become an automatic part of who each student is.

REFERENCES

Alexander, P.A., & Jetton, T.L. (2000). Learning from text: A multidimensional and developmental perspective. In M.L. Kamil, P.B. Mosenthal, P.D. Pearson, & R. Barr (Eds.), *Handbook of reading research* (Vol. 3, pp. 285–310). Mahwah, NJ: Erlbaum.

Allington, R.L. (2001). *What really matters for struggling readers: Designing research-based programs*. New York: Longman.

Anderson, J.R., & Schunn, C.D. (2000). Implications of the ACT-R learning theory: No magic bullets. In R. Glaser (Ed.), *Advances in instructional psychology: Educational design and cognitive science* (Vol. 5, pp. 1–33). Mahwah, NJ: Erlbaum.

Anderson, R.C., Wilson, P., & Fielding, L. (1988). Growth in reading and how children spend time outside of school. *Reading Research Quarterly, 23*, 285–303.

Beane, J.A., & Brodhagen, B.L. (2001). Teaching in middle schools. In V. Richardson (Ed.), *Handbook of research on teaching* (4th ed., pp. 1157–1174). Washington, DC: American Educational Research Association.

Cotton, K. (2001). *The schooling practices that matter most*. Alexandria, VA: Association for Supervision and Curriculum Development.

Csikszentmihalyi, M., & Schneider, B. (2000). *Becoming adult: How teenagers prepare for the world of work*. New York: Basic Books.

Darling-Hammond, L. (1997). *The right to learn: A blueprint for creating schools that work*. San Francisco: Jossey-Bass.

Deci, E.L., with Flaste, R. (1995). *Why we do what we do: The dynamics of personal autonomy*. New York: G.P. Putnam's Sons.

Dembo, M.H., & Eaton, M.J. (2000). Self-regulation of academic learning in middle-level schools. *The Elementary School Journal, 100*, 473–490.

Gaskins, I.W. (1998). There's more to teaching at-risk and delayed readers than good reading instruction. *The Reading Teacher, 51*, 543–547.

Gaskins, I.W. (2000). *Word detectives program for 5th grade and above: A program for adolescent struggling readers who are experiencing decoding and spelling difficulties.* Media, PA: Benchmark Press.

Gaskins, I.W., Anderson, R.C., Pressley, M., Cunicelli, E.A., & Satlow, E. (1993). Six teachers' dialogue during cognitive process instruction. *The Elementary School Journal, 93*, 277–304.

Gaskins, I.W., & Elliot, T.T. (1991). *Implementing cognitive strategy instruction across the school: The Benchmark manual for teachers.* Cambridge, MA: Brookline Books.

Jackson, A.J., & Davis, G.A., with Abeel, M., & Bordonaro, A. (2000). *Turning points 2000: Educating adolescents in the 21st century.* New York: Teachers College Press.

Langer, J.A., Close, E., Angelis, J., & Preller, P. (2000). *Guidelines for teaching middle and high school students to read and write well: Six features of effective instruction.* Albany, NY: National Research Center on English Learning and Achievement.

Lee, V.E., & Smith, J.B. (1999). Social support and achievement for young adolescents in Chicago: The role of school academic press. *American Education Research Journal, 36*, 907–945.

Murphy, J.M. (1996). *A follow-up study of delayed readers and an investigation of factors related to their success in young adulthood.* Unpublished doctoral dissertation, University of Pennsylvania, Philadelphia.

National Institute of Child Health and Human Development. (2000). *Report of the National Reading Panel. Teaching children to read: An evidence-based assessment of the scientific research literature on reading and its implications for reading instruction* (NIH Publication No. 00-4769). Washington, DC: U.S. Government Printing Office.

Noddings, N. (1992). *The challenge to care in schools: An alternative approach to education.* New York: Teachers College Press.

Pearson, P.D. (1999). A historically based review of *Preventing Reading Difficulties in Young Children. Reading Research Quarterly, 34*, 231–246.

Pianta, R.C. (1999). *Enhancing relationships between children and teachers.* Washington, DC: American Psychological Association.

Pressley, M. (1998). *Reading instruction that works: The case for balanced teaching.* New York: Guilford.

Pressley, M. (2001, December). *What I have learned up until now about research methods in reading education.* Address given at the 51st meeting of the National Reading Conference, San Antonio, TX.

Pressley, M., El-Dinary, P.M., Gaskins, I.W., Schuder, T., Bergman, J.L., Almasi, J., et al. (1992). Beyond direct explanation: Transactional instruction of reading comprehension strategies. *The Elementary School Journal, 92*, 513–555.

Roeser, R.W., Eccles, J.S., & Sameroff, A.J. (2000). School as a context of early adolescents' academic and social-emotional development: A summary of research findings. *The Elementary School Journal, 100,* 443–471.

Rycik, J.A., & Irvin, J.L. (2001). Introduction. In J.A. Rycik & J.L. Irvin (Eds.), *What adolescents deserve: A commitment to students' literacy learning* (pp. 1–9). Newark, DE: International Reading Association.

Schmoker, M. (1996). *Results: The key to continuous improvement.* Alexandria, VA: Association for Supervision and Curriculum Development.

Shepard, L.A. (2000). The role of assessment in learning culture. *Educational Researcher, 29*(7), 4–14.

Strauss, S.E., & Irvin, J.L. (2001). Exemplary literacy learning programs. In J.A. Rycik & J.L. Irvin (Eds.), *What adolescents deserve: A commitment to students' literacy learning* (pp. 114–119). Newark, DE: International Reading Association.

CHILDREN'S LITERATURE CITED

Goodman, B. (1997). *More chills: 12 more chilling tales and exciting adventures.* Lincolnwood, IL: Jamestown.

Hobbs, W. (1989). *Bearstone.* New York: Avon Books.

CHAPTER 8

With a Little Help From My Friends: Peer Tutors and Struggling Fifth-Grade Readers

Douglas Fisher, Nancy Frey, Lynne Thrope, and Julie Jacobson

> As fifth grader Erik walked into the after-school reading club room, he recognized the expression of excitement on Sayoko's face. Sayoko, his second-grade tutee, immediately reached into her backpack for the new book she wanted to share with Erik.
> "Look Erik, I got a new book we can read. It's about a pig and the circus."
> The two of them begin to read *Olivia Saves the Circus* (Falconer, 2001). This isn't a book that Erik would typically choose to read himself. However, given his role as a tutor in the after-school reading club, he is willing to focus on this book so that he can help Sayoko read. Erik, a current fifth grader, reads well below grade level. What he may not realize is that the help he gives to Sayoko is also reinforcing his own reading habits and skills.

Keene and Zimmermann (1997), Fearn and Farnan (2000), and Templeton (1997) maintain that language learning is more than a process of integrating sounds, words, and grammatical formations. A focus on higher order thinking skills, they assert, provides opportunities for students to analyze and interpret text. It is this type of cognitive activity that is at the heart of academic study. The behaviors that are key to academic literacy include the ability to provide explanations, logical arguments, grounded interpretations, and abstract analyses. Through opportunities for interpreting texts, explaining and justifying conclusions, making predictions based on the text, hypothesizing outcomes or related situations, comparing and evaluating ideas, and talking about how these objectives are accomplished, students

Adapted from Jacobson, J., Thrope, L., Fisher, D., Lapp, D., Frey, N., & Flood, J. (2001). Cross-age tutoring: A literacy improvement approach for struggling adolescent readers. *Journal of Adolescent & Adult Literacy*, *44*, 528–547.

discover an enhanced purposefulness to the reading experience. In addition, readers are more effectively prepared for future reading and writing activities. In addition to fostering cognitive activity, these behaviors also form the basis for social interactions in classrooms.

One way that teachers provide students with the opportunity to engage in critical thinking skills, as well as collaborative activities, is through peer tutoring. Many teachers throughout the United States have attempted to design tutoring programs to accommodate their students' individual needs (e.g., Fischer, 1999/2000; Maheady, Mallette, Harper, Sacca, & Pomerantz, 1994). Peer tutoring has resulted in students' enhanced enjoyment of working with partners, increased requests for help, expanded friendships that extend beyond the tutoring setting, and improved attitudes about writing (Potter, 1997; Taylor, Hanson, Watts, & Justice-Swanson, 1997; Utay & Utay, 1997; Zukowski, 1997).

A type of tutoring that has gained increased attention in recent years is cross-age tutoring (Giesecke, 1993; Jacobson et al., 2001; Newell, 1996). The process of cross-age tutoring involves an older pupil, under a teacher's guidance, who helps one or more younger students to learn or practice a skill or concept. The successful engagement of students helping one another can supplement classroom instruction for both tutors and their tutees. Cohen (1986) explains that planning instruction for others facilitates long-term retention and aids in students' familiarity with text. Through purposeful engagement, cross-age tutoring provides learners with an authentic reason for practicing in order to improve their reading performance (Haluska & Gillen, 1995; Juel, 1991). According to Gaustad (1993) and Cobb (1998), cross-age tutoring is beneficial because the process allows tutors expanded opportunities to review material, to contemplate the purpose as well as the intended outcome of a task, and to improve communication skills. In addition, cross-age or peer tutoring has been found to promote positive reading attitudes and habits (Caserta-Henry, 1996; Newell, 1996).

One-to-one tutoring programs, such as peer and cross-age tutoring, can result in emotional and academic benefits for the tutee as well (Haluska & Gillen, 1995; Potter, 1997). Tutees can benefit from individualized instruction in which tutors scaffold information and adapt the strategies they use to the younger learner's pace, learning style, and level of understanding. In addition, tutees can receive immediate feedback, answers to questions, and correction within a tutoring format.

The benefits to the tutees, through effective modeling, include learning study skills such as concentrating on material and organizing work to be completed. Much of the published evidence on cross-age tutoring has focused on the literacy outcomes for younger learners (e.g., Caserta-Henry, 1996; Henriques, 1997; Zukowski, 1997).

In the research for this chapter, we were particularly interested in determining the success of peer tutoring for the older students, the tutors. We wondered if cross-age tutoring would be beneficial for less proficient readers in the upper elementary and middle school grades. The remainder of this chapter focuses on the implementation of cross-age tutoring for less proficient readers and the outcomes of cross-age tutoring for these students.

The After-School Reading Club

The after-school reading club was implemented in an elementary school that consisted of just more than 1,500 students. Of these 1,500 students, 76% were English language learners, 99% qualified for free or reduced-price lunches, and 28% read at grade level.

The tutoring program involved both upper elementary and primary-grade students. The upper elementary school students were fifth graders who tutored 75 students in grades 1 and 2. Although many fifth graders in this school peer tutor during the after-school reading club, the specific focus of our work was on the expansion of reading skills for 24 less proficient fifth-grade students, 9 girls and 15 boys, who attended one of the after-school reading club classes. These 24 students all qualified for free lunch, spoke languages other than English at home with their families, and tested at least two grade levels below their peers on both performance and standardized measures.

Before tutoring sessions began, the tutors practiced reading individually and together in small groups. These fifth graders were taught strategies through direct instruction, demonstration lessons, and guided practice. Strategies included reading for meaning, becoming independent in word recognition through the use of decoding and self-monitoring strategies, learning to spell by focusing and repeating sounds in words, spelling the sounds through direct association with letters, attending to letter order, using high-frequency words, selecting books at appropriate reading levels, and using metacognitive reading strategies. They were also given opportunities for independent learning and were continually supported in their reading and instructional efforts by the teacher. Each day, the after-school reading club teacher read aloud grade-level literature including *Frindle* (Clements, 1996), *Just Juice* (Hesse, 1998), and *Riding Freedom* (Ryan, 1998). In addition to these read-alouds, the teacher structured her two-hour per day, three-day per week after-school reading club class around cross-age tutoring (based on the format provided by Thrope & Wood, 2000):

Day 1: The text to be used as the base of instruction for the tutees was introduced. Students discussed personal familiarity with texts and predicted the tutees' prior knowledge of the story, as well as related topics. The teacher modeled specific instructional strategies that the fifth graders would use with younger students, including word identification and comprehension skills. After viewing the entire lesson that they would conduct, the tutors practiced the teaching techniques that were modeled. Each tutor read his or her book to a peer in the class. As they read, tutors were asked to identify five difficult words. Partners then worked together to determine an appropriate definition for each word through context, through a glossary, or by using the dictionary. The tutees used sticky notes to place on the text as reminders for instructional techniques they wanted to use or for questions that they wanted to ask tutees in order to check comprehension.

Day 2: Tutors met with their tutees and taught the lesson to at least two younger peers. After the lessons, the students practiced reading aloud as both tutors and tutees shared the book.

Day 3: In an effort to provide students with opportunities to reflect on their own and the tutees' learning experiences, whole-class discussions were conducted. Students were encouraged to identify their successes as well as the challenges they had experienced the previous day. Then, each student recorded his or her individual reflections in a tutors' journal. The students often commented on the tutees' attitudes, motivation, cooperation, and interest as well as their overall achievements.

The philosophy of the after-school reading club was that optimum learning occurs in an environment of intrinsic purposeful engagement through supportive instructional methods (e.g., DeCosta, 1987). We believed that struggling readers needed instruction in reading strategies to help them learn to decode, to talk about the meanings of unfamiliar words, to understand what good readers do when they read, and to anticipate possible challenges they might encounter when reading.

We hypothesized that as the fifth-grade struggling readers gained expertise as tutors, they would be motivated to read and to try the strategies that they were suggesting to younger students.

At the beginning of the year, the teacher developed sample lessons for the fifth-grade students to use with their tutees. For example, the following lesson, based on *The House That Jack Built* (Mayo, 2001), provides students with five steps to implement:

1. Explain to your tutee that reading can help develop vocabulary and general knowledge of the world. Ask the tutee about the word *malt*. Discuss how the word *malt* can be used for grain like barley that grows in the field. Also ask the tutees what other words mean the same as *house* (*home*, *condo*, *apartment*, etc.).

2. Read to the tutee the book *The House That Jack Built*.

3. Explain to your tutee that many words in English share spelling patterns and that by learning the patterns, people can read more fluently and at a faster pace. Ask the tutee to write down on his or her individual dry-erase board all the words from the book that end in *–orn* or *–at*.

4. Ask the tutee to write one more word that ends with *–orn* and *–at* that was not in the book.

5. Explain that rereading and organizing a story sequence is a strategy that good readers use. Reread the book *The House That Jack Built* to the tutee, this time providing pictures of the items discussed in the text that he or she can put in order as the text is read.

The following six-step lesson was used with the book *Five Creatures* (Jenkins, 2001). These strategies were often drawn from a list of "Things Good Readers Do" that was posted on the wall of the reading club classroom (see Figure 8.1).

1. Explain to your tutee that previewing reading material to both determine prior knowledge and build knowledge can help with comprehension. Introduce the book *Five Creatures* by looking through it together. Do not read the words of the book at this time; only talk about what the pictures tell. Have the tutee make predictions about what is happening on each page. Helpful questions you may ask include the following:

- What are the characters doing?
- How is this character feeling about the situation? What clues helped you answer that?
- What is happening on this page?
- What do you think will happen next?

2. Explain that people can experience difficulty when they read if they cannot pronounce a word, or if they are unfamiliar with a word's meaning, such as the words *creature*, *human*, or *newspaper*. Read each difficult word to the tutee. Then ask him or her to read each word.

3. Have the tutee write each word on a 5"x7" card. Also have him or her write a definition of the word and draw a picture that illustrates the word's meaning. Ask the tutee to describe the picture. Finally, ask the tutee to write one sentence using the word on the back of the card.

4. Explain that monitoring and editing are important activities. Tell the tutee that through editing and revising, we can check for correct language use. Make sure that the tutee wrote a good sentence. Ask yourself, "Was I able to read his or her writing?" Check for correct spelling, punctuation, and capitalization. You can suggest more interesting words, if the sentences need them.

5. Read aloud the book *Five Creatures* to the tutee.

6. Tell the tutee that his or her thoughts and opinions about the text are important. Share your thoughts about a character or about a theme you have identified in the story. Ask the tutee to write a journal entry about the feelings he or she had about the book.

FIGURE 8.1

THINGS GOOD READERS DO

- Use their knowledge to make sense of new information
- Predict the content of the text and monitor predictions
- Ask questions about the text before, during, and after reading
- Make connections between text and self, text and world, and text and other texts
- Use "fix-up" strategies when meaning breaks down
- Reread
- Skip words and try to figure out the sentence
- Look up words in the dictionary
- Visualize
- Write summaries or retell the text to another person

As the school year progressed, many of the tutors began developing their own lesson plans for their tutees, with the assistance of the reading club teacher. For example, two students planned a lesson on *Stick Out Your Tongue! Fantastic Facts, Features, and Functions of Animal and Human Tongues* (Bonsignore, 2001). The students identified five steps in their lesson plans for the second graders (based on Ogle, 1986):

1. Ask the tutee, "What do you know about tongues?" Also ask, "What do you want to learn about tongues?" There should be at least 10 thoughts in each column.

2. Read the book *Stick Out Your Tongue* to the tutee.

3. Use the compare/contrast diagram. Above the word *different*, write the words *humans* and *animals*. In the *human* circle, ask the student to write at least three things that tell only about human tongues (they can use the book). Do the same in the *animal* circle. Make sure that the tutee writes things that are unique to each one. In the middle circle marked *alike*, write three things that tell about the characteristics that animal and human tongues share.

4. Ask the tutee to tell you about the differences between human and animal tongues. Ask some additional comprehension questions from the book.

5. Ask the tutee to describe anything new that he or she learned about tongues. Write these on the chart under "What I Learned."

Another pair of tutors decided to use the book *The Class Artist* (Karas, 2001) as the focus of a lesson they developed for their tutees. This lesson had seven components:

1. Introduce the book *The Class Artist* by chatting through it together with the tutee. Do not read the words of the book at this time, only talk about what the pictures tell you. Have the tutee make predictions about what is happening on each page. Helpful questions are as follows:
   - Who is the character?
   - What is the character doing?
   - How is the character feeling about the situation? What clues helped you answer that?

- What is happening on this page?
- What do you think will happen next?

2. Tell the tutee that there are some difficult words in the book *The Class Artist* that have to be learned before reading the book. These words are either difficult to pronounce or difficult to understand. Read each difficult word to the tutee, and then ask him or her to read each word.

3. Have the tutee write each word on a 5"x7" card. Also have him or her write a definition of the word and draw a picture that tells what the word means. Ask the tutee to tell you about the picture that he or she drew. Have the tutee write one sentence using the word on the back of the card.

4. Edit and revise the sentences. Make sure that the tutee wrote a good sentence. Ask yourself, "Was I able to read his or her writing?" Check for correct spelling, punctuation, and capitalization. Suggest more interesting words if the sentences need them.

5. Read aloud to the tutee the book *The Class Artist*.

6. Talk with the tutee about the book while working on an art project together.

7. Ask the tutee to write a journal entry about the feelings he or she had about book.

One of the favorite activities that the tutors completed with their tutees was writing words for wordless books. The after-school reading club teacher introduced the book *Window* (Baker, 1991) to her students. Originally, she had planned to invite tutors to write simple text for this wordless book and then invite the tutors to read their composed text to their tutees. Interestingly, the tutors wanted to take the book and co-write the words with their tutees. This lead to an increase in requests for wordless books. The teacher was able to collect several from the school library, including *Time Flies* (Rohmann, 1994), *Why?* (Popov, 1996), *Moonlight* (Ormerod, 1982), *The Snowman* (Briggs, 1978), and *I See a Song* (Carle, 1973).

Examining Outcomes

The literacy-related outcomes for the struggling fifth-grade readers were evaluated on three measures: the Student Oral Language

Observation Matrix (SOLOM), the Diagnostic Reading Assessment (DRA), and the Stanford Diagnostic Reading Test (SDRT). On each of these measures, student scores were higher in the group that tutored compared with similar groups of students who did not peer tutor. In addition, the 24 students in the reading club on peer tutoring had statistically significant increases in their reading achievement over the course of the year—more than two years' growth during the year.

Although we are unable to conclude that the cross-age tutoring alone resulted in these changes, we do believe that the various intervention strategies, including the implementation of direct reading instruction, each student's personal responsibility for teaching another child, and the opportunity for reflection on their progress through journal writing, influenced the literacy growth of these students. In addition to the test scores, our observations also suggest that the fifth-grade students improved their literacy skills and became much more interested in talking about books. We noticed, for example, that during the tutors' read-aloud time, they increasingly demonstrated appropriate examples of rhythm, rhyme, stress, and intonation as they modeled the skills for their tutees.

In one example, during an early observation of a tutor, Jessica, the observation notes indicate that Jessica "makes many mistakes during her read-aloud of *Stand Tall, Molly Lou Melton* (Lovell, 2001), including mispronunciations of the words *shortest*, *proudly*, and *alongside*. She also has several mis-starts and speaks in a monotone voice as she reads to her tutee." Five months later, observation notes indicated that she read the book *Chrysanthemum* (Henkes, 1991) with only four word errors—*envious, begrudging, discontented*, and *jaundiced*. The notes indicate that Jessica "reads with enthusiasm and interest. She stops several times to ask questions of her tutee."

In a second example, during a tutor named Anthony's read-aloud of *Click, Clack, Moo: Cows That Type* (Cronin, 2000), the observational notes from October are similar to those about Jessica. The observer wrote: "Anthony doesn't show much emotion when he reads and he reads slow—like he's trying to get all the words right. All the words sound the same. Even the exclamation marks don't cue him to read the text any differently. He doesn't make this very interesting for his tutee." By the end of the school year, observational data suggested that Anthony had significantly improved his fluency skills. The observer watched Anthony read the book *Fly Away Home* (Bunting, 1991) and noted that he made "no errors in reading the text. His speed has increased, as has his intonation. He seems to like reading much better and is really engaging his tutee. He pauses periodically to ask questions to make sure that his tutee understands the story. It seems that Anthony also understands the story."

In addition to the changes in reading fluency and attitudes toward reading, observational data suggested that the fifth-grade struggling readers paid much more attention to words, their meanings, and their spellings. For example, during a November observation of Taylor and her reading of the book *Miss Spider's Tea Party* (Kirk, 1994), the observer noticed that Taylor was stopping each time a word ended with *–ay, –ight, –oom,* or *–ook*. When Taylor and her tutee had finished reading the book, the observer noted that "Taylor asked her tutee to go back through the book and make a list of words that ended with *–ay, –ight, –oom,* or *–ook*. Taylor then added to each of the columns of words two additional words that were not in the book. The two of them then created sentences using the words that they had written down."

Another example of the attention to words paid by struggling readers who tutored was Brandon's use of the book *Grandfather's Journey* (Say, 1993) in March. As Brandon read the book with his tutee, they made a list of words that were difficult, including *journey, astonished, riverboat, sculptures,* and *factories*. Brandon asked his tutee to write each word on a 5"x7" card and then had the tutee write a definition of each word and draw a picture that told what the word meant. Following this activity, Brandon and his tutee agreed on a sentence that contained each word. As the observer noted, "Brandon likes the dictionary work with his tutee. They find the definitions of the words together. Brandon still makes spelling errors when he writes sentences but accepts assistance from his tutee." Brandon and his tutee seemed to really enjoy making cards and can often be found writing down difficult words from books so that they can make flash cards. It should be noted that this strategy for word study was introduced by the after-school reading club teacher and modeled several times. Brandon selected this strategy as one he could use with his tutee.

In addition to the test scores, assessments, and observations, we also collected assessment information by asking the tutors about their experiences in tutoring. The tutors consistently reported that the cross-age experience was beneficial, motivating, and enjoyable. Many of the students used adjectives such as *fun, great, useful,* and *challenging* to reflect the positive nature of their experience. As Jessica said, "I like teaching. I think I'll be a teacher when I grow up." It was not uncommon for the tutors to report that the after-school reading club was one of their favorite activities. As Brandon said, "I like being the teacher and helping. It makes me feel good to do that."

What Did We Learn?

We believe that there were several factors related to the successes experienced by these 24 fifth-grade struggling readers. It is important to note that we are not sure that the entire effect was related to cross-age tutoring, per se. We believe that the structure of the after-school reading club was key to students' successes. Tutoring was the foundation of the club, and we believe that this experience provided the students with an authentic reason for wanting to improve their literacy skills. This accountability seemed to work where previous student-level accountability systems (e.g., failing grades, retention) did not. Taken as a whole, we believe that the peer tutoring effort was successful for several key reasons.

First, the students listened to books being read to them by a competent reader, the teacher, on a regular basis. In addition, these students were able to hear the book read aloud a second time. This is consistent with previously published research, including the work of Ouellette, Dagostino, and Carifio (1999), which indicates that read-alouds are an effective strategy for improving the comprehension of less fluent readers.

Second, we believe that the structure of the club made picture books and wordless books "okay" books for older students to study and learn. The performance expectation of reading the book to younger students and knowing all the words was likely an important factor. However, we believe that using the picture books and wordless books provided these less fluent, but older, readers with models of text that they needed but were uncomfortable using due to social pressures. Other teachers and researchers have found the use of picture books and wordless books useful with older students, including Carr, Buchanan, and Wentz (2001), Cassady (1998), Mitchell and Pullum (1998), Mundy and Hadaway (1999), and Robb (1998).

Third, we believe that the club also provided students an opportunity to reread their texts. The evidence for repeated reading or rereading is strong (e.g., Bossert & Schwantes, 1995; Fowler, 1998; Green, 1997/1998; Lewman, 1999). However, teachers are sometimes reluctant to encourage struggling readers to reread texts they find difficult. The after-school reading class provided us a chance to address this literacy strategy with minimal resistance from the students.

Finally, we believe that the club, structured in this way, provided important modeling of effective reading strategies for the students. Not only were they taught strategies that they could use but they also were expected to model these strategies for younger students. This required the students to internalize the strategies and forced the students to use them. This transference, we believe, was key in the success of the students and would not have been accomplished without a cross-age tutoring component.

REFERENCES

Bossert, T.S., & Schwantes, F.M. (1995). Children's comprehension monitoring: Training children to use rereading to aid comprehension. *Reading Research and Instruction, 35*, 109–121.

Carr, K.S., Buchanan, D.L., & Wentz, J.B. (2001). Not just for the primary grades: A bibliography of picture books for secondary content teachers. *Journal of Adolescent & Adult Literacy, 45*, 146–153.

Caserta-Henry, C. (1996). Reading buddies: A first-grade intervention program. *The Reading Teacher, 49*, 500–503.

Cassady, J.K. (1998). Wordless books: No-risk tools for inclusive middle-grade classrooms. *Journal of Adolescent & Adult Literacy, 41*, 428–433.

Cobb, J.B. (1998). The social contexts of tutoring: Mentoring the older at-risk student. *Reading Horizons, 39*, 50–75.

Cohen, J. (1986). Theoretical considerations of peer tutoring. *Psychology in the Schools, 23*, 175–186.

DeCosta, E. (1987). *Integrative motivation and the development of linguistic proficiency in second language education: A dual learning concept.* Paper presented at the annual meeting of the International Association of Applied Linguistics, Sydney, Australia. (ERIC Document Reproduction Service No. ED301051)

Fearn, L., & Farnan, N. (2000). *Interactions: Teaching writing and the language arts.* New York: Houghton Mifflin.

Fischer, C. (1999/2000). An effective (and affordable) intervention model for at-risk high school readers. *Journal of Adolescent & Adult Literacy, 43*, 326–335.

Fowler, D. (1998). Balanced reading instruction in practice. *Educational Leadership, 55*(6), 11–12.

Gaustad, J. (1993). Peer and cross-age tutoring. *ERIC Digest, 79*. Office of Educational Research and Improvement. (ERIC Document Reproduction Service No. ED354608)

Giesecke, D. (1993). Low-achieving students as successful cross-age tutors. *Preventing School Failure, 37*, 34–43.

Green, M. (1997/1998). Rapid retrieval of information: Reading aloud with a purpose. *Journal of Adolescent & Adult Literacy, 41*, 306–307.

Haluska, R., & Gillen, D. (1995). Kids teaching kids: Pairing up with cross-grades pals. *Learning, 24*(3), 54–56.

Henriques, M.E. (1997). Increasing literacy among kindergartners through cross-age training. *Young Children, 52*(4), 42–47.

Jacobson, J., Thrope, L., Fisher, D., Lapp, D., Frey, N., & Flood, J. (2001). Cross-age tutoring: A literacy improvement approach for struggling adolescent readers. *Journal of Adolescent & Adult Literacy, 44*, 528–547.

Juel, C. (1991). Cross-age tutoring between student athletes and at-risk children. *The Reading Teacher, 45*, 178–186.

Keene, E.O., & Zimmermann, S. (1997). *Mosaic of thought: Teaching comprehension in a reader's workshop*. Portsmouth, NH: Heinemann.

Lewman, B. (1999). Read it again! How rereading—and rereading—stories heightens children's literacy. *Children and Families, 8*, 12–15.

Maheady, L., Mallette, B., Harper, G.F., Sacca, K.C., & Pomerantz, D. (1994). Peer-mediated instruction for high-risk students. In K.D. Wood & B. Algozzine (Eds.), *Teaching reading to high-risk learners: A unified perspective* (pp. 269–290). Needham Heights, MA: Allyn & Bacon.

Mitchell, D., & Pullum, T. (1998). Using children's literature to spark learning. *English Journal, 87*, 94–97.

Mundy, J., & Hadaway, N.L. (1999). Children's informational picture books visit a secondary ESL classroom. *Journal of Adolescent & Adult Literacy, 42*, 464–475.

Newell, F.M. (1996). Effects of a cross-age tutoring program on computer literacy learning of second-grade students. *Journal of Research on Computing in Education, 28*, 346–358.

Ogle, D.M. (1986). K-W-L: A teaching model that develops active reading of expository text. *The Reading Teacher, 39*, 564–570.

Ouellette, G., Dagostino, L., & Carifio, J. (1999). The effects of exposure to children's literature through read aloud and an inferencing strategy on low reading ability fifth graders' sense of story structure and reading comprehension. *Reading Improvement, 36*, 73–89.

Potter, J. (1997). New directions in student tutoring. *Education + Training, 39*(1), 24–29.

Robb, L. (1998). Helping reluctant readers discover books. *Book Links, 7*(4), 51–53.

Taylor, B.M., Hanson, B.E., Watts, S.M., & Justice-Swanson, K. (1997). Helping struggling readers: Linking small-group intervention with cross-age tutoring. *The Reading Teacher, 51*, 196–209.

Templeton, S. (1997). *Teaching the integrated language arts* (2nd ed.). Boston: Houghton Mifflin.

Thrope, L., & Wood, D. (2000). Cross-age tutoring for young adolescents. *The Clearing House, 73*, 239–242.

Utay C., & Utay J. (1997). Peer-assisted learning: The effects of cooperative learning and cross-age peer tutoring with word processing on writing skills of students with learning disabilities. *Journal of Computing in Childhood Education*, *8*, 165–185.

Zukowski, V. (1997). Teeter-totters and tandem bikes: A glimpse into the world of cross-age tutors. *Teaching and Change*, *5*, 71–91.

CHILDREN'S LITERATURE CITED

Baker, J. (1991). *Window*. New York: William Morrow.

Bonsignore, J. (2001). *Stick out your tongue! Fantastic facts, features, and functions of animal and human tongues*. Atlanta, GA: Peachtree.

Briggs, R. (1978). *The snowman*. New York: Random House.

Bunting, E. (1991). *Fly away home*. New York: Clarion.

Carle, E. (1973). *I see a song*. New York: Scholastic.

Clements, A. (1996). *Frindle*. New York: Aladdin.

Cronin, D. (2000). *Click, clack, moo: Cows that type*. New York: Simon & Schuster.

Falconer, I. (2001). *Olivia saves the circus*. New York: Simon & Schuster.

Henkes, K. (1991). *Chrysanthemum*. New York: Mulberry.

Hesse, K. (1998). *Just juice*. New York: Scholastic.

Jenkins, E. (2001). *Five creatures*. New York: Farrar, Straus & Giroux.

Karas, G.B. (2001). *The class artist*. New York: Greenwillow.

Kirk, D. (1994). *Miss Spider's tea party*. New York: Scholastic.

Lovell, P. (2001). *Stand tall, Molly Lou Melton*. New York: Putnam.

Mayo, D. (2001). *The house that Jack built*. New York: Barefoot Books.

Ormerod, J. (1982). *Moonlight*. New York: Viking Penguin.

Popov, N. (1996). *Why?* New York: North-South Books.

Rohmann, E. (1994). *Time flies*. New York: Crown.

Ryan, P.N. (1998). *Riding freedom*. New York: Scholastic.

Say, A. (1993). *Grandfather's journey*. Boston: Houghton Mifflin.

CHAPTER 9

Taking Computers Out of the Corner: Making Technology Work for Struggling Intermediate-Grade Readers

Melanie R. Kuhn and Lesley Mandel Morrow

I didn't really know much about the computer. I don't have one at home. (Katrina, age 9)

I didn't know anything about computers. I know what they are used for, but I never had one myself, and I didn't really know how to use them. (Wendy, age 12)

I learned you can play games and learn how to write better when you use the computer. You can also write to people and hear back from them really soon, even if they are really far away. (Dominique, age 8)

I really didn't know there was so much to know and learn on the Internet. It would have taken so much more time to look for the information we needed about the farm in the library. We probably wouldn't have found as much either. (Bonifacio, age 12)

These comments were offered by children at the end of a cross-age project in which children living in two different cities (New Brunswick, New Jersey, and Detroit, Michigan) learned to use technology to learn together about farms and farming. In the course of the project, children in grades 1 and 6 had opportunities to correspond with each other as e-mail pen pals; they e-mailed questions to a farmer in Missouri who served as their "farming consultant." They researched the Internet for information about farming and presented what they learned in a PowerPoint presentation. The culminating activity was a three-way interactive television session with the farmer in Missouri, the first graders in New Brunswick, and the sixth graders in Detroit.

During the course of this project, our beliefs about the potential for technology to enhance students' learning opportunities were confirmed and reinforced. However, as the children's comments suggest, we also were reminded of how few opportunities many children have to learn about and learn through technology. In this chapter, we explore ways for classroom teachers to make better uses of the technology that is now so widely available.

W hen discussing technology as an aid to literacy learning in general and struggling upper-elementary readers in particular, there are two questions we consider to be useful in guiding our discussion: First, what can be done to support literacy development using instructional technology that cannot be done without it? Second, how can instructional technology be used to make literacy accessible to intermediate-grade struggling readers? Given that instructional technology (referred to in this chapter as IT), defined broadly, has significant potential to aid students in their reading and writing in ways that traditional, print-based tools cannot (e.g., Merrow, 2001; Reinking, 1998), it strikes us as extremely important to identify ways in which IT can be used uniquely and effectively within the classroom. Additionally, although IT can be useful for all learners, some of the modifications that can be made through technology are especially beneficial for students who experience difficulty with their reading and writing. Having had discussions with a number of teachers and researchers who consider instructional technology to be a primary focus, we present a number of strategies and suggestions in this chapter that have been anecdotally demonstrated to be effective in the classroom and that we hope will inspire additional research in this field.

Instructional Technology as a Literacy Learning Tool

When computers first entered schools, they were hailed by many as a tool that would enable students to learn in ways previously unimagined (e.g., Hawisher & Selfe, 1999; Synder, 1999; Wenglinsky, 1998). These machines would be highly motivating, they would allow students access to information that was unavailable through traditional sources, and they would promote a greater depth of understanding by allowing students to learn in ways that were only beginning to be envisioned (e.g., Papert, 1984). However, it soon became apparent that neither the simple presence of computers in the classroom nor the sheer amount of information to which they enable access would be enough to guarantee that students would more readily engage in learning (Balajthy, 1996; Merrow, 2001). In fact, initial attempts to introduce technology were often hindered by application difficulties in the classroom (e.g., Rickelman & Caplan, 2000; Travers, 1999).

Despite the initial difficulties experienced in implementing IT in the classroom, the effective use of computers and the Internet is increasing in schools across the United States (Rowand, 2000). One of the most fundamental reasons for this change is that, while computers have become increasingly sophisticated, they also have become increasingly user-friendly (Travers, 1999). Additionally, as technology has become increasingly prolific within our culture, both teachers and students are more at ease with it. Nonetheless, according to a recent U.S. Department of Education survey (Smerdon et al., 2000), a large number of teachers feel inadequately prepared to exploit the full potential of computers within their classrooms.

The purpose of this chapter is to discuss ways in which computer-based technologies can be effectively integrated into the literacy curriculum, with particular attention to the ways computer technology may mediate the literacy needs of struggling intermediate-grade readers. Our hope is that this chapter will prove helpful to teachers who are searching for better ways to integrate computers and the Internet into their literacy instruction routines. To meet this goal, we will discuss the ways in which computers can add unique elements to various aspects of the curriculum. We also will present some exemplars that make use of computer-based instruction across various subject areas while maintaining a literacy focus. The exemplars are intended to provide a basis for conversation and exploration rather than a prescription for implementation.

Using Instructional Technology to Support Literacy Development

Struggling readers in the intermediate grades typically differ from capable readers in three important ways: they lack fluency in reading, they have less developed vocabulary knowledge, and they experience greater difficulty in comprehending required texts. Instructional technology may provide important ways to support students' development in each of these areas.

Fluency Development

One of the most frequently observed differences between struggling readers and their more skilled peers in the upper-elementary grades is the struggling reader's lack of fluency (Allington, 1983; Chall, 1996; Kuhn & Stahl, 2000). Fluent reading consists of not only automatic and accurate word recognition but also of those features that lead to an expressive rendering of text. Such expressive reading incorporates prosodic features such as appropriate stress, pitch, and phrasing and allows readers to replicate many of the qualities present in oral language. However, struggling readers often have difficulty making the transition from purposeful decoding to fluent reading. There are a number of factors that contribute to this lack of fluency, including the practice of round-robin reading, in which readers interact with text as fragments rather than as a unified whole (Opitz & Rasinski, 1998); leveled grouping, in which struggling readers have only other nonfluent readers to serve as models (Allington, 1983); and the use of texts that are almost exclusively beyond the students' zone of proximal development (Rasinski & Padak, 1996).

There are a number of approaches designed specifically to develop fluent reading, including repeated readings (Samuels, 1979); echo, choral, and paired reading (Kuhn & Stahl, 2000); and audiotaped books (Carbo, 1978; Chomsky, 1976). One unique way that computer-aided instruction can expand on these strategies is through the use of "talking books," that is, CD-ROMs that present an animated version of text. Although the basic format of assisted reading with talking books is similar to assisted reading with audiotaped books, there are two ways in which the computer-aided texts differ from the audiotape format. The first and most obvious difference is the provision of animation, as well as narration, in the computer-aided version. However, a second difference with particular implications for the development of fluent reading involves the presentation of the text itself. In addition to enabling the student to see the text while listening to the read-aloud, a computer-aided rendition also allows the text to be highlighted in meaningful phrases as it is being read expressively. This ensures that the reader focuses on phrase units that maintain the meaning of the story.

Vocabulary

A second area in which significant differences are evident between struggling readers and their more skilled peers is that of vocabulary development. Most learners who experience difficulty in reading have a significantly smaller vocabulary than their peers with higher levels of reading achievement (Nagy, 1988; Stahl, 1999; Stanovich, 1986). Stanovich (1986) argues that the gap between high- and low-performing readers increases, rather than remains constant, over the course of a student's career. The primary reason for this increasing gap involves differences in the reading experiences of the two types of readers. As struggling readers experience difficulties when reading, they are less likely to read, and as a result, they have less exposure to text. As a consequence of their limited exposure to text, they encounter fewer new words and concepts, which, in turn, contributes to difficulty with future reading. Able readers, on the other hand, read more, are exposed to and subsequently acquire new words and concepts, and as a result, find future reading easier. As noted by others cited in this book, Stanovich (1986) referred to this cycle of learning as the Matthew Effect—that is, a context in which the rich get richer and the poor get poorer.

Nagy, Herman, and Anderson (1985) indicate that most vocabulary development occurs at an incidental level rather than through direct instruction. In other words, it is the exposure to new words that takes place through the process of reading itself that leads to the eventual incorporation of most new words into our vocabularies. It would, therefore, seem that to increase students' vocabularies we must increase the amount of text they read. This can be done, at least partially, by making the words and concepts presented in the text accessible to students. A unique way in which electronic texts can assist struggling readers is through their potential to make text more transparent by providing immediate access to the meaning of a word. Computer technology allows the definition of a word or phrase to be embedded into any text. The key words themselves can then serve as hot buttons, allowing students to click on them in order to determine the definition of an unknown or unclear word. Such immediate access to the meaning of a word can make difficult terms understandable, potentially contributing to the students' comprehension of a passage. Further, having immediate access to a word's meaning can help readers not only in their ability to understand the particular text they are reading but also, potentially, to transfer this increased understanding of the term to future texts.

Comprehension

Most educators agree that the ultimate goal of reading is the construction of meaning and that the primary goal of all literacy instruction is to ensure that this occurs. However, it is necessary to recognize that successful comprehension is an interactive process (Keene & Zimmermann, 1997; Pearson, Roehler, Dole, & Duffy, 1992; Pressley, 2000). That is, in order to construct meaning from a given text, readers must combine information presented directly in the passage with information they already possess. Given the importance of reader-based knowledge in constructing meaning, insufficient knowledge of a subject or topic can negatively affect learners' understanding of what they read. As such, it is necessary to design literacy instruction in a way that assists students who may have insufficient background knowledge about a particular subject or topic to successfully read and understand a focal text. One of the most effective ways to aid comprehension of material that deals with unknown or unfamiliar concepts is to provide information regarding that concept prior to reading (e.g., Cooper, 2000; Guillaume, 2000; Strickland, Ganske, & Monroe, 2002).

The Internet provides a unique way for learners to explore an extensive range of background information connected with any given concept. For example, if students were reading about the settling of the British colonies in America, it would be easy for them to simultaneously research what the settlements were like on several levels. They could find out about the type of food, clothing, and lifestyles settlers experienced through a virtual tour of Plimoth Plantation (http://pilgrims.net/plimoth plantation/vtour). Further, they could look at the kind of settlement that was occurring in the rest of the Americas during this period, including finding out about the first Thanksgiving, or "La Toma," that took place in New Mexico in 1598 (http://www.neta.com/~1stbooks/texas2.htm). Similarly, students could easily identify what was occurring in the European countries that were responsible for these settlements. For example, they could find examples of the type of art that was being created across Europe during this period by looking at the National Gallery in London (http://www.nationalgallery.org.uk) or the Prado Museum in Spain (http://museoprado.mcu.es/prado/html/ihome.html). Or students could identify the kinds of inventions and scientific or mathematical advances that were taking place during these years. Not only does the Internet provide easy access to all this information but also the visual and audio elements that often accompany the text on websites make it easier for students who might shy away from a print-only source of information to construct an understanding of the material.

Using Instructional Technology to Make Literature Accessible to Struggling Readers

The general category of "literature" is one that is well suited to IT in general and the Internet in particular. There are numerous ways in which websites, CD-ROMs, and DVDs are compatible with the study of literature. One of the primary advantages is the capability of these technologies to incorporate both audio and visual resources into the presentation of content, thereby making the material more accessible to learners across a range of reading levels. This can be especially useful for struggling readers who might otherwise find the assigned material inaccessible without substantial support.

In addition to numerous resources directly connected to the texts themselves, the Internet provides wonderful ideas for lesson plans and extension activities. For example, when we looked up the Newbery Award-winning book *From the Mixed-up Files of Mrs. Basil E. Frankweiler* (Konigsburg, 1977), we found several sites related to the story. Many of these were designed for teachers planning lessons or units developed around the book (e.g., http://www.sdcoe.k12.ca.us/score/fris/fristg.htm, http://cspace.unb.ca/nbco/pigs/novel/social2.html). However, a number of sites also could be used directly by students. These sites provided connections to various aspects of the book, including items described in the Metropolitan Museum of Art (http://www.metmuseum.org and http://www.k111.k12.il.us/king/mixed_up.htm); the outline of a scavenger hunt based on the adventures of Claudia and James (http://www.yahooligans.com/tg/basil.html); and a proposal that students compute how much it would cost the runaways to conduct their 1968 journey both today and 20 years hence, using resources available through the Internet (http://www.hobart.k12.in.us/webquests/jonesquest/filequest.html). Such connections could easily serve to make the text seem more meaningful to a struggling reader. For example, it may be much easier to understand where Claudia hid her violin case once you have seen a picture of the sarcophagus described in the text than it would be by simply looking up the term in the dictionary. Likewise, for students who have not been to a large city, it is likely they would have a better understanding of how easy it is to get overlooked in this environment if they have access to maps of New York (http://maps.yahoo.com/py/maps.py?&Pyt=Tmap&addr=&csz=New+York+City, NY). This would allow them a sense of the relative distances the two protagonists were covering. Further, live-action photos of New York from a webcam on Fifth Avenue would let them view the hustle and bustle firsthand (http://riotingmanhatton.com/old_riot_site/webcam.html). Each of these potential extensions of the story holds the possibility of engaging struggling readers in a way the text alone might not.

Another way in which the Internet can engage struggling readers is through the design of a website that presents information about a particular text, an example of which was created by Linda Christianson based on the novel *Stone Fox* (Gardiner, 1980) (http://www.edgar.k12. wi.us/edgar/stonefox.htm). This site provides ways for students to research a topic that is connected to the story—in this case, the tribes of Native Americans indigenous to the state of Utah—while further allowing the students to represent what they have learned publicly. Such a project has the potential to motivate struggling readers in ways that more traditional forms of presentation—for example, a book report or research report—may not. Such research also provides students with an opportunity to work either independently or collaboratively in order to expand their knowledge. Finally, the creation of a webpage can, in itself, allow students and teachers access to a new form of learning that expands their understanding both of the technology they are developing and of what can be constituted as text.

Using Instructional Technology to Make Content Area Literacy Accessible to Struggling Readers

As students become increasingly proficient readers, the focus of their literacy instruction starts to center on their developing ability to learn from new material (Chall, 1996). Traditionally, the focus on reading and writing in the content area began in the upper-elementary grades and continued throughout students' middle and high school years. This shift created a phenomenon referred to as the fourth-grade slump—a time when many students experienced a drop in both their reading performance and their reading interest. The fourth-grade slump is often explained by the fact that as students enter the upper-elementary grades, they are confronted with a type of learning that differs fundamentally from that which they have encountered before fourth grade. In the upper-elementary grades and beyond, there is a shift in emphasis from reading genres that are generally familiar to students—that is, narratives, in which most of the concepts are part of the students' schema and most of the words are already part of their oral vocabulary—to reading genres that are generally unfamiliar to students, that is, nonfiction, in which the concepts and vocabulary are generally new. Without proper support, this shift can be problematic both for those students who are already experiencing difficulties learning to read and write and for some who had not previously encountered such difficulties. One way in which teachers can ease this transition is by minimizing the abruptness of the shift; this can be done by introducing students in the primary grades to content area materials as part of their early literacy development (Cooper, 2000; Duke, 1999; Guillaume, 2000). It is likely that such early support will allow learners to develop a better sense of reading and writing across the content areas. Despite teachers' best efforts, however, some learners will continue to encounter difficulties with nonfiction texts even when introduced to them throughout the primary grades; in these situations, instructional technology can be extremely effective at providing both scaffolding and opportunities to explore various content in a highly motivating manner (Roe, 2000).

For example, numerous reference texts are available in CD-ROM format; perhaps the best known are the interactive encyclopedias, among them *Compton's Multimedia Encyclopedia*, which offers an online subscription service, and *Grolier Multimedia Encyclopedia* (both available at http://www.broderbund.com), as well as the *World Book Encyclopedia* (http://www2.worldbook.com). These resources provide learners with multiple facets of a given listing. This means that if a student wants to learn about the international space station, it might be possible to view blueprints of the spacecraft from a number of angles, see a video clip of a space shuttle docking with the space station, and hear an interview with one of the astronauts who has actually lived in orbit for an extended period of time. The presentation of such a varied array of information, coupled with the fact that the text is supplemented by non–text-based resources, has the potential to provide students with a clearer understanding than might be developed through traditional reference materials.

In addition to commercially available informational resources, the amount of content area information available via the Internet is virtually limitless. For example, the research on the space station discussed earlier could be supplemented with information gathered directly from NASA's website (http://www.nasa.gov). The site has a series of activities designed for students, along with extras such as video feeds, which allow students to observe a series of regularly updated events connected with the space program as well as numerous other links. In fact, it is easily possible to find enough information on the Internet to consider it a stand-alone reference source. A case in point occurred when we looked up *geography*. We found several sites that provide information relevant to the topic; among them were the About

Geography website (http://geography.about.com/?once=true&)—the "Fun, Games & Humor" link is especially recommended; Geography World (http://members.aol.com/bowermanb/101.html), which has a plethora of information on the subject; and the *National Geographic* website (http://www.nationalgeographic.com), which has a special section for children, as well as an education section.

Again, the interactive nature of these sites, coupled with the non-text sources of information, has the potential to engage students with their research to a greater degree than would have been the case using more traditional methods. The Internet also has the advantage of being able to update the information it provides virtually instantaneously. As a result, it presents material in a real-time format that traditional print-based texts are unable to match. For example, an online atlas can keep up with the creation and dissolution of nation-states in ways that simply are not feasible with a printed book that must go through an extensive process prior to publication.

However, it is important to acknowledge drawbacks that may occur when students deal with resources that have such an ephemeral nature. First, there is no guarantee that the websites themselves will continue to be accessible after a given period of time. Second, it is difficult to confirm information that is ever-changing. For example, when attempting to find details of a news item from the previous day's news coverage on a number of websites, we discovered that the information was no longer searchable. Although similar difficulties occur with other nonprint media such as radio and television, print-based resources have always been considered to be permanent (Reinking, 1998), and libraries have acted as repositories for copies of dated material. For example, most university libraries and larger city libraries keep copies of old newspapers for several months, after which the information is transferred to microfilm or microfiche. There is no equivalent for archiving websites. In order to compensate for this, it may be necessary to print out a hard copy of any information considered to be important enough to use as a reference. Although doing so changes the nature of the cited material by turning it into an artifact, it allows learners to have a permanent version of whatever it is they are seeking.

The third drawback is that there is ongoing concern about student access to potentially inappropriate websites (e.g. Dillon, 1999; Kinzer, 2000). There are a number of possible ways to address this concern. First, there are several sources that provide software designed specifically to minimize the chances of students wandering onto, or intentionally searching for, objectionable sites. Among them are programs found at http://www.bess.com, http://www.netnanny.com, http://www.pearlsw. com/school/index.html, and http://www.solidoak.com. A second alternative is to allow students to use only search engines from sites such as Yahooligans (http://www.yahooligans.com), Ask Jeeves for Kids (http://www.ajkids.com), or Lightdog (http://www.lightdog.com) that were designed with some safeguards already in place. A third option is for a teacher to conduct a topic search and to bookmark acceptable pages, making it clear to students that only bookmarked sites should be used in assignments. Finally, teachers can print out appropriate material for an assignment and provide the hard copy for their students, thereby eliminating students' direct access to the Internet altogether. However, doing so also eliminates the students' opportunity to interact with a site, simultaneously denying access to the type of potential opportunities discussed throughout this chapter. For example, http://www.howstuffworks.com is designed specifically to take advantage of the multifaceted nature of the Internet by providing viewers with the opportunity to view animation that will create a deeper understanding than could be provided simply through still illustrations or words. The three-dimensional nature of this site would be lost should students have access only to a hard copy of an illustration.

Using Instructional Technology to Help Struggling Readers Develop a Critical Stance

It is commonly known that although there is a great deal of information available on the Web, not everything that is accessible has equal validity or credibility. For example, when exploring sites for a unit on global warming, we found two sources of information that look at first glance as though they would present similar content: http://www. globalwarming.org and http://www.globalwarming.net. However, upon exploring the sites, we found that the two present radically opposing perspectives. The former discusses the way in which the "problem" of global warming has been sensationalized, with hot buttons such as "Why We Shouldn't Sweat Global Warming" and "The Cooler Head Coalition." The latter site, on the other hand, presents a series of links that clearly adopts the perspective that global warming is a problem; the site presents connections that allow the reader to become involved in possible solutions. Additionally, we found a third site designed by the

Environmental Protection Agency (http://www.epa.gov/globalwarming), which states that one of the site's goals is the provision of "a more objective approach through the presentation of accurate information on the very broad issue of climate change and global warming in a way that is accessible and meaningful to all parts of society—communities, individuals, business, public officials and governments."

The issue of bias is not new to the Internet; it also exists in content area classes, where a single textbook is often the primary, if not the only, source of information for the student (Bigelow, 1989; Hoffman, 1992). Although bias in the texts that schools use for instructional purposes is worrisome under any circumstances, it is especially troubling when dealing with the Internet. (On the Internet, it is far easier to present information as fact, regardless of the accuracy of interpretation or the reliability of the information than it is in print media, where delineated standards, such as fact-checking, have been adopted by most publishers.)

It is, therefore, necessary to teach students to make judgments about the accuracy of their print resources and the biases, stated or unstated, that each presents. Central to this issue is teachers' ability to help students develop a critical stance by teaching them to systematically and routinely examine the accuracy and biases of a given text. We can begin by noting Chall's (1996) caution that a practice of using a single source of any type may unwittingly lead students to believe that what is written or said is necessarily true. By using multiple resources with varying perspectives on a given subject, teachers demonstrate to students the necessity of examining the basis for particular perspectives and taking an evaluative stance as a reader. To do this, however, it is necessary not only to present students with multiple texts but also to scaffold the texts in ways that allow students to become comfortable questioning the author, looking for the biases in any text, and confirming the information presented with facts from alternative resources.

For example, comprehension and vocabulary strategies can be modified to help scaffold the reading of multiple texts, whether print-based or presented via new technologies. Using the structure for semantic feature analysis (Johnson & Pearson, 1984), students could review a series of websites and compare the various definitions, conditions, and conclusions presented on a given topic, such as global warming (see Figure 9.1). After having students complete a semantic feature analysis individually or in small groups, teachers can lead a large-group discussion regarding the various definitions and facts presented by each resource. This will encourage students to question the notion that everything in print is true or unbiased, and to weigh the evidence and form their own opinions. Another useful strategy for evaluating ideas in print is the jot chart format, suggested by Hadaway & Mundy (2000) to outline important facts across various subjects or components of a subject to see if a pattern emerges (see Figure 9.2). A third example is the Circle of Questions strategy recommended by Sampson, Sampson,

FIGURE 9.1

SEMANTIC FEATURE ANALYSIS FOR GLOBAL WARMING

	carbon emission	deforestation	ozone depletion
www.globalwarming.net			
www.globalwarming.org			
www.epa.gov/globalwarming			
www.rainforest-alliance.org			

FIGURE 9.2

JOT CHART FORMAT FOR RESEARCH ACTIVITY

	Floods	Hurricanes	Tornadoes
Define this weather disaster.			
What are the causes?			
What are the effects on people and property?			
Identify any trends that indicate that global warming may affect this weather disaster.			

FIGURE 9.3

FORMAT FOR CIRCLE OF QUESTIONS

The teacher draws a circle and writes the topic inside it. After completing an informational text, the teacher divides students into groups of five. Students serve as

- Timekeeper • Reporter • Recorder • Encourager • Leader

Students have three minutes to list as many questions about the topic as they can think of.

Students share their questions, and the teacher writes around the circumference of the circle.

The class reviews the questions and divides them into categories.

Each group selects a different category to become "experts" in, rereading the text to find the answers.

Recorders write the answers and note where the information was found.

Reporters share the information with the class.

Unanswered questions are used as the basis of further research, with each group identifying a different website and recording that site's answers to the questions.

Answers are again shared, and different perspectives are noted and discussed.

---

and Linek (2000), which encourages students to ask questions about a given text and to explore the topic further if all their questions cannot be answered fully from the original source (see Figure 9.3). Each of these strategies has the potential to create an atmosphere in which learners feel comfortable questioning the information that is being presented in a given text—a practice that is essential if students are to develop into truly independent learners.

Conclusion

In conclusion, we began this chapter by asking two questions: (1) What can be done to support literacy development using technology that cannot be done without it? and (2) How can technology make literacy accessible to intermediate-grade struggling readers? Throughout the chapter, we sought to answer the questions with specific examples that included the use of multiple types of instructional technology. We hope our suggestions will provide teachers with activities that they can integrate into their own classrooms. We also hope these ideas will serve as a starting point for the creation of additional strategies that make use of instructional technology as an effective support for the literacy development of students. Finally, we hope the ideas and suggestions we have presented have deepened teachers' awareness and understanding of the many ways instructional technology can improve and support teaching and learning in general.

REFERENCES

Allington, R.L. (1983). Fluency: The neglected reading goal. *The Reading Teacher*, *37*, 556–561.

Balajthy, E. (1996). Using computer technology to aid the disabled reader. In L. Putnam (Ed.), *How to become a better reading teacher: Strategies for assessment and intervention* (pp. 331–343). Englewood Cliffs, NJ: Prentice-Hall.

Bigelow, B. (1989). Discovering Columbus: Rereading the past. *Language Arts*, *66*, 635–643.

Carbo, M. (1978). Teaching reading with talking books. *The Reading Teacher*, *32*, 267–273.

Chall, J.S. (1996). *Stages of reading development*. Orlando, FL: Harcourt Brace.

Chomsky, C. (1976). After decoding: What? *Language Arts*, *53*, 288–296.

Cooper, J.D. (2000). *Literacy: Helping children construct meaning*. Boston: Houghton Mifflin.

Dillon, K. (1999). Nasties on the net: Media hype or major concern for schools? In J. Hancock (Ed.), *Teaching literacy using information technology: A collection of articles from the Australian Literacy Educators' Association* (pp. 89–106). Newark, DE: International Reading Association.

Duke, N. (1999). *The scarcity of informational texts in first grade*. Ann Arbor, MI: Center for the Improvement of Early Reading Achievement (CIERA).

Guillaume, A.M. (2000). Learning with text in the primary grades. In R.D. Robinson, M.C. McKenna, & J.M. Wedman (Eds.), *Issues and trends in literacy education* (2nd ed., pp. 247–264). Boston: Allyn & Bacon.

Hadaway, N.L., & Mundy, J. (2000). Children's informational picture books visit a secondary ESL classroom. In D.W. Moore, D.E. Alvermann, & K.A. Hinchman (Eds.), *Struggling adolescent readers: A collection of teaching strategies* (pp. 83–95). Newark, DE: International Reading Association.

Hawisher, G., & Selfe, C. (1999). Reflections on research in computers and composition studies at the century's end. In J. Hancock (Ed.), *Teaching literacy using information technology: A collection of articles from the Australian Literacy Educators' Association* (pp. 31–47). Newark, DE: International Reading Association.

Hoffman, J.V. (1992). Critical reading/thinking across the curriculum: Using I-Charts to support learning. *Language Arts*, *69*, 121–127.

Johnson, D.D., & Pearson, P.D. (1984). *Teaching reading vocabulary* (2nd ed.). New York: Holt, Rinehart.

Keene, E.O., & Zimmermann, S. (1997). *Mosaic of thought: Teaching comprehension in a reader's workshop*. Portsmouth, NH: Heinemann.

Kinzer, C. (2000). *Addressing issues of Internet safety: An electronic classroom Web watch*. Available: www.readingonline.org/electronic/elec_index.asp?HREF=/electronic/webwatch/safety/index.html

Kuhn, M.R., & Stahl, S.A. (2000). *Fluency: A review of developmental and remedial practices*. Ann Arbor, MI: Center for the Improvement of Early Reading Achievement (CIERA).

Merrow, J. (2001). Double-click: Threat or promise? *Ed. magazine*, *45*(1), 22–25. Available: http://www.gse.harvard.edu/news/features/merrow03012002.html

Nagy, W.E. (1988). *Teaching vocabulary to improve reading comprehension*. Newark, DE: International Reading Association.

Nagy, W.E., Herman, P., & Anderson, R.C. (1985). Learning words from context. *Reading Research Quarterly*, *20*, 233–253.

Opitz, M.F., & Rasinski, T.V. (1998). *Good-bye round robin: 25 effective oral reading strategies*. Portsmouth, NH: Heinemann.

Papert, S. (1984). New theories for new learnings. *School Psychology Review*, *13*(4), 422–428.

Pearson, P.D., Roehler, L.R., Dole, J.A., & Duffy, G.G. (1992). Developing expertise in reading comprehension. In S.J. Samuels & A.E. Farstrup (Eds.), *What research has to say about reading instruction* (2nd ed., pp. 145–199). Newark, DE: International Reading Association.

Pressley, M. (2000). Comprehension instruction in elementary school: A quarter-century of research progress. In B.M. Taylor, M.F. Graves, & P. van den Broek (Eds.), *Reading for meaning: Fostering comprehension in the middle grades*. New York: Teachers College Press; Newark, DE: International Reading Association.

Rasinski, T.V., & Padak, N. (1996). Five lessons to increase reading fluency. In L. Putnam (Ed.), *How to become a better reading teacher: Strategies for assessment and intervention* (pp. 255–265). Englewood Cliffs, NJ: Prentice-Hall, Inc.

Reinking, D. (1998). Introduction: Synthesizing technological transformations of literacy in a post-typographic world. In D. Reinking, M.C. McKenna, L.D. Labbo, & R.D. Kieffer (Eds.), *Handbook of literacy and technology: Transformations in a post-typographic world* (pp. xi–xxx). Mahwah, NJ: Erlbaum.

Rickelman, R.J., & Caplan, R.M. (2000). Technological literacy in the intermediate and middle grades. In K.D. Wood & T.S. Dickinson (Eds.), *Promoting literacy in grades 4–9: A handbook for teachers and administrators* (pp. 306–316). Boston: Allyn & Bacon.

Roe, B.D. (2000). Using technology for content area literacy. In S.B. Wepner, W.J. Valmont, & R. Thurlow (Eds.), *Linking literacy and technology: A guide for K–8 classrooms* (pp. 133–158). Newark, DE: International Reading Association.

Rowand, C. (2000). Teacher use of computers and the Internet in public schools. *Education Statistics Quarterly*, *2*(2), 72–75.

Sampson, M.B., Sampson, M.R., & Linek, W. (2000). Circle of questions. In T.V. Rasinski et al. (Eds.), *Teaching comprehension and exploring multiple literacies:*

Strategies from The Reading Teacher. Newark, DE: International Reading Association.

Samuels, S.J. (1979). The method of repeated reading. *The Reading Teacher, 32,* 403–408.

Snyder, I. (1999). Integrating computers into the literacy curriculum: More difficult than we first imagined. In J. Hancock (Ed.), *Teaching literacy using information technology: A collection of articles from the Australian Literacy Educators' Association* (pp. 11–30). Newark, DE: International Reading Association.

Stahl, S.A. (1999). *Vocabulary development.* Cambridge, MA: Brookline Books.

Stahl, S.A., Hynd, C.R., Britton, B.K., McNish, M.M., & Bosquet, D. (1996). What happens when students read multiple source documents in history? *Reading Research Quarterly, 31,* 430–456.

Stanovich, K.E. (1986). Matthew effects in reading: Some consequences of individual differences in the acquisition of literacy. *Reading Research Quarterly, 16,* 32–71.

Strickland, D.S., Ganske, K., Monroe, J.K. (2002). *Supporting struggling readers and writers: Strategies for classroom intervention 3–6.* Portland, ME: Stenhouse; Newark, DE: International Reading Association.

Travers, J. (1999). Everything is connected: An information technology program comes together. In J. Hancock (Ed.), *Teaching literacy using information technology: A collection of articles from the Australian Literacy Educators' Association* (pp. 66–77). Newark, DE: International Reading Association.

Wenglinsky, H. (1998). *Does it compute? The relationship between educational technology and student achievement in mathematics* (Practicum paper). Princeton, NJ: Educational Testing Service. (ERIC Document Reproduction Service No. ED425191)

CHILDREN'S LITERATURE CITED

Gardiner, J.R. (1980). *Stone Fox.* New York: Harper Trophy.

Konigsburg, E.L. (1977). *From the mixed-up files of Mrs. Basil E. Frankweiler.* New York: Yearling Books.

Supporting Students in Grades 3 and Beyond as They Learn Through Text

CHAPTER 10

From Trade Books to Textbooks: Helping Bilingual Students Make the Transition

Wanda B. Hedrick, Janis M. Harmon, and Karen D. Wood

Ms. Carson teaches fourth grade in a suburban school district in a sprawling city of more than 4 million people. The majority of her students come from homes in which the parents have professional careers and are upwardly mobile. Although most of her students seem to enjoy reading and actively participate in daily independent reading, she notices that many have confused looks on their faces when she asks them to read passages from their social studies and science textbooks. Their participation in class discussions about what they read in these texts pales in comparison to the energy and enthusiasm evident in class trade-book discussions.

Meanwhile, Mr. Donatelli, another fourth-grade teacher, works in an inner-city school in the same city as Ms. Carson. His students come from homes of low socioeconomic status and areas of town where many families need federal assistance. Although some of his students enjoy reading trade books, many are below grade level in reading achievement and have already adapted a disinterested and apathetic stance toward reading trade books. This attitude also permeates how they read expository texts.

Another resident of this city is Ms. Reis, who also teaches fourth grade. Her school is located on the east side, where the majority of the residents are second language learners. Her bilingual class contains students who have been in the district's bilingual program for several years. Most are making good progress toward becoming fluent in English. Like the students in both Ms. Carson's class and Mr. Donatelli's class, Ms. Reis has a few fourth graders who are avid readers of trade books, but most struggle with reading, especially their content area textbooks.

Many fourth graders across this city are experiencing a downturn or slump in their reading progress.

As noted by Kuhn and Morrow in the previous chapter, the fourth-grade slump has long been recognized in the professional literature as a time when students' performance and progress in reading often begins to decline (Chall, Jacobs, & Baldwin, 1990; National Assessment of Educational Progress, 1994). One of the reasons offered for the decline in achievement scores of students in the fourth grade is that they have not had sufficient practice, exposure, and training in the reading of expository text in the early grades to adequately prepare them for the demands this type of reading requires (Caswell & Duke, 1998; Duke, 2000; Newkirk, 1989; Pappas, 1993). As neophyte readers, they lack an understanding of the way in which expository text is organized and structured. Most of these students have just acquired the ability to learn to read when they are asked to read to learn from informational texts in varied disciplines (Armbruster, Anderson, & Ostertag, 1989).

Another reason offered for the underachievement of many struggling readers is the overemphasis of teacher-controlled interactions (Allington, 1991; Cazden, 1988; McDermott & Aron, 1978). Students who are already overwhelmed by the material to be read often become passive participants in class activities that are dominated by teacher talk. Therefore, it is evident that methods are needed that enable students to read and talk about text, both narrative and informational (Gambrell & Almasi, 1996; Roser & Martinez, 1995). Previous chapters in this book have addressed the ways the Book Club approach (McMahon & Raphael, 1997; see also chapters 4 and 5 of this book) can be used to engage students in collaborative book talk in response to narrative text. In each of these cases, the Book Club approach was used within the context of language arts periods. We see the value of using book clubs in the content areas as well and have developed a means of addressing these needs called the Talking About Books (TAB) Book Club Approach (Harmon & Wood, 2001). The TAB Book Club Approach integrates reading, talking, and writing in several ways that help students comprehend informational texts as they work in small groups.

We found that, with ample modeling, struggling readers can be taught how to verbalize their thinking about what they read (Harmon & Wood, 2001). The TAB Book Club Approach provides needed support for this new activity by first engaging students in different levels of discussion. Second, students read the texts themselves and then go through the process of gathering information and interpreting what they find. Third, students write about their interpretations and learn about ways to extend and share their ideas with others.

We also postulated that instructing students to understand the differences in the structure of narrative and information texts and then teaching them how to respond to textbook selections using a book club or literature circle, or responsive model, in the form of the TAB Book Club Approach would enhance their comprehension and strategic processing of expository text. Figure 10.1 depicts what we call the trade book to textbook transfer, which is achieved through analysis of both narrative and information text using a book club responsive model of instruction. This illustration indicates the reading strategies needed for analyzing text structures and for constructing meaning across trade books and textbooks.

FIGURE 10.1

TRADE BOOK TO TEXTBOOK TRANSFER

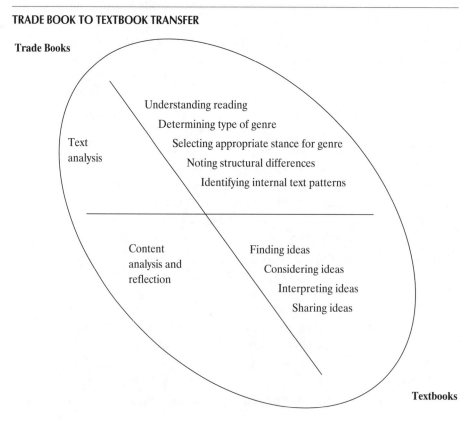

Trade Books

Text analysis

Understanding reading
Determining type of genre
Selecting appropriate stance for genre
Noting structural differences
Identifying internal text patterns

Content analysis and reflection

Finding ideas
Considering ideas
Interpreting ideas
Sharing ideas

Textbooks

In this chapter, we describe our work in a fourth-grade bilingual classroom located in a large, urban, southwestern U.S. school district. We engaged students in extensive modeling and training in the differences between narrative and expository text, coupled with training and analysis on how to write and read expository content, through interactive small-group and whole-class discussions and presentations. The following section of this chapter describes the lesson sequence involved in making the trade book to textbook transfer.

The Trade Book to Textbook Lesson Sequence

The following lesson sequence presents one variation of the TAB Book Club format in which the purpose of the instruction is to help students develop an awareness and a clearer understanding of how to read textbooks. In order to stimulate students' thinking about and understanding of reading, the introductory session asks them to identify the varied circumstances in their environment in which they are engaged in some form of reading. The next session begins with activities and discussions to help students differentiate between narrative and expository texts and then leads into the ways in which textbooks can be read. Next, the focus is on different text patterns (e.g., cause/effect, compare/contrast, sequence, etc.) and how recognition of these patterns can support comprehension. The TAB portion of the framework comes at the end of the lesson, when students actually engage in textbook reading, apply expository reading strategies, and then move beyond to grapple with text ideas.

Understanding Reading

We began the lesson sequence with a focus on reading in general. We activated student background knowledge by posing the following questions for class discussion:

What is reading?

What are some things you read outside of school?

Why do you read them?

To stimulate students' thinking, we displayed several photographs of sites in the community containing print, such as billboards, school signs, and signs from commercial establishments. After quickly recognizing these artifacts, the students contributed examples of their own. The discussion then shifted to reading inside the classroom. Although students claimed that reading outside school was for entertainment, they felt that the primary purpose for school reading was to "do work." School reading, according to the students, included reading posters, rules, calendars, information books in the library, and Accelerated Reader tests to "see what you know."

Understanding Differences in Text Structures

For this segment of the lesson sequence, the fourth-grade bilingual teacher displayed a fiction book and an information book related to the current social studies lesson on the Texas War for Independence. The fiction book was *The Mystery at the Alamo* (Warner, 1997), and the information book was *Texas: From Sea to Shining Sea* (Fradin, 1992). Class discussion began with a focus on the following questions:

What do you know about stories (narratives)?

What makes a story a story?

What must authors include in a story to make it a story?

What do you like about stories?

Regarding the first question, knowledge of stories, the fourth graders interpreted the question in light of what they had previously learned about story structure. They mentioned that stories had "main ideas"; "an introduction, event #1, event #2, event #3, and a conclusion"; "a main character that could be a person, animal, or fish"; "problems and solutions"; and "paragraphs and conclusions." Students' understanding of story appeared to be influenced by the writing instruction provided by the teacher. This instruction paralleled the tasks students would be asked to do on the upcoming state-mandated writing test. Nevertheless, the students contended that they liked stories, especially ones that were funny, scary, action-packed, and realistic.

The next set of discussion questions focused on information books:

What are information books?

What must authors include in an information book to make it an information book?

What do you like about information books?

The students noted that information books had "no problem" and "no characters" and that authors included information, illustrations, and descriptions of events and people. Some reasons for liking information books included "they give you stuff you want to know," "information books help you learn for a test," "they tell answers to questions," and "they give facts."

After this discussion, students were divided into five groups of three or four students each in order to work together comparing and contrasting the external features of the books *The Mystery at the Alamo* and *Texas: From Sea to Shining Sea*. Each group had a copy of the books to examine. The groups discussed the similarities and differences between the books, and a volunteer scribe in each group took notes. After the discussion, the groups used their notes to complete a Venn diagram of the findings, then they shared this information with the whole class. Figure 10.2 is a compilation of the students' findings.

As a change of pace, the students then used sentence strips to make labels for the external features of each type of text. With each

FIGURE 10.2

SIMILARITIES AND DIFFERENCES BETWEEN NARRATIVE TEXTS AND INFORMATIONAL TEXTS

Narrative Texts (e.g., *The Mystery of the Alamo*)	Both	Informational Texts (e.g., *Texas: From Sea to Shining Sea*)
Fiction	Title	Nonfiction
Drawings	Books	Timeline
Characters	Table of contents	Map
List of other Boxcar Children's Books	Illustrations	Glossary
Fake Alamo	Author	Index
	Page numbers	Introduction
		Photographs
		Real Alamo
		Big captions under pictures
		Key

student wearing a label, groups then portrayed different types of texts by arranging themselves in the order in which the text features appear in a fiction or informational book (i.e., title page, copyright page, table of contents, etc.). The class had to guess what type of book each group portrayed. We included this activity in the lessons to reinforce the learning and to maintain student interest and motivation (Hoyt, 1992).

Once the students understood the differences between fiction and information books, the next step was to have them examine the similarities and differences between the information book and their social studies textbook. Following the same procedure that was used with the comparison between the fiction book and the information book, the students discussed the similarities and differences and then completed another chart with the information. A compilation of student responses is presented in Figure 10.3.

FIGURE 10.3

SIMILARITIES AND DIFFERENCES BETWEEN INFORMATION BOOKS AND SOCIAL STUDIES TEXTBOOKS

Same	Different (Textbook has)
Index	Biographical dictionary
Glossary	Questions
Table of contents	Place to write your name
Captions	Gazetteer
Maps	Dictionary of geographic terms
Map keys	Infographic
Numbered pages	More chapters
Nonfiction	More pictures
History	More authors
Boldfaced words	Songs
Illustrations	Reference section
Titles	Biographical information
Capitalization	List of vocabulary words
Texas facts	Chapter review section
Real pictures	
Timeline	
Credits/Acknowledgments	

Text Awareness and Analysis

After the students examined and discussed the external features of fiction books, information books, and textbooks, they were ready to participate in a discussion about the ways in which readers engage in reading these different books. This segment of the lesson sequence included both class discussions and some dramatizing. First, the teacher explained and modeled how the reading of the books might be different. After this explanation, the students worked in groups to develop a list of strategies to help them read a textbook. The students then created a class list that contained the following information about how to read a textbook:

- You can look at and read captions first.
- You can look at maps first.
- You can skip around in the textbook and in the information book.
- You cannot skip around in a story.
- You can start a textbook at the front if you want to.
- You have to read a lot more of the textbook if you are going to answer the questions.

After this discussion, two groups of students were each given five sections of a segmented fairy tale to hold up for the class to see. Each section of the story was written on a separate poster. One group held up the sections in the correct order, and the other group scrambled their sections. The class had to read all the posters and decide which presentation of segments made sense. Two other groups were then given sections of a textbook chapter, again displayed in different order. The class read both presentations and decided that each one was an acceptable way to read the information. With this inductive approach, the teacher reinforced the idea that expository text does not necessarily need to be read in sequential order as does narrative text.

Text Analysis—Internal Features

Teaching internal text patterns is a challenging and sometimes daunting task because some patterns, such as cause/effect and compare/contrast, present great cognitive demands on students (Armbruster, Anderson, & Ostertag, 1989; Harvey, 1998). At this point in the lesson sequence, we realized that one way to address internal structures was through writing and visual representations, two modes that the students understood. Although it is one of the most difficult for students to learn, we selected the cause/effect text pattern because many of the passages in the social studies textbook reflected this pattern. We then used the following procedure to teach the cause/effect pattern:

1. Begin a class discussion about cause and effect using simple, everyday examples that are familiar to the students. In this lesson, the teacher walked through the door and pretended to trip over a chair. This example led to a discussion about what happened (the effect—the teacher tripped) and why it happened (the cause—because she didn't watch where she was walking).

2. Create or find a graphic representation to use as an example. Our graphic representation was the herringbone pattern recommended in reading methodology textbooks (Johns & Lenski, 2001). This pattern, which looks like fish bones, is commonly used to represent cause and effect text patterns. The teacher filled in the mapping with the effect (tripped over the chair) and the cause (not watching where she was going).

3. Continue the class discussion by asking students to provide examples of a cause and having others provide a realistic effect. Then reverse the process, asking for effects and having students give the causes. One example given by a student in this fourth-grade class was " I got bit by a dog." To have the students think about possible effects of being bitten by a dog, the teacher probed for effects and noted that some students provided causes, such as "he hit the dog." To clarify this confusion, the teacher used direct instruction to point out the differences between a cause and an effect by having students consider the order in which events occur. In this way, students were able to successfully respond to this example. The highlighting of student talk using relevant examples revealed the misconceptions and confusion the students had about cause and effect. The teacher then visually presented the information on the chalkboard. After several examples of cause and effect patterns, the students were ready to move on to the writing portion of the lesson.

4. Have the children write a paragraph based on a completed visual representation. For this step, the teacher modeled the writing procedure by using a familiar topic and context for the children: making a sandwich. In collaboration with the students, the teacher completed a herringbone map with the effect ("the teacher has sandwich ingredients") and a variety of causes ("the class was learning how to write a "how to" paragraph"; "the class was learning how to make a sandwich"; and "the students were going to be tested on this writing on the state assessment"). Once the visual was complete, the teacher then discussed turning the visual into a paragraph. She mentioned that writers often use specific clue words that are associated with cause/effect patterns, and she then led a discussion that ended with a list of teacher-suggested and student-generated clue words on the chalkboard: *because, so, since, why, as a result, for this reason,* and *if, then.* Using the visual and the list of clue words, the teacher instructed the student groups to write a paragraph while she wrote her own on chart paper. She encouraged students who were confused to attend to her as she modeled the writing task. After the student groups finished their paragraphs, each group read their paragraph aloud while the others raised their hands every time they heard a clue word.

5. *Use the same graphic representation to organize the information learned recently in a content area.* The teacher found three examples of cause/effect patterns in previous social studies chapters and used them as a basis for a scavenger hunt. The student groups were given a worksheet (see Figure 10.4) to complete for the three cause/effect patterns. The visuals on this worksheet contained variations of the herringbone design for cause and effect to represent the content of the passages. In this way, students would be able to see that cause and effect patterns can be represented in different ways in texts but still contain the underlying relationship between concepts. This enabled students to experience the variability of text information and to transfer use of the basic cause/effect to different contexts. After discussing their findings in a whole-class format, the teacher and the students together wrote a paragraph based on the first cause/effect pattern on the worksheet. Then the groups wrote their own paragraph for the second cause/effect pattern and noted similarities and differences among paragraphs when they shared them with the whole class.

TAB Book Club

In the TAB Book Club approach, students engage in finding ideas, considering and interpreting ideas, and extending and sharing ideas as they negotiate text ideas with what they know and with what others in the group know (Harmon & Wood, 2001). The implementation of this

FIGURE 10.4

WORKSHEET: CAUSE/EFFECT TEXT PATTERNS

Social Studies Scavenger Hunt

Page 125

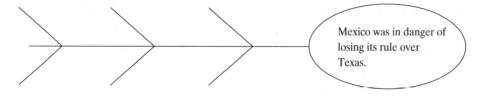

Coronado and his expedition returned to Mexico without gold.

Page 136, first paragraph under the heading "The Big Picture." Find a cause/effect pattern and draw your own graphic organizer here.

Read "Different Ways of Life" on page 161.

Mexico was in danger of losing its rule over Texas.

approach can vary considerably and still maintain the integrity of the TAB approach as students negotiate and construct meanings through group discussions as well as individual and group writing. In this lesson sequence, the components emerged in spiral fashion as student groups first gathered information about a specific textbook passage using the cause/effect text pattern as a lens from which to construct meaning. Through talk, the groups considered the text ideas, reflected on the meaning of the author's message, and negotiated ways to represent their own ideas in the final written product. Through writing, they had opportunities to respond and reflect individually to the text information and to work collaboratively with other group members in creating a collective reaction to text-based ideas.

Understanding and Interpreting What the Authors Say

Following the first step of the TAB Book Club framework, the teacher assigned the student groups a section of a textbook chapter on Texas Independence and asked them to reread their designated section. (The teacher had previously read the chapter to the class in preparation for this step.) Each group was given a cause/effect organizer to complete for its chapter section. The organizer contained both a visual representation of a cause/effect pattern related to the text and also two open-ended prompts designed to elicit personal reflection about the content (see Figure 10.5 for an example). This organizer became the focal point for guiding group discussion about the topic as well as student reactions to the concepts. The social construction of meaning that emerged from these discussions became the basis for writing about the topic.

Using the recorded information on the organizer, student groups continued to discuss as they negotiated not only what to include in the writing but also who would be the scribe. For example, while acting as scribe for her group, Maria hesitated to write Jose's ideas when she realized that he was not articulating the ideas clearly enough to enable her to put them down on paper. She was concerned that these ideas did not represent the group's consensus. Furthermore, as the most capable student in the group, Maria struggled with trying not to dominate the discussion and trying not, as scribe, to include only her ideas in the paragraph.

After the students completed the paragraphs, the teacher collected the students' work to compile a computer-generated "textbook chapter." The rough draft of this chapter contained the students' paragraphs typed in typical textbook formatting with double columns,

FIGURE 10.5

CAUSE/EFFECT ORGANIZER FOR WINNING INDEPENDENCE

"The Big Picture"

Page 174

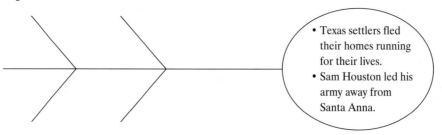

- Texas settlers fled their homes running for their lives.
- Sam Houston led his army away from Santa Anna.

Paragraph:

How does this information make you feel?

What does this information make you think about?

sidebars, subheadings, and spaces for illustrations and captions. During a subsequent class session, the student groups edited and made revision suggestions for their sections of the textbook chapter. In particular, students wrote headings for their sections, made decisions about illustrations, selected various typographical formats such as color and font size, and changed the locations of text and pictures. After the teacher made these revisions, the student groups then made minor editorial changes for the final copy. At the same time, individual students read the entire "chapter" and made written responses about what the information meant to them and how it made them feel. Some student responses included the following:

> **Arturo:** I feel as a Texan very excited about Sam Houston winning a battle against Santa Anna. As a Texan I feel pleased about the Battle of San Jacinto. As a Texan I feel great about Sam Houston defeating Santa Anna.

> **Lizzeth:** It makes me feel scared of war. It makes me feel scared because we can have a war and lose. I hope if we have a war we get our freedom.

> **Jesus:** It makes me feel like the general of Sam Houston. It also makes me feel like a person in the war. It makes me feel proud of Sam Houston.

> **Jessica:** How do I feel about the war? I feel really ashamed that other people think of war. I feel really ashamed of Afghanistan.

> **Joshua:** It made me surprised because Santa Anna was caught off guard. I feel glad because Sam Houston traded Santa Anna for Texas freedom. Because I wouldn't be living right now.

This final activity enabled the students to reflect on and respond to the chapter's historical events on a personal level. From these examples, we noted that some children made connections to current world events, others to individual feelings about war in general, and still others to historical repercussions of the Texas War for Independence to the present day.

Although the lesson sequence concluded with the students' personal responses to the text information, we believe that a focus on multiple historical perspectives would have enriched these responses. An important culminating task would be to ask students to respond to the following scenario from different perspectives:

Pedro and Juan Delgado live with their parents on a small farm south of San Antonio. Their father is a soldier in Santa Anna's army. The family had recently moved to the Mexican state of Texas to farm the land; they did not own any land in Mexico. The Guadalupe River runs through their property, giving water for crops and animals. They are hoping that their relatives from Laredo will be able to join them on a nearby farm. But settlers from Tennessee who also live near the river do not want more Mexicans moving there. Instead, they are hoping to buy the land to have their slaves plant more cotton.

How do you think the Delgados feel?

How do you think the Tennessee settlers feel?

Who should have the land?

Students could then come together in groups to discuss their responses and write a group reaction statement to the Mexican perspective and to the U.S. perspective.

Key Features of the TAB Lesson Sequence

Several distinctive features in this lesson sequence provide the support struggling readers need to handle the demands of expository texts. These features are applicable to any intermediate (or higher) grade level in which strategic reading of content area texts is critical. First, student engagement is important to the success of these lessons. This engagement includes opportunities for participation through various means of expression, such as talk, writing, and even drawing. Although content area lessons rarely include group talk that is not dominated by the teacher, the social dimension of learning is crucial as students learn from and support each other in collaborative groups. These groups add a rich layer of meaning to student talk. This opportunity to share in group discussions varies considerably from the kind of talk evident in whole-class discussions. Yet both situations offer students opportunities to articulate their thoughts and ideas about a given topic. In this TAB lesson, students had many opportunities to talk about not only social studies concepts but also the text features that differentiate stories from informational texts, especially school textbooks. In addition to oral expression, content area lessons can provide rich opportunities for students to use other forms of expression as a way of learning, such as writing and drawing. In the TAB lessons, the students created visual representations to organize their thoughts, wrote about text ideas and their personal responses to this information, illustrated their understandings through drawings, and designed a tangible product of their learning with their own computer-generated "textbook chapter."

Another feature is the importance of highlighting reading strategies. Teachers need to maintain a focus on strategic reading, reminding students that readers must attend to what makes sense and what does not as they construct meaning. This is an especially challenging task for teachers who work with struggling readers or teachers who work with English language learners. To help students develop this metacognitive awareness, teachers can support reading strategies such as predicting, asking questions, making important connections, and summarizing as students grapple with text ideas. Also, teachers can use direct instruction to continually highlight both external and internal text structures to help students develop a clearer understanding of how expository reading differs from narrative reading. Armed with this knowledge, students then become coconstructors of meaning with the teacher and their peers, acting as vital participants in both whole-class and small-group discussions. Over time, in different content areas, teachers can continue to provide gentle reminders to help students to maintain an awareness of these text differences. Children whose first language is not English can especially benefit from a focus on these text structures as they develop conceptual understandings in the different content areas.

Finally, students need time to reflect on and internalize the concepts presented in the content lesson as they write in their journals and then share their feelings and opinions in group sessions. In our view, it is through these types of interpretive activities that students integrate newly acquired content knowledge into their existing schemas and create new mental models to accommodate this knowledge.

Summary

Our preliminary work in helping students to develop metacognitive awareness of text structure differences in narrative and expository material, and using the literary response techniques typically applied to narrative material with expository text, indicates an increase in students' understanding of, sense of control over, and ability to comprehend both types of discourse. We believe the use of both narrative and expository material in the form of trade books to transition students to the reading of textbooks has the potential to help diverse learners as well as students of all ability levels increase their understanding.

REFERENCES

Allington, R.L. (1991). The legacy of "slow it down and make it more concrete." In J. Zutell & S. McCormick (Eds.), *Learner factors/teacher factors: Issues in literacy research and instruction* (40th yearbook of the National Reading Conference, pp. 19–29). Chicago: National Reading Conference.

Armbruster, B.B., Anderson, T.H., & Ostertag, J. (1989). Teaching text structure to improve reading and writing. *The Reading Teacher, 43*, 130–137.

Caswell, L.J., & Duke, N.K. (1998). Non-narrative as a catalyst for literacy development. *Language Arts, 75*(2), 108–117.

Cazden, C.B. (1988). *Classroom discourse: The language of teaching and learning.* Portsmouth, NH: Heinemann.

Chall, J.S., Jacobs, V.A., & Baldwin, L.E. (1990). *The reading crisis: Why poor children fall behind.* Cambridge, MA: Harvard University Press.

Duke, N.K. (2000). 3.6 minutes per day: The scarcity of informational texts in first grade. *Reading Research Quarterly, 35*, 202–225.

Gambrell, L.B., & Almasi, J.F. (Eds.). (1996). *Lively discussions! Fostering engaged reading.* Newark, DE: International Reading Association.

Harmon, J.M., & Wood, K.D. (2001). The TAB Book Club Approach: Talking (T) About (A) Books (B) in content area classrooms. *Middle School Journal, 32*(3), 51–56.

Harvey, S. (1998). *Nonfiction matters: Reading, writing, and research in grades 3–8.* York, ME: Stenhouse.

Hoyt, L. (1992). Many ways of knowing: Using drama and oral interactions to enhance reading comprehension. *The Reading Teacher, 45*, 580–584.

Johns, J., & Lenski, S. (2001). *Improving reading: A handbook of strategies* (3rd ed.). Dubuque, IA: Kendall/Hunt.

McDermott, R.P., & Aron, I. (1978). Pirandello in the classroom: On the possibility of equal educational opportunity in American culture. In M.C. Reynolds (Ed.), *Future of education for exceptional students: Emerging structures* (pp. 41–64). Reston, VA: Council for Exceptional Children.

McMahon, S.I., & Raphael, T.E. (Eds.). (1997). *The Book Club connection: Literacy learning and classroom talk.* New York: Teachers College Press; Newark, DE: International Reading Association.

National Assessment of Educational Progress. (1994). *Reading report card for the nation and the states.* Washington, DC: Author.

Newkirk, T. (1989). *Critical thinking and writing: Reclaiming the essay* (Monographs on Teaching Critical Thinking, No. 3). Urbana, IL: National Council of Teachers of English.

Pappas, C.C. (1993). Is narrative primary? Some insights from kindergartners' pretend readings of stories and information books. *Journal of Reading Behavior, 25(1)*, 97–129.

Roser, N.L., & Martinez, M.G. (Eds.). (1995). *Book talk and beyond: Children and teachers respond to literature.* Newark, DE: International Reading Association.

CHILDREN'S LITERATURE CITED

Fradin, D.B. (1992). *Texas: From sea to shining sea*. Chicago: Children's Press.
Warner, G.C. (1997). *The mystery at the Alamo*. Morton Grove, IL: Albert Whitman.

CHAPTER 11

Using Reading Guides With Struggling Readers in Grades 3 and Above

Michael C. McKenna, Lisa W. Davis, and Susan Franks

Ms. Williams' fifth graders are relatively good decoders, but many of them find their science text difficult to understand. Its vocabulary is challenging, its organization (including innumerable figures and sidebars) is confusing, and its factual content is overwhelming at times. Ms. Williams has tried a number of approaches to help her students contend with these problems. She has tried various questioning strategies during postreading discussions. She has conducted chapter previews to acquaint the students with the organizational patterns. She has provided extensive background knowledge prior to asking her students to read the text. Such strategies have proved only partially effective, however. They fail to target the crux of her students' problem, which involves acquiring factual information from their science text. Ms. Williams is at her wit's end. She is tempted to sidestep the text entirely and simply present its contents through lecture, demonstration, and discussion. She is concerned, however, about her students' limited ability to learn through text. Avoiding the text would help her students achieve mandated science objectives, to be sure, but it would shortchange their development as readers. What should she try next? We believe that Ms. Williams' class would benefit from reading guides, an evidence-based instructional strategy that encourages students to comprehend challenging nonfiction.

A reading guide, also called a study guide, is a list of questions and other tasks to which students respond while reading. The purpose of such guides is to focus students' attention, to help them process content, and to model strategic reading. Guides can be used with any type of reading selection, but we are concerned in this chapter with the most challenging material children face—expository prose. Our intent is to make a case for the use of reading guides by teachers in the intermediate grades. To do so, we will describe reading guides in detail, offer suggestions for their construction and use, briefly examine their research base, and attempt to anticipate and address possible teacher objections.

One type of reading guide, the anticipation guide, consists of a list of statements to which the reader must respond prior to reading a selection. Figure 11.1 presents a brief anticipation guide for this chapter. Before you read the remainder of this chapter, we invite you to place a check mark in the "Before Reading" column next to each of the statements with which you tend to agree.

Anticipation guides are useful whenever the content of a reading selection targets possible misconceptions that students may bring with them as they begin to read (Dufflemeyer, 1994). Such guides represent one of several types that Wood, Lapp, and Flood (1992) have cataloged and discussed in detail. It has been our experience, however, that fitting guides into discrete categories may be too limiting. Later in this chapter, we will describe an approach to creating reading guides that is flexible and invites teachers to be creative.

FIGURE 11.1

CHAPTER ANTICIPATION GUIDE

Before Reading	After Reading		
_____	_____	1.	Publishers of most commercial textbooks supply reading guides that can be used by teachers.
_____	_____	2.	The effectiveness of reading guides has been supported by virtually every research study on record.
_____	_____	3.	Reading guides are more appropriate for use in the middle grades than in the upper-elementary grades.
_____	_____	4.	Reading guides are intended to support independent reading and usually work best when students complete them outside of class.
_____	_____	5.	Creating a reading guide would probably require too much time on my part.

How Well Do Guides Work?

Researchers have investigated the effectiveness of guides in numerous studies. Alvermann and her colleagues found that reading guides were one of the few content literacy strategies supported by every investigation that had been conducted (Alvermann & Moore 1991; Alvermann & Swafford, 1989). Most of these studies, however, involved students in the middle grades and higher. They also focused on the comprehension of particular selections. Consequently, the results were fairly predictable: Middle schoolers' (i.e., grades 6–8) comprehension of a particular reading selection tends to be better with a guide than without a guide, especially when the measure of comprehension is based on information targeted by the guide.

Although encouraging, these studies do not do enough to persuade us that guides should become a mainstay of instruction. In a recent study funded by the Eisenhower Program (Franks, McKenna, & Franks, 2001), we wanted to find out whether guides could be used prior to the middle school grades and also whether their use leads to improved comprehension ability with reading that is done when guides are not available. According to Chall's (1983/1996) stage model of reading development, most children have attained sufficient fluency by the time they enter third grade to support the reading of nonfiction. This means that reading guides may be an appropriate instructional strategy for children of this age, although we know of few third-grade teachers who use them. Guides may, in fact, be an ideal approach because of the support they provide to children who are just beginning to learn through text.

In our study, third-grade teachers developed four reading guides based on selections from their science textbooks. They used the guides with their students at various points during the school year, carefully coaching students in how to complete the guides. Following the use of the fourth guide, the students were asked to read an unfamiliar science passage that was unrelated to any of the concepts they had studied during the year. This time they were given no guide, and yet they significantly outperformed comparable students who had not been instructed with reading guides during the year.

Our study provided evidence that children as young as grade 3 can benefit from reading guides and that the effects are not limited to the selections covered by the guides. Rather, they appear to result in better comprehension *ability*, not just improved comprehension of the selections themselves. This is an important distinction, one that argues strongly for the regular use of reading guides as a means of building better comprehenders.

We believe that guides influence comprehension ability by modeling the strategic processes proficient readers use as they tackle challenging new material. Good readers pose questions as they read, they make notes to themselves, and they may reorganize key concepts in order to better understand them. When teachers assist students as they complete reading guides, they help sharpen these processes and confirm their importance.

Constructing a Reading Guide

Very few commercial publishers provide ready-to-use reading guides to accompany their textbooks. The few we have seen have a standardized look and exhibit little creativity. In nearly all cases, then, if you wish to use a reading guide, you must first construct it. This may be a somber prospect for busy teachers, but there is a bright side. As reading guides are best used as in-class activities, the time you spend creating them can be thought of as instructional planning time. That is, instead of planning a customary lesson, you can construct a guide in roughly the same amount of time. You will not need to do further planning for that class session, as the students will be reading during class time to complete the guide.

What is the best way of creating an effective guide? Because guides vary with the selection and with a teacher's purposes, there is no blueprint to follow. A one-size-fits-all approach simply will not work. We can, however, offer these general suggestions for constructing an effective reading guide:

1. Analyze the material. Read the selection carefully in order to decide what to emphasize. Think about the thought processes the students must use to fully understand the material. For example, if a science textbook chapter presents the three major classifications of rocks, then you might want to include a three-column chart in the guide.

2. Identify information to support assessment items. Look ahead to a chapter or unit test that will assess the extent to which your students have mastered the content of the selection. Make sure that the guide is aligned with this assessment and does an adequate job of preparing students for it.

3. Make the guide interesting and interactive. A simple list of questions will not do. Look for ways of varying the tasks you present to students, and look for tasks that require them to translate material from the printed selection into some other form. For example, completing charts, building diagrams, answering questions in their own words, and writing brief responses to prompts are a few of the ways that real interaction can be encouraged.

4. Monitor the length and difficulty of the guide. It is important that a reading guide not be an intimidating document. It should be easier to read than the selection itself, of course, and it should contain plenty of blank space for the students to complete tasks. It should also be fairly brief and might cover only a section or so of an entire chapter. (There is not enough time for students to complete reading guides for all of the nonfiction reading they will do.)

5. Include page numbers and subheadings where answers can be found. These provide signposts that are useful to students as they work through a reading guide. Students will need to go back and forth between book and guide, and they will need to keep their bearings as they do so.

6. Include comprehension aids. Try to anticipate possible difficulties your students will face as they read. A good reading guide should do more than focus attention and set purposes for reading. It also should assist students as they encounter possible pitfalls. For example, a guide might provide quick definitions or synonyms for key terms. It might include bridging comments that link new content with previously covered material. It might provide clarifying statements that paraphrase or summarize a difficult passage. It might also give indications that some of the material is either extremely important or might be skipped or skimmed over. This is precisely the kind of advice that will encourage independent strategic reading on the part of your students in the future.

7. Use a word processor to create the guide. By creating the guide as a word processing document, you will be able to edit your guide for future use if you find that certain portions of it do not work well. Word processing also can help you enliven the guide by using a variety of fonts and point sizes. Some technologically savvy teachers may wish to go the extra mile and use desktop publishing software to create guides, but we believe that using a standard word-processing package can produce perfectly acceptable guides.

8. Review your own purposes. When you have completed a draft of your guide, reexamine it critically to discern whether or not it will accomplish your own instructional purposes. Ask yourself whether a student who successfully completes the guide will possess the level of content mastery you expect.

After constructing a guide, it is a good idea to complete it yourself. Doing so not only provides you with a "key" as you assist students but also alerts you to trouble spots you may have overlooked previously. Now, the guide is ready to present in class.

Figure 11.2 presents a possible reading guide that covers this chapter. (We have tried to follow our own advice to be creative.) Use it as an example of how a reading guide might look. We encourage you to complete it as well. If you do, introspect and ask yourself whether the guide improved your comprehension and resulted in greater interaction with the material.

FIGURE 11.2

READING GUIDE FOR THIS CHAPTER

In your own words, define *reading guide* (pp. 208–209).

List three purposes of reading guides:

1.

2.

3.

Define *anticipation guide*:

How Well Do Guides Work? (p. 210)

Check all statements that are true:

_____   Reading guides tend to improve comprehension of a reading selection.
_____   Reading guides tend to improve comprehension ability.
_____   Reading guides have been successfully used in grade 1.
_____   Reading guides have been successfully used with nonfiction.

(continued)

FIGURE 11.2 (continued)

Constructing a Reading Guide (pp. 211–213)

Why is there no blueprint to follow in constructing a reading guide?

Jot down what you think is the most important thing to remember for each step in writing a guide:
1. Analyze the material.
2. Identify information to support assessment items.
3. Make the guide interesting and interactive.
4. Monitor the length and difficulty of the guide.
5. Include page numbers and subheadings where answers can be found.
6. Include comprehension aids.
7. Word-process the guide.
8. Review your own purposes.

Why is it a good idea to complete a guide you have written yourself?

Teaching With a Reading Guide (p. 215)

Why make transparencies of your guide?

Why not use guides with every nonfiction selection?

Complete the chart below by listing possible teacher objections to guides in the left-hand column. In the right-hand column, provide arguments that address these concerns. We have discussed some of each in the chapter, but you may be able to think of more.

Possible Teacher Objections to Guides	Counterarguments

Teaching With a Reading Guide

Reading guides are likely to be unfamiliar to your students. Do not assume that students will be able to complete a guide without assistance. Younger developing readers and older struggling readers will need considerable support if they are to succeed. This means initially completing one or more guides together, as a class. Make transparencies and complete them with student input as you make your way through a selection in class. Think aloud as you use a transparency marker to complete the guide. Make visible the thought processes you use to respond to questions and other tasks required by the guide.

Provide the students with their own copies of the guide and monitor their performance, even though they may simply be copying from the screen at first. Once students understand how guides operate, begin to assign guides without class processing. Students will still complete each guide in class, but you can transfer more of the responsibility to them. Nevertheless, you will need to continually monitor their efforts.

Completing guides also affords an opportunity for collaboration. Students might work with partners or in small groups, but we advise you not to attempt to group students until the nature of guides is well understood. When and if you do move to partnering and group work, do so experimentally. It is important that roles are defined clearly, that all students participate, and that the "mix" is right.

Remember that guides cannot be used with every nonfiction selection your students read. Fortunately, even the occasional use of guides can have a profound influence on the way students approach reading to learn. It is difficult to imagine a better investment of class time.

A Final Word

Take a moment to reconsider the five statements in the anticipation guide in Figure 11.1 at the beginning of this chapter. Use the second column to record your postreading responses. Have your opinions changed? We suspect that one or more of them have. Anticipation guides of this sort can be effective whenever new content may be at odds with prior notions. We believe that a brief anticipation guide works well at the beginning of a full reading guide. Had we actually provided a stand-alone version of the guide displayed in Figure 11.2, we would have placed these five statements at the beginning of it. After you had completed the rest of the guide, you would have been instructed to return to the statements to consider them anew.

REFERENCES

Alvermann, D.E., & Moore, D.W. (1991). Secondary school reading. In R. Barr, M.L. Kamil, P.B. Mosenthal, & P.D. Pearson (Eds.), *Handbook of reading research* (Vol. 2, pp. 951–983). White Plains, NY: Longman.

Alvermann, D.E., & Swafford, J. (1989). Do content area strategies have a research base? *Journal of Reading, 32,* 388–394.

Chall, J.S. (1996). *Stages of reading development.* New York: McGraw-Hill. (Original work published 1983)

Dufflemeyer, F.A. (1994). Effective anticipation guide statements for learning from expository prose. *Journal of Reading, 37,* 452–457.

Franks, S.T., McKenna, M.C., & Franks, G. (2001, April). *Using action research to increase elementary students' reading comprehension in science.* Paper presented at the annual meeting of the American Educational Research Association, Seattle, WA.

Wood, K.D., Lapp, D., & Flood, J. (1992). *Guiding readers through text: A review of study guides.* Newark, DE: International Reading Association.

CHAPTER 12

Stories From the Classroom: Understanding and Scaffolding Children's Research Processes

Joyce E. Many

I am sitting in the back of a classroom of 10- and 11-year-olds in Aberdeen, Scotland, taking notes for an ethnographic study on children's processes as they learn to do research. A student carrying an oversized book catches my eye. His name is Ian. Ian has been working for six weeks on a project focusing on leaders during World War II. He pulls out a sheet of paper from his desk and hunches over the pages of his resource. He is beginning a section on a new leader, and I can predict his process; it is one this young researcher had used before. First, Ian will laboriously copy paragraph after paragraph onto a sheet of paper. Next, using his copied text, he will begin line-by-line paraphrasing of this information into his report booklet. When he has finished putting all the information "into my own words," as Ian would say, then he will go on to the next world leader he plans to study. *(Story drawn from ethnographic data from Many, Fyfe, Lewis, & Mitchell, 1996)*

This story shares a glimpse of what conducting research meant to Ian. To those of us who have taught intermediate-grade children to do research, the processes he used may include some elements that are familiar and others that seem unusual. Often what many teachers say when we introduce students to research is "read information and then put it into your own words"—a dictum that Ian had learned. We teachers stress repeatedly the warning not to copy, and, indeed, close scrutiny of Ian's final project report absolved him of any suspicion of plagiarism. Ian worked laboriously to change complex sentences into simple sentences. He removed pronominal references. He reworded each line one step at a time. Ian also demonstrated other practices that many teachers encourage. He worked with a clear plan in mind. He brain-stormed about leaders he might address, writing their names on a plan-ning web. His final project booklet contained 21 pages of information and drawings related to Adolph Hitler, Winston Churchill, Roosevelt, Joseph Stalin, Benito Mussolini, and Chiang Kai-Shek. Ian's story also raises some questions, however. Why did he first copy all information verba-tim from his resource onto a separate sheet of paper? Did he use multi-ple sources of information? What did Ian learn from this activity?

To help teachers think through these issues, in this chapter I share stories drawn from data gathered in two ethnographic studies. Both studies examined classroom situations in which children were involved in the process of conducting research over extended periods of time. In the first inquiry, the one in which I met Ian, the self-directed nature of a Scottish classroom provided me with an opportunity to describe processes children use to work from text and their impressions of what it means to do research (Many et al., 1996). The second study (Many, 2002) was conducted in a school with a diverse student body in the southern United States. Data were collected in the third/fourth and fifth/sixth-grade classrooms during interdisciplinary units over the course of a year. The teachers and I discussed the children's processes, and the teachers worked to scaffold the conceptual understandings and strategy use of their students. The stories I share from these classrooms will illustrate what the teachers and I learned as we considered how to help struggling readers be involved in meaningful inquiry.

Meaningful Research: Constructing a Personal Understanding of Information

What does it mean to do research? Actually, it can mean different things to different students and to different teachers. When one sits and thinks about what one believes it means to do research, one might find that one can define it in a range of ways, depending on the purposes for the research. For some, research means accumulating information. Take, for instance, the process of Claudia, an 11-year-old in Ian's class.

> Claudia sits at a long table near the back of room with two other students. All of the students in her class are involved in a three-month interdiscipli-nary unit on World War II, and each is also conducting a personal research project on a self-chosen topic related to the war. Claudia has just completed

her project, "Aberdeen at War," a 17-page booklet of writings, drawings, and photocopied information. I have talked with Claudia throughout her research process and have compared her project booklet to the source texts that she has used. Claudia's primary focus in putting together her World War II research project is to find "something interesting" that her teacher will want to share with the class.

Although Claudia follows her teacher's direction to create a planning web for her topic, her method of doing research has involved thumbing through books and finding something interesting to include, or finding out what her classmates were doing and doing something similar in her project booklet. Thus, Claudia often "finds" information through serendipity rather than as the result of a concentrated search. The strategies of working from text that Claudia uses are primarily photocopying, verbatim copying, and drawing and labeling. On a number of occasions, including on her initial brainstorming on her planning web, she includes information she likes regardless of whether it has a direct connection with her topic itself. As I talk with Claudia, however, she is very pleased with her booklet. Assessing her project, she notes, "I think I did quite good. I find it interesting...I don't have as much as other people do [but] I think I did quite good." As we talk, Claudia comments that she wouldn't change anything about her work. She clearly feels that she has been successful in fulfilling her own expectations of what it means to do research. *(Story drawn from ethnographic data from Many et al., 1996)*

To Claudia, research meant collecting interesting information. To Ian, research meant something else entirely. Research was putting things in your own words, a process of transferring information from an author's source text to your own report. Many teachers who graded Ian's efforts would have surely awarded his final project an A. His work stayed on topic, addressed a vast amount of detailed information about a variety of world leaders, and was carefully laid out with illustrations and pictures to supplement his report. If a teacher turned an eye to Ian's processes, however, a number of questions might arise. Ian seemed to have problems using the table of contents and index of his text. His procedure of first copying out relevant passages verbatim was a coping strategy he had learned because of difficulties he had encountered in finding his place in the large text from one day to the next. Ian also showed little interest in working from multiple sources; to him, research was about rewriting information from a source and putting it in his own words. As his text obviously had plenty of information, he did not see a need to go to other resources. Finally, although Ian's product was impressive, he had difficulty talking freely about what he had learned. As I watched Ian interact with his peers during small-group discussions about world leaders, he seldom shared information unless he was reading directly from his project booklet. He seemed to have transferred the information into "his own words" without building his own understanding of the content itself.

The perspective on research I address in this chapter differs from the notion that Claudia demonstrated (the idea that research is collecting or accumulating information) and from Ian's impression (that research involves transferring information). Rather, I consider research as a transformation process leading to personal understanding. Such an inquiry perspective involves different research processes and different strategies for working from text. The contrasts between these different impressions of what it means to do research and of ways of working are shown in Figure 12.1.

As illustrated, when students view research as transforming information, they are involved in a complex set of research processes, including planning, searching, finding, recording, reviewing, and presenting. These processes do not occur in a linear fashion; rather they are recursive throughout the research investigation. This recursive nature is illustrated in the following story about Allison, another student in Ian and Claudia's class.

> I am sitting at the table where I take notes and talk to students during my daily visits to the classroom. Allison walks to my table and says "hi." Ms. Lindsey, her teacher, has told me she is pleased with the work Allison is doing on her

FIGURE 12.1

STUDENTS' TASK IMPRESSIONS, RESEARCH PROCESSES, AND STRATEGIES IN WORKING FROM TEXTS

	Task Impressions		
Ways of Working	Accumulating information	Transferring information	Transforming information
Research Subtasks	Finding, recording	Searching, finding, recording	Planning, searching, finding, recording, reviewing, presenting
Strategies Used to Work From Sources	Photocopying Verbatim copying Drawing and labeling	Sentence-by-sentence reworking Read-remember-write	Cut and paste synthesis Discourse synthesis

research on Anne Frank. I ask Allison how "Anne Frank" is going. She responds, "I'm not doing just Anne Frank. I'm doing Jewish customs and history too." I ask her if she will talk with me about her project, and together we look at her planning web. In the center of her web are the words Anne Frank. On rays extending out from the center, she has written, "Introduction to Anne Frank, Jewish symbols, Jewish customs, religion, Jewish history, the annex, things I like about Anne Frank's diary, Life in hiding, Life under the Nazis, Concentration camps." She explains, "I'm writing about Jews and what they were like and what they went through and all that." "How did you come up with these things?" I ask. She responds, "By reading bits of the book [Diary of Anne Frank], I decided 'Things I like about Anne Frank's Diary'...I had this book from the library and it said the stuff that the Nazis did, making rules they had to obey, and I got that idea from that book." Pointing to the section on the concentration camps, she notes, "[I got that] from that big book on Anne Frank [an informational text]. Ms. Lindsey gave me the idea for the Jewish customs and religion. I don't have anything on Jewish history yet." *(Story drawn from ethnographic data from Many et al., 1996)*

As Allison continued her search for information, she drew from numerous books on Anne Frank as well as general texts with information about the Jewish religion, the Nazis' treatment of the Jews, and concentration camps. She sent away for, and received, information from the Anne Frank Foundation and Museum. To Allison, doing project work involved finding many books about her topic and writing about what she knew after reading them. It involved identifying what she wanted to learn and searching for sources that might reveal that information. It involved looking at the table of contents of a book to identify specific sections of interest and taking notes. It also involved changing and adapting plans in light of what she learned along the way. Allison viewed research as transforming information. She was involved in a recursive process of planning and then searching for and finding information. She developed ways to record and review her information and to consider if she had addressed her topic sufficiently. She thought through how to present that information effectively to the people she considered her audience.

For teachers, the stories of Allison, Ian, and Claudia raise important questions. What can teachers do to help all children be involved in research that leads to personal understanding? How do teachers scaffold students' research processes? What strategies do students need to be able to use to conduct such research? How in particular do teachers help struggling readers? I believe that teachers need to consider specific ways to support students as they engage in research. I had an opportunity in my second ethnographic study to work with two teachers, Joy Ward and Susan Henderson, who continually involved students in on-going research projects throughout the course of their school year. These teachers used instructional conversations to scaffold their students' perspectives on what it means to do research and on the processes involved, and to scaffold their students' use of specific strategies to work from text. In the following section, I share stories from these classrooms to illustrate how the teachers helped their third- through sixth-grade students learn both content and processes.

Supporting Students' Efforts to Learn Through Research

The students in the upper-elementary classrooms (third/fourth and fifth/sixth grades) have been studying the Caribbean. The teachers have read The Cay out loud with students from both classes. Today, the third- and fourth-grade children are spread out around their classroom, working on their individual research. Joy, their teacher, is sitting at a large table with Curtis, an 11-year-old student from her class. Curtis is doing a research project on reggae and has been talking to Joy about what he has learned. Looking over the packet of work he has turned in, Joy says, "You have information from one source. This is the information-gathering phase. If you have only one source, how do you know if this is true?" Joy flips through some pages that Curtis has printed off the Internet and notes a few pictures that would be good to use in the project. She continues, "There is nothing here that belongs to you. The part where you are telling me all this stuff, it is not in this package. There is nothing here that tells me what you know." She notes that he has talked to her about his project, so she knows he has learned some things, but what he has handed her does not show what he knows. She explains, "This is stuff that anyone could have printed out. Your dad could have printed it out while you were asleep. This doesn't show what you know."

Joy elaborates on the difference between printing out information and doing something that shows what Curtis has learned. In essence, he needs to "make it his own." Raising the question of how a person can be certain of the accuracy of the information retrieved from the Internet, Joy then explains, "I want you to read an encyclopedia or let me know that you have read an article and show me that you know that this [the information from the Internet] is true. I could put something on the Internet, and I don't know anything about reggae. If you read this and then you read something else that matches, then you may find this could be true. But, just printing it off the

Internet doesn't show me what you know, and just telling me it is true is not enough. Unless you look up the source of who put that information there, or you compare the information with other sources and find that it says the same thing, you cannot be certain that the information is accurate. *(Story drawn from ethnographic data from Many, 2002)*

In this instructional conversation, Joy was providing Curtis the support and guidance he needed. Conversations like these are vital aspects of the curriculum in this school, which is grounded in a social-constructivist perspective toward literacy learning. The teachers believe social interaction is the key to children's knowledge construction (Vygotsky, 1934/1978). They use instructional conversations in one-on-one, small-group, and whole-class settings to scaffold students' progress to new developmental levels.

According to Vygotsky, students' actual developmental level refers to what a learner can understand or can perform independently. What a learner can do with the support of a teacher can be described as being at the learners' level of potential development. The distance between these levels is deemed to be the zone of proximal development and to be the area in which instructional scaffolding occurs. Through scaffolding, a teacher provides the assistance a learner needs (Roehler & Cantlon, 1997). Such scaffolding enables learners to develop understandings or use strategies of which they would not have been capable on their own (Meyer, 1993; Palincsar, 1986). As the learner gains more competence and moves toward independence, the support can be withdrawn gradually (Bruner, 1986, 1990).

During the year of observing in these multiage classrooms, I was able to look closely at how Joy and the fifth- and sixth-grade teacher, Susan, scaffolded students' research processes. This involved supporting students' growing understanding of what it means to do research, the research processes involved, and the use of specific strategies the children needed to work from text. The processes Joy and Susan used moved from those using substantial teacher support (modeling, supplying information, clarifying, and assisting) to processes inviting more student participation (questioning, prompting, and focusing attention) and, finally, to processes requiring the most student involvement (encouraging self-monitoring, labeling, and affirming).

In Joy's conversation with Curtis, she uses two scaffolding processes, clarifying and supplying information. Clarifying involves explaining concepts or strategies to which a student already has been introduced. Since the beginning of the year, the class had been involved in conducting various research investigations. The importance of sharing what one knows through one's research projects had always been implicit in the curriculum, and each unit ended with students presenting their research to the class. For this particular interdisciplinary unit on the Caribbean, though, students had begun to turn to the Internet as a resource to a far greater extent than they had on previous research projects. Like Curtis, many children had cut and pasted information from websites or simply printed out relevant pages. Joy's explanation that these printed-out pages did not show what Curtis knew helped to clarify the fact that even if a student read and could talk about what was printed off the Internet, handing in such information did not illustrate personal understanding.

The second scaffolding procedure Joy uses with Curtis involves supplying information. Over the previous month, Joy, Susan, and I had discussed how use of the Internet was underscoring a need for students to engage in critical literacy (Many, 2000). For example, although the Internet provides a virtually limitless resource of information, readers must systematically consider the authenticity of information drawn from this resource. Joy's discussion of the importance of verifying the truth of information from the Internet supplied Curtis with new information to consider. The strategy she suggested, turning to additional sources as a cross-checking mechanism, was new to him. After this conversation, Joy decided to bring up these issues with students in both classes. As shown in the following story, Joy uses a range of scaffolding procedures to help the students understand the strategies they need to use when drawing from resources for their research inquiries.

> The third/fourth- and fifth/sixth-grade classes have come together for a sharing session. The students circle the classroom, sitting cross-legged on the floor. Joy explains that in the past few days it had become clear that something Curtis had done was a problem and that she realized that others were having the same problem, too. She asks Curtis to share with the class. Curtis begins, "I got a bunch of papers off the Internet and tried to turn it in to Joy and she wouldn't accept it—because my dad could have printed it off. I know a lot of stuff but the stuff I have been saying is not in there." Joy continues, "It is like he can talk to me about his project—but nothing he has [turned in] has shown me what he knows about it."
>
> Joy walks to the bookshelf and picks up a physics book. She hands the book to Susan and notes, "I can't just hand this book to Susan and say that this book is what I've learned about teaching physics." Joy goes on, leading the

students to see how handing Susan this book does not show what she, Joy, has learned. Joy is in the process of preparing a new unit to teach the kids about physics. Drawing from her work to prepare the unit, she explains, "I haven't taught this before so I need to research how to teach physics." She tells them that to research physics, she would not just look at one book. She picks up another text on the shelf and says, "I would look at this other book and the one that Tori and I found." Tori, a fourth-grade student, gets that text and brings it to Joy. Joy says, "When I think about how I am going to teach physics to you all, I am going to look through all three of these and get ideas. And I am going to call up someone I know who knows about physics and I will ask, 'If I am teaching kids about physics, what things should I consider?' When I come to you and we are about to start physics, I will give you a summary of what I have found out and I will ask you what we might learn together. I have never taught this before to kids your age and I am doing a research project."

Joy continues, "Now, suppose I took this book and Alexander [a sixth-grade student known for his intelligence] doesn't think much about it. And maybe someone else also thought it might not be a good source. If I just taught right out of this book, would that be a good decision? I don't know if stuff in this book is right. Just because it is a book doesn't mean that I know everything in it is right." Joy reads some reviews off the back cover of the book and together the class talks about the fact that these reviews are designed to sell the book. They decide that even if these reviews are good, one would need to be cautious because the publisher wouldn't have put a bad review on the outside cover. The class decides she would need another way to judge whether the information in the book is accurate.

Joy goes on to the next book. "Suppose I got out this book and it says that everything in this other book isn't true? What would I do?" The kids volunteer things that she could do to decide which book is correct. Together they brainstorm that she could talk to a mechanic, read another book, look at the computer, talk to more people, and look at more sources.

Then Joy goes back to the example with Curtis: "I asked Curtis to talk about this because there are other people who have had similar experiences. We need to look at both what we know about the things and where we are getting the information we are telling. If you know a lot of information you need to transmit it and let us hear it and share it." Alexander jumps in, "Remember when I was doing research on jazz? It said a date and I looked in another book and the date was completely different in the second book. I still don't know which date was right."

Joy agrees, "That is right. Sometimes we get conflicting information." To help the students understand how they could decide on sources they might use, she begins to use examples the students can relate to: "If you stopped someone on the playground and wanted to know the rules for soccer, who would you ask?" The students answer by naming different people in the school.

Through Joy's questions, they explain they said these names because these students are good in soccer. Joy then explains that these students are seen as experts. She then goes on to use other examples, asking students whom to ask for other problems, such as how to build play structures and how to play tag. The students share their ideas for each by naming someone who knows or plays that thing a lot. Joy then goes on, "You have some authentic information about how to decide who to go to when you have questions. If I read something about the person who wrote this book [holding up the teaching physics book again] and found out he was a professor at a college, then I might think he knows a lot about it. If I read that he changed tires at a gas station..." (She pauses, and the students shake their heads and murmur, "no.") "...then he might still know about it." Her voice stresses the word might with an indication that she is not as sure about his knowledge in contrast to the college professor. "What if he lived on a desert island for the past 20 years?"

They discuss how physics is a rapidly changing field and that it would be important to have up-to-date information. Joy stresses, "You have to find out where the person got the information. How do you know they know?" She continues, "It is the same way with sources from the Internet. I could write something about reggae and put it on the Internet." Curtis jumps in, "But you don't know anything about reggae." Joy nods, smiling, "The person who put the pages on the Internet might not either. How would you know?" Remembering their discussions, Curtis volunteers, "You should read something else to make sure it is true." Joy agrees, "Good idea. Read something else and see if it matches." *(Story drawn from ethnographic data from Many, 2002)*

In this story, Joy is building the students' overall impression of research as transforming information. She clarifies that research involves learning and then sharing what one knows. The importance of developing a personal understanding is stressed throughout the instructional conversation. She also uses other scaffolding processes to develop students' abilities to search and find information and to review the authenticity of their sources. She uses modeling as she draws from her own experience of researching physics in preparation for the classes' upcoming unit. She uses scaffolding processes such as questioning and prompting to have students consider how they might deal with conflicting information between sources. She continues to elicit student involvement through questioning and prompting as she has the classes consider ways to verify the credentials of authors and the authenticity of information. Finally, when Curtis responds with what a person should do to verify information from the Internet, she labels and affirms his recommendation.

In addition to developing students' understanding of research processes and what it means to do research, teachers in this study also worked with readers who needed support in using basic strategies in reading, working from text, and writing. The range of the strategies these teachers scaffolded can be found in Figure 12.2.

The scaffolding of the strategies used independently occurred most frequently as teachable moments that arose in one-on-one and small-group situations. Research investigations were integral to the social studies and science curriculum; therefore, substantial class time was spent with the students engaged in such activities. As the students worked, the teachers held conferences with individuals, discussing their topics and their research processes. As shown in the following story, this approach allowed the teachers to understand their students' difficulties and to provide support and guidance that struggling students needed to develop effective strategies.

> Earlier in the day, Susan's class went to the library to look for resources for their investigations into types of shelters. As Susan hands out small pads of adhesive notes that students can use to mark important passages in their texts,

FIGURE 12.2

SCAFFOLDING STUDENTS' USE OF STRATEGIES

Reading Strategies	Using context Scanning Map reading Decoding and pronunciation
Working From Text	Searching for and locating information Identifying relevant, authentic, and accurate information Understanding text format Using computers Note taking
Writing and Composing Strategies	Planning Labeling Drafting Revising Editing Publishing

she asks, "Tell me something about the process this morning. What was helpful?" Glenda responds, "The computers because you didn't have to go through the aisles to find something." Susan agrees, but then notes, "Sometimes when you find a section then you can find a lot of books there that can help." "One of the things that was frustrating," comments Rita, "was that sometimes you couldn't find what you wanted when you got to the shelf." Susan leads the class in considering things that were beneficial or frustrating. They discuss the words they had brainstormed before they had gone to the library. The words were examples of things they might look up. Susan notes that some of their words were very specific instead of general and that the very specific words probably wouldn't have a whole book listed for them. She then encourages the students to take some time and begin reading through their books.

As the students begin to look through their books, Glenda catches Susan's eye. Glenda is eager to begin writing. Susan encourages Glenda to take the next 15 minutes to read her book. Unsure whether she is supposed to just read, Glenda asks again. Susan explains, "I want you to just take it in, just read and take it in."

Susan notices that June is not reading about her project. Taking a book from the center of the table, Susan sits down with June and says, "Let's see if we can find something in here." She has June put her fiction book away, and she begins to leaf through the resource with June looking on. June's investigation is to find out about the shelters used by an African tribe. Susan asks if June has found out whether it is a tribe in Kenya. June doesn't know. She says she has been on the computer twice but hasn't found anything. Susan tells June to look through the book while Susan finds an additional resource. While Susan is examining another book, she finds a picture related to Rita's research, a cloth igloo. As she shows it to Rita, Glenda exclaims, "Ooh, look!" Glenda and Susan hunch over her book and then call June to come over. They have found where June's tribe is located. All three look closely at the page, and Susan says, "June, you have a job to do. Go find an atlas and look up Johannesburg." She then asks June to repeat to her what she should do. When June can't, Susan repeats that she should get an atlas, and she clarifies what to look for. June asks where the atlas is, and Glenda asks if June wants her to help. Together, Glenda and June go to find the atlas.

When they return, Glenda and June begin thumbing through pages in the atlas. Susan notes, "There is an easier way to do this," and she reminds June of the index at the back. She grabs a book and calls attention to the word Johannesburg, writing the word down on an adhesive note. She places the note in front of June and then tells June to look in the index and find the latitude and longitude for Johannesburg.

Susan circulates through the room and then returns to June. She calls June's attention to the guide words at the top of the pages in June's atlas. The atlas June is using is very large, about 2 feet tall. They lay it down on a table, and Susan reads the guide words and calls attention to the letters. As June begins to look at the proper page, Susan places the adhesive note on the page. When June finds the word, Susan explains that the numbers tell her the map that it is on, the page number, and the letters, M2. Susan uses the note to help June focus on the correct number in the index. Then June looks to find the page. When she gets to the page, Susan prompts her to find M2. She shows her the M, and they find the 2 together. Then Susan goes to get the book Glenda was using, so they can find how far her tribe lived from Johannesburg. They look back and forth from the small map in Glenda's book to the large atlas. Susan calls attention to the curve of the land on the small map and to how the page on the large atlas does not show that curve. She explains they will have to go to the next page to find that curve of land.

Then Susan notes, "Here is what we could have done. If we are looking for a tribe, then an area might have been named for that tribe. What could we have done?" Susan draws attention to how they looked up Johannesburg, and she prompts June to consider, "What could we have done to look up the area we are trying to find?" June guesses they could have looked up the name of the tribe. Susan tells her to use the guide words to look up the name of the tribe. June flips through a large number of pages very quickly. She seems to be using the guide words to some extent, but when she gets close to the pages she needs, she begins to look down column after column on a number of pages. Susan comes by again and talks to her about whether she has found anything similar to the name of the tribe. Together they decide there is nothing in the index. Susan begins talking about the clues they have identified at this point. They know the tribe is located near Johannesburg and Swaziland. She notes that the name of the tribe is probably too specific to find a whole book on it. They will probably have to find a book on South Africa in general. She suggests that June also look at the old National Geographic magazines they have available.

In this story from Susan's fifth/sixth-grade classroom, we see her provide the assistance June needs to be able to work with sources. The support Susan provides allows the student to pursue her investigation and to work with texts she is unable to use independently at this time. At times, Susan prompts and focuses June's attention, encouraging her involvement. When needed, Susan clarifies the process or assists June directly to ensure her continued progress. Susan also provides opportunities for June to attempt to use strategies on her own but stays closely attuned to June's difficulties so that she can offer the support June needs to continue her investigation.

The stories from these classrooms provide increased understanding of children's impressions of research and the processes and strategies students use when they set out to conduct inquiries. The instructional conversations running through these stories also illustrate the ways teachers can support children's efforts to investigate information. Drawing from these stories, I would like to highlight five support strategies that teachers who work with struggling readers might consider when working to scaffold students' abilities to do research.

Support Strategy 1: Give Students Time to Roam

Typically, the first step students encounter when teachers assign a research project is the need to decide on a topic. The first support strategy that teachers need to remember, especially when working with struggling readers, is to ensure that students have an opportunity to explore the subject in general before settling down to a focused investigation. In her work with Curtis, Joy referred to this as the information-gathering phase. Susan prompted her students to refrain from taking notes and instead to spend time reading and "just taking in" information. I would offer that, particularly when working with an unfamiliar topic, students should go through a process similar to Claudia's as she collected interesting information. The research processes at this point focus on simply finding information. Students might photocopy or print out information from a wide variety of resources, collect artwork, and check out numerous books. Only after they have begun to develop background knowledge in a topic can students begin to form meaningful questions, review their resources for relevant information, and search purposefully for additional information to answer their questions.

Support Strategy 2: Help Students Find a Range of Sources

One advantage children had in both the contexts discussed in this chapter is that their teachers encouraged the use of a wide range of sources and supported their students' development of strategies to gather information from these sources. In most classrooms, typical sources for research reports include encyclopedias and expository texts. Although texts of this nature may be available on a range of readability levels, struggling readers often have difficulty reading such texts. In looking at the strategies the Scottish students used to work from text, it was clear that when readers tried to use complex resources, they chose less demanding strategies for working from the text, such as line-by-line paraphrasing or verbatim copying. Even students who typically worked to synthesize information from across multiple texts would fall back on these strategies when they encountered texts that were difficult for them. However, teachers in these schools also encouraged use of interviews, works of art and music, and historical fiction. Such resources enabled less proficient readers to learn information from a variety of means, and students proved capable of drawing from such sources effectively when giving research presentations or creating products based on what they had learned.

In addition to encouraging students to use both typical and novel sources of information, the teachers' use of class time for personal research investigations ensured that students had the support they needed when working from text. Ms. Lindsey, the Scottish teacher, continually recommended specific texts for individual students to consider. Joy conferenced with students regularly, guiding their planning and replanning, their ability to search for new texts, and their consideration of the importance of cross-checking the accuracy of information as well as of verifying the credibility of the authors. Susan circulated throughout her classroom, identifying teachable moments by watching her students' attempts to use the indexes of books, to conduct searches on the Internet, to use guide words, and to highlight relevant information in text. By staying aware of their students' needs, conceptions of research, research processes, and strategy use, these teachers were able to support their struggling readers' abilities to find and effectively use relevant sources of information for their investigations.

Support Strategy 3:
Make Note Taking a Read-Understand-Write Strategy

If students are going to use their research investigations to develop personal understanding, one key strategy that needs to be taught explicitly is the ability to take notes through a read-understand-write approach. Although students may photocopy or verbatim-copy during the information gathering phase, or even do line-by-line paraphrasing of information as they rework specific sentences, such strategies do not ensure that they construct meaning from their research. As Joy remarked to Curtis, someone else could print information off the Internet for students. Even if the students are directly involved, activities such as cutting and pasting from Internet sources does not mean individuals have learned any information. Both Susan and Joy used whole-class minilessons to model how to read and glean key points from resources. Teachers also can provide students with scaffolding by first having students listen to information and write down key points, and then having them work in similar ways from written texts. Although many teachers do have students create notecards as they conduct research investigations, the key emphasis of ensuring that students are developing an understanding of what they are learning is crucial to research as an meaningful inquiry process.

Support Strategy 4: Have Students Consider the Source

A fourth support strategy that is vital in today's society is the practice of having students carefully consider the source of their information. This need is explored in the stories from Joy's class as she discusses the issue of author credibility with Curtis, and later as she discusses with the students her own process of conducting research on physics. As Joy stresses, critical consideration of the author's credentials is vital. In the past, students typically may not have encountered such an emphasis until they were studying in colleges and universities. Often, teachers in the early years (particularly those who have attempted to have elementary and middle school students conduct their first research projects) have been content to simply encourage students to use other resources besides an encyclopedia. If students did find multiple published sources on their topics, these teachers felt that they were successful. However, in today's world, children and adults have access to a limitless supply of resources on any topic. Many of the documents they encounter, though, have often not gone through any type of review process for quality or for accuracy of content. Consequently, for the students of today, the ability to critically evaluate the credibility and authenticity of information should be considered a basic literacy skill (Many, 2000). As Joy explains and then models, such critical literacy skills involve strategies such as cross-checking information by comparing sources and considering the background and credibility of the author or the site itself.

Support Strategy 5: Consider What Is of Value

Finally, the stories from these classrooms remind teachers that if they are going to support students' research processes, they need to begin by looking closely at what they value. Is the production of grammatically correct, polished final products high on a particular teacher's list? Is the teacher interested in having students turning in a set of notecards and a formal report? Does it matter if students can talk about their work and answer questions about what they have learned? Is the teacher concerned about whether students have been willing to take risks with new strategies in working from texts? Does the teacher wonder what his or her students think research is all about?

What teachers value shapes what they expect from students, what they reward with praise and high grades, and ultimately what students learn from the research activities teachers have them carry out. To illustrate, consider the excerpts in Figure 12.3 from the research products produced by three of the Scottish students, Jean, Ian, and Allison.

FIGURE 12.3

COMPARISONS OF EXCERPTS FROM FINAL PRODUCTS

Jean's Project	Ian's Project	Allison's Project
In world war 2 women had to do men's work when they wear fighing a war men work on farm's and factories they had hard Jobs to do. So when men went to war the women had to there work for them. The women had to feed little baby's if they had baby's they would have to do the men's work at the same time. They had to tidy up the house as well as doing the other things as well as doing the house work. The women have hard work when the mean area at war. And if the men come home they are very happy to see them. The women had baby's gass mask's.	Benito Mussolini was the son of a outspokenly socialist blacksmith from central Italy. He use to be a socialist journalist. When he joined the army he rose to the rank of the corporal. In 1919 Benito Mussolini founded the Fascist party, so named from its fasci di combattimentor ("combat groups"). Mussolini spoke from the benches of the extreme right. Nobody dared to sit there. At the same time was Mussolini was in the parliament black-shirted supporters had created a reign of terror on the streets. The post war Italy was suffering from the acute economic social and political unrest.	Nazis first set up Concentration Campus they were some kind of prisons in 1939 there were three kinds of camps in Astora and Germany and in other Countries Some Concentration Camps became Exterminations camps people were murdered or worked to death most people were killed in the gas chambers Eight million people were murdered in concentration Campus six million of them were Jews Jews were taken to concentration Camps by Germas. Children were taken away from there familys and put to separate Concentration Camps Anne and her sister died in a Concentration Camp with a dises called Typho Margot died with it and then a couple of days later Anne died with it to.

If teachers primarily value products, they might praise Ian's work to the highest extent. Careful checking would indicate that Ian had not plagiarized from his source; he had, rather, carefully written the information in his own words. His report is carefully edited and polished. When teachers look at Jean's and Allison's work, they might note the less complex sentence structure, the frequency of misspelled words, and a less impressive range of content.

If, however, teachers have been closely attuned to the processes their students were using, they would appreciate struggling reader Jean's ability to draw from multiple oral sources of information to develop her understanding of children's experiences during the war. Her dedication in taping her grandparents' discussions of their memories of wartime events and then listening to the tapes and constructing a written report was considerable. Despite her difficulties with reading and writing, she drew from both their conversations and the information presented in class to create a written document illustrating what she had learned.

Turning to Allison, teachers' examination of her processes would have helped them appreciate her efforts to synthesize information from three different texts to create this section of her report. Looking at her report in comparison to Ian's, however, one sees a less polished product. If teachers focus primarily on the final product, and perhaps reward Ian with the higher grade, they are in danger of limiting students' development of more complex strategies in working from texts. In order to truly synthesize across multiple sources, students must move away from sentence-by-sentence reworking to a strategy such as read-understand-write. However, at least initially, students' resulting products are more likely to contain grammatical inconsistencies and spelling errors, simply because the structure of the text no longer matches that of the original source text. Consequently, if teachers value research as a means for developing personal understanding through inquiry, they will have to be cognizant of, reward, and praise developments in process as well as products.

Summary

The stories from these classrooms offer an opportunity to explore how children come to know what it means to do research. Teachers must begin with an understanding of students' task impressions and the processes and strategies needed to carry out meaningful investigations. Second, they need to create opportunities in their classes to frame instructional conversations around their students' research projects. Through such conversations, teachers can provide the scaffolding necessary to support struggling readers' attempts to become involved in meaningful inquires.

REFERENCES

Bruner, J.S. (1986). *Actual minds, possible worlds*. Cambridge, MA: Harvard University Press.

Bruner, J.S. (1990). *Acts of meaning*. Cambridge, MA: Harvard University Press.

Many, J.E. (2000). How will literacy be defined in the new millennium? *Reading Research Quarterly, 35*, 65–67.

Many, J.E. (2002). An exhibition and analysis of verbal tapestries: Understanding how scaffolding is woven into the fabric of instructional conversations. *Reading Research Quarterly, 37*, 376–407.

Many, J.E., Fyfe, R., Lewis, G., & Mitchell, E. (1996). Traversing the topical landscape: Exploring students' self-directed reading-writing-research processes. *Reading Research Quarterly, 31*, 12–35.

Meyer, D.K. (1993). What is scaffolded instruction? Definitions, distinguishing features, and misnomers. In D.J. Leu & C.K. Kinzer (Eds.), *Examining central issues in literacy research, theory, and practice* (42nd yearbook of the National Reading Conference, pp. 41–53). Chicago: National Reading Conference.

Palincsar, A.S. (1986). The role of dialogue in providing scaffolded instruction. *Educational Psychology, 21*(1–2), 73–98.

Roehler, L.R., & Cantlon, D.J. (1997). Scaffolding: A powerful tool in social constructivist classrooms. In K. Hogan & M. Pressley (Eds.), *Scaffolding student learning: Instructional approaches and issues* (pp. 6–42). Cambridge, MA: Brookline Books.

Vygotsky, L.S. (1978). *Mind in society: The development of higher psychological processes* (M. Cole, V. John-Steiner, S. Scribner, & E. Souberman, Eds. and Trans.). Cambridge, MA: Harvard University Press. (Original work published 1934)

Note: Page numbers followed by *f* indicate figures; those followed by *t* indicate tables.

identification of, 120–121; instructional approaches for, 18–19, 21–22; in
middle school, 137–155 (*see also* middle school intervention program);
numbers of, 14; portable assessment for, 10–22; in third grade, 117–133
(*see also* third grade intervention program). *See also* reading problems
STUDY GROUPS: in Teachers' Learning Collaborative, 95–99, 98*f*, 113
STUDY GUIDES. *See* reading guides
SUPPLYING INFORMATION: as scaffolding procedure, 224–226

T

TAB BOOK CLUB APPROACH, 191–205; implementation of, 199–205; internal
text patterns and, 197–199; interpretation of, 199–205; lesson sequence
in, 193–205; reading strategies in, 205; student engagement in, 204–205;
student-generated textbook chapter in, 201–203; text awareness/analysis
and, 196–204; text structure differences and, 194–196, 195*t*
TALKING ABOUT BOOKS (TAB) APPROACH. *See* TAB Book Club Approach
TEACHERS' LEARNING COLLABORATIVE, 94–114; assessment systems of,
107–112, 111*f*; Book Club and, 95, 99–100; Book Club *Plus* and, 95–96,
100–112 (*see also* Book Club *Plus*); cultural diversity and, 100;
curriculum framework of, 100–107; curriculum reform and, 112–114;
differentiated instruction and, 96; diverse viewpoints in, 95, 97; goals of,
97; history of, 95, 99–100; "I Can" statements for, 112; as learning
community, 113–114; Literacy Circle and, 96, 100; "Our Storied Lives"
curriculum in, 103; professional development via, 96; public discourse
and, 113; study groups in, 95–99, 98*f*, 113; support for, 96; teacher
influences and, 97–99, 98*f*; teacher training and, 99
TEACHING: diagnostic, 14. *See also* literacy instruction
TECHNOLOGY. *See* instructional technology
TEXAS: FROM SEA TO SHINING SEA (FRADIN), 194, 195, 195*t*
TEXTBOOKS: Book Club approach for, 191–205 (*see also* TAB Book Club
Approach); culturally relevant, 41–42; diagnostic teaching for, 20–21;
fourth-grade slump and, 179, 190, 191; reading guides for, 208–216 (*see
also* reading guides)
TEXTS: content area, 179–180; for cross-age tutoring, 161, 162–163, 165;
culturally relevant, 41–42, 53, 54*t*; electronic (*see* instructional
technology); readability formulas for, 130–131; for Readers Theatre, 53,
54*t*; reference, 179–180
THIRD GRADE INTERVENTION PROGRAM, 117–133; ability grouping and, 120,
130–133; differentiated instruction in, 122; end-of-year results of,
125–127; essential components of, 132–133; flexible grouping in,
121–122; identification of struggling readers for, 120–121; mid-year
results of, 125; monitoring progress in, 124; outcomes with disadvantaged
students, 128–129; outcomes with middle-class students, 125–127; planning